THE MAIN STREAM OF JACOBITISM

THE MAIN STREAM
OF JACOBITISM

BY

George Hilton Jones

Assistant Professor of History
Washington College

HARVARD UNIVERSITY PRESS

Cambridge, Massachusetts

1 9 5 4

This book is dedicated
to two of my great benefactors

ELIZABETH HILL

AND

ROBERT HEILMAN

PREFACE

I have many acknowledgements to make. The Rhodes Trust has generously supported my studies from 1947 to 1950. Mr. H. C. Allen, of Lincoln College, Oxford, supervised my work on an earlier draft of this book, accepted as a doctoral dissertation by the examiners of Oxford University. I have also to acknowledge the gracious permission of Her Majesty the Queen to use the Stuart Papers in the Royal Archives at Windsor Castle. Without the two hundred and more volumes of manuscript in that collection which fall into the period which I have undertaken to study, and which yet remain uncalendared by the Historical Manuscripts Commission, my work would have been impossible. The Bodleian Library, in which most of my other work was done, is staffed with the most patient people I know. I am also grateful to the archivist at Windsor, Miss Mary Mackenzie, M.V.O., and to those of the British Museum, the Public Record Office, and the Archives of the French Ministry of Foreign Affairs at Paris, and to the Sterling Memorial Library at Yale University, for courtesies and assistance. Dr. Nicholas Riasanovsky and Mr. Foster Provost have kindly read the book in manuscript and made a number of suggestions. For these I return my thanks. The four lines of verse on p. 246 are taken from "Little Gidding," by T. S. Eliot. I am indebted to Mr. Eliot and to his publishers, Harcourt, Brace and Company, for permission to quote.

Unless otherwise stated, dates of events recounted in this volume are given in the style used in the country in which they occurred. Some dates are given in both styles — e.g. March 29/ April 9, 1704. Old Style, in use in England and Russia, is abbreviated to "O.S."; New Style, in general use elsewhere, to "N.S." The New Style date can be found, before 1700, by adding ten days to the date in Old Style; after the end of February in that year, eleven days must be added, to offset the day in the Old Style calendar added to February. Old Style dates can be calculated by a similar subtraction from the New Style date, care being used in the case of dates near to February 29/March 10, 1700. The beginning of the year given here is always January 1, except when both years are given for dates between January 1 and March 25. G. M. Trevelyan has pointed out that different beginnings of the year are only incidentally connected with the two styles. In my own experience, the Tuscan government used the New Style, while dating the year from the Incarnation (March 25) just as England did, although, of course, March 25 fell later by ten or eleven days, depending on the century.

G. H. J.

CONTENTS

THE MAIN STREAM OF JACOBITISM

I

REVOLUTIONERS AND JACOBITES

Compounders and Non-Compounders

(1 6 8 8 – 1 6 9 4)

1. THE REVOLUTION

The seventeenth century was above all an age of kings. A king in any European country was an object of reverence and awe, if not of fear, and the citizens of the important republics of Venice and the United Netherlands felt an esteem for monarchs not exceeded by that owed as a duty by born subjects. Despite the great example of Charles I's royal catastrophe, even to some extent because of it, there existed a feeling of the hedging divinity which persisted into the succeeding age, on some levels of society, with undiminished vigor. Nevertheless, we must not exaggerate the potency of respect when opposed by necessity, or mere expedience: the eighteenth century was to see a number of disputed successions, in which the right was very much in doubt, and left to determination by might; foreign powers, though monarchical, intervened according to their interests, while private persons chose sides, if it came to civil war, in the same way. Thus the English, Spanish, Polish, Austrian, and Bavarian successions were in turn disputed by force of arms, and only the unlooked-for stamina of the infant King Louis XV kept France from similar divisions and their consequent turmoil.

Therefore the abandonment of King James II by his fellow monarchs in 1688 was not an astonishing rarity. His father had experienced a like apathy among the others anointed by the Lord. It was no surprise to the son that the only king who supported his claim was the one who lost most by his deprivation, a loss which his restoration would balance.

Other kings and princes lost little. Against the open violation of the principle of monarchy in England, they set the curtailment of the power for aggression of their neighbor Louis XIV, who had offended or frightened most of them by that constantly expanding appetite for the possessions of others which made possible, and necessary, the dominance of French military power. The Franche-Comté he took from the king of Spain in 1678. In the period following the Peace of Nijmegen, a number of smaller annexations, under the title of "reunions," deprived some small lordships of their independence, and gave the alarm to Germany, so much of which, while it was disunited, consisted of states as powerless as those annexed. The unprovoked capture of the very important imperial city of Strassburg, placing France in a position to impose its will upon South Germany, was the climax of these seizures. The Holy Roman Empire, a loose collection of states large and small, was in no condition to resist at that time, the year 1681, or to assist Spain later, when the Spanish Netherlands were diminished by the occupation in time of peace of Courtrai and Luxemburg.

Spain and the Empire were shown to be defenseless — Spain distressed by financial difficulties and the misgovernment attendant upon the reign of an invalid king; the Emperor distracted by a long war with the Turks, during which the capital of his hereditary dominions was besieged by the enemy. The impotence of these powers was the worse in that England would not or could not honor her agreements with the offended nations: Charles II did not desire a parliament to meet before his brother's succession had been secured, for fear that that succession might be prevented, and because he was bound by secret ties to the aggressor, who supplied from the French treasury the money lost to Charles by his persistence in rule without check by the money-granting body of the country. And when the states on the continent sought to bind themselves together, England's inaction made doubtful the adherence of the Dutch. In a way, then, a union of interest and vindictive sentiments led other governments than that of France to greet the fall of James II with satisfaction, because James was seen as the successor of Charles in his Francophil sympathies. It was to be one of the bitterest complaints of the Catholic Jacobites, that the Pope himself, being consulted before it occurred, acquiesced in the overthrow of England's last Catholic king.[1]

The subjects of the king had their own quite independent motives in departing from the traditional hereditary succession, to which probably a great majority of the population had been committed at one time. It is to be observed that the Catholic rulers of Spain, Savoy, and the Empire, and the Protestant re-public of the Netherlands were united by extra-religious consid-erations against the hyper-Catholic Louis XIV, who was himself the accomplice of the Turk, and the Catholic James II, whom the other powers regarded as a French satellite. The English, on the other hand, were alienated from their king by his views on religious subjects, i.e., the relative positions of the Anglican and Roman Catholic communions — views some of which incidentally appeared to involve unconstitutional action.

To this state of mind the English were brought from the one more general at the accession of James II, when, furnishing an index of popular feeling, the unfortunate, and undeserving, Monmouth landed in the West, received only local and ineffec-tual support, and saw his misled supporters bloodily routed and herded off to execution or transportation. Not only could this be, but it has even yet to be shown that the merciless suppres-sion of the "Bloody Assizes" led to an immediate revulsion. Only a few, acquainted with the leniency of an earlier time, remarked, as did Robert Harley, that not one was pardoned.[2] James II might have been as well established in popular favor as ever his brother Charles had been, had he been contented with that, but he would not be condescended to with toleration: he would set the course of the nation for himself, and he would have no interference by either Parliament or the Church of England with matters which he reserved for himself. The affair of Magdalen College, the Declaration of Indulgence, the trial of

---

[1] Carte MS. 231, fol. 31–a v.
[2] Historical Manuscripts Commission (henceforth to be cited as H.M.C.) *Report* XIV, appendix, part III, 388.

the seven Anglican bishops, and the disagreeable use of the writs of *quo warranto* to fill municipal governing bodies with his own sympathizers have all been discussed beyond my limits by greatly gifted historians of many schools. A general field of agreement exists that James II threw away an opportunity to rule England well and with good will for the gaining of politico-religious ends — Catholic schools, suspension of anti-Catholic penal laws, Anglican consent to the enlargement of the bounds of Catholic life, and the recall of charters oppressive to Catholics of the boroughs. His haste aroused fear: among Whigs that his power would execute a political persecution; among Tories that a religious persecution would be the reward of conscientious obedience. These fears were a powerful cohesive agent among the otherwise disunited and mutually exclusive parties for a joint opposition to the king.

The birth of James II's son, the Prince of Wales, whose succession might be expected to prolong the period of arbitrary and Catholic rule beyond the king's own lifetime, occurred in the midst of the excitement which accompanied the trial of the bishops and, by increasing it, precipitated the fall of his father. There is now no doubt of the legitimacy of the child, since much evidence, and that not trivial, has been found to set against the foolish, but effective, charge that he was brought to the queen, who was counterfeiting childbirth, in a warming pan.[3] The boy was to be educated as a Catholic, of course, now that James was his own master. Mary, Princess of Orange, and Anne, Princess of Denmark, half-sisters to the young prince, had both been reared as Protestants by Charles II, and had been married to Protestants. It was the hope of the Anglicans, alarmed by the events of the years 1686 to 1688, that one of these ladies would succeed their father, and restore the established church to its former position.

The prospect of a Catholic heir was repugnant to the heiresses-presumptive, as well as to the populace, for religious reasons; for Mary and Anne were as devout in their religious views as James

[3] Judith Collingwood's declaration, April 12, 1713, printed in C. E. Lart, *Parochial Registers of Saint-Germain-en-Laye* (London, 1910–12), II, 141–42. See also H.M.C. *Report* XIII, app. II, 53.

was in his. Time had led the princesses to expect the throne as the right of one or other of them; the number of brothers and half-brothers whom they had seen to be born, to decline, and to die under the vigorous care of the royal nurses had seemed to establish a prescription. It was a blow to be put from the throne by a child, a half-brother, and a Catholic too. Anne, the younger, could not be a direct danger to her brother's right, although she added her spite to the irritation of her co-religionists; [4] Mary, on the other hand, was married to a foreign prince, William of Orange, whose power, though limited, was truly the determining factor in Dutch politics, since he was the leader of the anti-French party in the United Provinces at a time when the opposed group had suffered an eclipse. He himself was near to the English throne by right of his mother, an English princess, and his desire to rule England is susceptible of underestimation. William was in a position, granted control of Great Britain, to form an alliance of which, as the principal influence in the policies of two of the great contracting parties, he would be the acknowledged head. He may have felt himself to be "a man with a mission," although his mission would have been a different one from that imagined by insular Church Tories of his time, or by equally insular Whigs, but he was elevated by his mission to the highest offices in two nations, and to a commanding power in European affairs.

James's behavior during the period of invasion only deepened the slough of distrust in which he wallowed: he called Parliament and revoked the call when he thought the danger to his throne ended by the temporary return of William's invasion fleet to port; he grudgingly reinstated the displaced fellows of Magdalen College; he dismissed Sunderland without giving his confidence to the sounder Secretary of State, Lord Middleton; finally he mishandled his army and saw his generals desert with large sections of it to the camp of the Prince of Orange. After this he returned to London, disbanded his army, and ran away, having previously sent to France his queen and his son, in the care of a Frenchman, the comte de Lauzun, who was present in

[4] Campana de Cavelli, ed., *Les derniers Stuarts à Saint-Germain-en-Laye* (Paris, 1871), II, 156.

England as an observer of the French foreign minister,[5] and who undertook what no Protestant Englishman would risk his life to do. James may have thrown the Great Seal of England into the Thames, but there is some doubt about that.[6] Brought back from arrest in Kent, where his attempt to escape had miscarried, he made off again, against the advice of his most faithful friends, on January 2 N.S., 1689. Two days later he landed at Ambleteuse in France. Here begins the history of Jacobitism.

2. MELFORT IN IRELAND

The danger of revolution had led some of the best-known Catholics to leave Great Britain before James. One of the first was John Drummond, Earl of Melfort, formerly Secretary of State in Scotland.[7] Lauzun retrieved his lost favor at the French court when he brought over Queen Maria near Christmas time.[8] The queen was a prize to Louis: if the King of England were to change his plans and send for his family to return to England, Louis intended that it should nevertheless be brought on to Vincennes; [9] use as political hostages was possible, perhaps by collusion with King James, who told Rizzini that one of his motives in sending his family away was "to have a legitimate subterfuge for never consenting to war against France." [10]

After the king's own departure many others followed: the Duke of Berwick, the Marquess of Powis, Lords Dover and Dumbarton, Admiral Strickland, and Charles Skelton.[11] Of these runaways, for the most part Catholics, there was formed a court at Saint-Germain-en-Laye, a former French royal palace not much used since the occupancy of Henrietta Maria of England during the Interregnum, to which place, as closer to Versailles,

---

[5] *Mémoires de St.-Simon*, ed. A. de Boislisle (Paris, 1879–1928), I, 122–125; Campana de Cavelli, II, 255n.

[6] Sir Hilary Jenkinson, "What happened to the Great Seal of James II," *Journal of the Society of Antiquaries of London*, 23:1–13 (April 1943).

[7] *Journal du marquis de Dangeau*, ed. Soulié (Paris, 1854–60), II, 231.

[8] *Ibid.*, II, 234; Campana de Cavelli, II, 427, 462.

[9] Campana de Cavelli, II, 453. The letter is misdated December 1 for January 1.

[10] *Ibid.*, II, 413.

[11] *Ibid.*, II, 461, 465; Dangeau, II, 297, 301, 311.

Louis XIV shifted the intended residence of his royal guests from Vincennes. With the court, James set up a government. As early as January 21 the Earl of Melfort entered into relations with the French court as a principal Secretary of State.[12]

It was intended almost from the first to win the revolted kingdoms back; the arrival of envoys of Tyrconnel, James's commander in Ireland, with assurances of loyalty for himself and the Catholic population[13] probably decided James to begin there. In anticipation of the attempt, Skelton and Colonel James Porter were sent on missions to the Emperor and Pope, begging for help from these Catholic rulers to their fellow Catholic in the reconquest of his dominions.[14] There was no mention of reconciliation.

King James, Lord Melfort, and an ambassador accredited to the government in Ireland by Louis XIV, the comte d'Avaux,[15] took ship at Brest, and arrived at Kinsale on March 11/21, 1689, proceeding in state to Dublin, where they made a public entrance on April 3. An Irish parliament was summoned to meet on May 7; but before the meeting the king desired to go north to the camp near Londonderry, to direct the siege of the principal remaining Protestant stronghold in Ireland. Tyrconnel and d'Avaux were opposed to this movement, because the king might lose prestige if he were compelled to raise the siege, and in any case would expose himself to needless danger. Promising to go no further than Armagh, James journeyed northward, then broke his word and went to Londonderry. The siege was broken up as had been predicted, but the king turned south again before that happened.[16]

This matter was the first cause of serious disagreement between Tyrconnel and d'Avaux on the one hand, and Melfort, who now possessed the king's confidence, on the other. D'Avaux had come to Ireland with instructions not completely in agreement with the Irish national and Catholic views which Tyrconnel

---

[12] Campana de Cavelli, II, 473.
[13] Dangeau, II, 329.
[14] Ibid., II, 333; Campana de Cavelli, II, 489.
[15] Instructions to D'Avaux, printed in James Hogan, Les Négociations de M. le comte d'Avaux en Irlande, 1689-90 (Dublin, 1934), 1.
[16] Ibid., 59, 85-86, 104.

held; particularly it was his duty to see that James was dissuaded from upsetting the Irish land compromise embodied in the Act of Settlement [17] of Charles II because of the great numbers of persons who would be alienated by having their land rights thrown into doubt by any disturbance of it. Yet Tyrconnel was the obvious balance to the strength of Melfort, whose policies were even further removed from those of the French king, and Tyrconnel was the obvious ally in the displacement of Melfort.

Melfort,[18] the younger brother of James, Earl of Perth,[19] had been prominent in Scotland for many years, particularly as Secretary of State while his brother was Chancellor. Under James II, the two brothers, both Catholic converts, had had influence in Scottish affairs far beyond that justified by their capacities or popularity. Melfort himself was an absolutist in upbringing and assumed quite naturally the headship, once in exile, of a bigoted and uncompromising group which was later to find the name of "non-Compounders." In Scotland he was so unpopular that his signature on a royal document in 1689 put "at least ten thousand hands out of the King's way," according to Lord Dundee. "Odious and insufferable . . . to his own Countrymen," was the description of Melfort appended by Thomas Sheridan.[20] The Irish detested Melfort for his argument that James II should so govern in Ireland, and so handle his army there, that he could with the least disadvantage transport it and himself to Scotland or England and conquer those nations as quickly as possible. To this argument Tyrconnel was directly opposed, as a subordination of Irish policy to English, with neglect of Irish interests as a necessary consequence.

The Irish parliament was Tyrconnel's ally, as some of its members were his puppets. The majority was Catholic, more than half of the Lords being absent, and was determined to establish an Irish Catholic predominance in Irish affairs. In James's

---

[17] *Ibid.*, 31.
[18] Born ca. 1650; created Earl of Melfort 1686; died January 1715.
[19] He was the fourth earl, and lived from 1648 to 1716.
[20] "Political Reflexions on the History and Government of England" (a MS. tract preserved at Windsor Castle), fol. 88. For Sheridan's authorship of this tract, see Appendix.

council Melfort, Tyrconnel, and d'Avaux, all Catholics, though disagreeing on some measures, drew up and presented for consideration acts which made that settlement certain.[21] Here d'Avaux followed French interests, to which an immediate and effective Irish diversion was desirable, whatever might happen in England as a result. Melfort and the king were somewhat at odds with this, because they wished to use Ireland as a stepping stone into Great Britain, but since the French support asked for [22] was not immediately forthcoming, they humored the Irish, and allowed the passage of the Irish legislation.

An act declaring the indefeasible right of the hereditary succession [23] was passed in the king's presence,[24] and probably with his complete approval. It contradicted the contract theory of government, posited the doctrines of divine right and non-resistance, and made a special point of affirming the king's absolute right to the command of the army, militia, and strong places as necessary to the obedience due to the king's "natural Person . . . within all Your Majesties Realms and Dominions." England's legislature had often given the law to Ireland; here was Ireland making a vengeful return. Unwise as it was, this act had the sanction of the small council which determined most measures of this parliament; the destruction of the Act of Settlement did not, but was passed regardless of the king's desire that ownership of land be left alone.[25] Even in his least perceptive frame of mind, James was aware that prominent Englishmen owning land in Ireland under the security of the Caroline act would be estranged from the cause of a monarch who brought, besides notions of government and religion which they did not like, chaos to the established system of property. Moreover, this repeal was an obstacle to the activities of James's friends in England, such as Lord Preston, already coming to be called "Jaco-

---

[21] Hogan, 89.
[22] Ibid., 61.
[23] Carte MSS. 181, foll. 60–63v.
[24] J. S. Clarke, ed., Life of James II, King of England . . . Writ of his own Hand, (London, 1816), II, 355–56.
[25] Charles O'Kelly, "Macariae Excidium," ed. T. C. Croker, Narratives Illustrative of the Contests in Ireland, (London, 1841), 30.

bites"; the money allowed them by King Louis for the cost of printed sheets and other expenses was thus wasted.[26]

In Scotland there was no need for secret activity, since a portion of James II's supporters had taken arms for him. The Revolution in England was followed at a short distance by one in Scotland, completed with a convention which made itself into a parliament (although the Scottish Convention Parliament, lacking a Triennial Act, sat for many years). This irregular assembly met at Edinburgh on March 14, 1689, but was so evenly divided that it was not at first apparent that the English Revolution would succeed in Scotland. Balcarres relates that the turning point was the arrival of a messenger named Crane on the third day of the session, with a letter from King James himself. The Jacobites, he says, were overjoyed, and crowded to hear the reading of the letter which they expected to be written "in terms suitable to the bad situation," but found it to be "Earl Melfort's hand and style," and fell into a tumult — "your [James's] enemies in joy and your friends in confusion." [27] Crane was ignorant, or pretended ignorance, of the reasons for the tone of the letter. The loyalists gave up hope of carrying the Convention and abandoned it; Balcarres, Lord Dundee, and the archbishop of Glasgow, empowered by a warrant from their master, called a new Convention to meet at Stirling [28] which the exigencies of the following months did not permit to meet anywhere or at all. The Duke of Gordon continued to hold the Castle of Edinburgh for a time in the name of "the old king," but eventually made terms.

Dundee summoned the Jacobites to arms, and began the campaign which ended with his life at Killiecrankie in July 1689. The Edinburgh rump continued to sit, and accomplished the Scottish Revolution: the new succession, the establishment of Presbyterianism, the abolition of the Lords of the Articles, and other measures to make the new order safe. Military action was still necessary, even after the death of Dundee. General Mackay, commanding the "Williamite" troops in Scotland, was opposed,

---

[26] Hogan, 16.
[27] *Memoirs touching the Revolution in Scotland, MDCLXXXVIII–MDCXC* (Edinburgh, 1841), 27–28.
[28] *Ibid.*, 29.

more than by the ability of his antagonists, by public sentiment in some parts of Scotland, especially the Highlands, and by disloyal subordinates of his own.[29] He commanded the Highlanders to submit, and was told to imitate General Monk; he mustered the heritors of Moray, and found them "not so fond of the change as might reasonably be expected of men so newly delivered from the greatest of all evils, temporal and eternal slavery." [30] Nevertheless, for lack of money and other support, General Buchan, the successor of Dundee, found it even harder to keep the field. At last, James allowed the loyal clans and his other friends to make terms.

In Ireland, James tried to do what he thought would keep up a party in Scotland, sending emissaries there at the beginning of the Killiecrankie campaign with copies of a declaration issued on April 1.[31] It was not vague, but all too clear, in promising to maintain the Protestant Church on its Episcopal footing, as established at the Restoration — a promise of dubious utility to his own side — and excepting from pardon "such as have voted against Us, Our Authority, and Right, or for the Prince of Orange in that late and illegal Convention held at Edenborough on the fourteenth of March." The declaration contained no promises to make new friends, and alienated some of the less loyal old ones by its obstinate tone. The counter-signature of Melfort contributed its share of irritation once more.

In April the French-Irish coalition in the small council was consummated by an agreement that Tyrconnel and his supporters were to consult d'Avaux before the execution of any measure.[32] Melfort's opposition to this combination was stubborn, and d'Avaux finally told Louis XIV that the employment of the earl was a disadvantage to the common cause.[33] Melfort, he said later, excited the opposition of the Duke of Gordon and the Earl of Seaforth by omitting to send them commissions in a general

[29] Hugh Mackay, *Memoirs of the War carried on in Scotland and Ireland, MDCLXXXIX–MDCXCI* (Edinburgh, 1833), 11, 37–38.

[30] *Ibid.*, 15, 19.

[31] Declaration to Scotland, Dublin, April 1, 1689. A copy is fol. 424 of Carte MSS. 181. See also Hogan, 48–49.

[32] D'Avaux to Louis XIV, Dublin, April 14, 1689, in Hogan, 54–55.

[33] *Ibid.*, 75, 104.

distribution he had made to the king's friends; this opposition was quickly communicated to their relatives and dependents. Moreover, the French general in Ireland, Rosen, found that Melfort was a poor supply officer, promising troops and arms when he could not send them or, Rosen thought, when he intended to neglect sending them.[34]

For the general confusion that Ireland presented to the eye in those days, Melfort seemed as much as any one person, and much more than was safe for himself, to be responsible, although it is now more difficult than it was to hold fixed opinions. At last, the Duke of Tyrconnel "had a petition presented to the king in the name of the Irish nation, demanding the removal of Melfort from the scene. The king, under the circumstances, believed that he could not refuse it to a nation which supported his interests so nobly. . . . Melfort was then sent to France, and from there to Rome, to reside as the king's minister at the Pope's court. The Chevalier Nagle, an Irishman and Attorney-General, was given the post of Secretary of State at the desire of Tyrconnel." So writes the Duke of Berwick.[35]

That is the short of it: Colonel Porter, later Vice-Chamberlain at St.-Germain, had been recalled from Rome on the advice of Louis XIV that his expensive maintenance contributed to no useful end.[36] Various persons, including Dundee, many members of the Irish parliament, Tyrconnel, and d'Avaux, having represented their dissatisfaction with Melfort as Secretary of State for Ireland, the earl was replaced by William Talbot, a nephew of Tyrconnel, in that post in July.[37] After this, d'Avaux redoubled his efforts to obtain Melfort's withdrawal from Ireland, where he remained too close to the king: he accused the earl of insufferable vanity, of faithlessness, and of negligence.[38] At last he obtained, or received without collusion, a *mémoire* outlining the malice and incompetence of the minister, supposed to have been written by an Irishman, which he had presented to James II at

[34] Rosen wrote to James II twice on this subject, on June 6 and July 10, 1689. Carte MSS. 181, foll. 197v, 198; foll. 214v–215v.
[35] Berwick, *Mémoires* (Paris, 1778), I, 86–87.
[36] Hogan, 178.
[37] *Ibid.*, 248–49; Carte MSS. 181, foll. 298–99.
[38] Hogan, 289, 293.

Dublin.[39] This may have been Berwick's petition presented by Tyrconnel. At the end of August the continued agitation against the minister was quieted by the resignation of his general powers, and the appointment of Sir Richard Nagle, formerly Attorney-General for Ireland, a member of the Irish Catholic faction.[40] On the evening of September 4, Melfort sailed from Ireland for France, not as envoy to Rome, but to Versailles.[41] D'Avaux thought his removal too late, and that on his reaching St.-Germain he would be the author of "new broils to be commenced on strands afar remote," [42] to steal a phrase; so well did the ambassador foresee the effect of Melfort's enraged descent on St.-Germain and Versailles. He could not predict the eventual relegation of the graceless fellow to Rome,[43] where Porter's mission had proved unprofitable, and where the post had been promised to Porter if it should again be held at all.[44] The chief profit, it seems fair to say, was in the removal of Melfort from scenes where he could do harm, without hurting James II, with whom the displaced minister was still in favor.

In title he remained Principal Secretary of State, and his activity in that office did not entirely lapse. What could have been the reasons for the prolongation of his influence can only be guessed. It seems that flattery, officiousness, and subservience to the king's exalted conception of prerogative played a great part both in keeping the earl in power beyond his time and in obtaining his later return to his master's court. That his conduct was generally hateful to his equals and subordinates is witnessed by his own admitted fear when he left Ireland that he would be assassinated by the Irish.[45]

He had, however, maintained relations with the loyalists in England, and had attempted to gratify the desire of the king to conciliate the Protestant interest in Ireland for the effects which

[39] *Ibid.*, 335–38.
[40] D'Avaux to Louis XIV, Dublin, Aug. 30, 1689, *ibid.*, 429.
[41] Melfort's warrant as envoy to France is dated Aug. 23 O.S., 1689. Entry book M 18 Windsor Stuart Papers (henceforth cited as W. S. P.), entry 58.
[42] Hogan, 434, 441.
[43] Clarke, II, 388–89; Melfort to James II, St.-Germain, Oct. 25, 1689, Carte MSS. 181, fol. 378v.
[44] Hogan, 533; Dangeau, III, 34–35.
[45] Hogan, 509.

could be expected of such a conciliation elsewhere. Preston and others distributed sheets to capture the English reading public, exhausting the funds first obtained for that purpose on such expostulations against the Revolution as "A letter from an absent Lord to one of his Friends at the Convention"; "A letter from a Gentleman in the Country . . . concerning the Coronation medal," and "A Letter from a Clergy-man of the Church of England to an Eminent Divine" — all dispersed in 1689.[46] Lord Dover, going over to France in July to ask King Louis to extend the war into England, was instructed to ask for more money for papers.[47] It is not certain whether Melfort's influence or a self-assertion of James II was responsible for the restraining order issued to the commanders of forts and garrisons in Ireland,[48] forbidding the execution of the rigorous commands of Rosen for the expulsion of all former supporters of William III from their homes. This order drew severe criticism from Rosen,[49] who was used to less merciful methods in France, and should, if known, have had corresponding praise from Englishmen. If Melfort was the author of it, he was wiser than he was generally believed to be. The Earl of Ailesbury, at any rate, apologizes for Melfort, and Dundee, in the very moment of asking him to resign, deplored the necessity of thus complying with public opinion. He was not "insufferable" to these two; it is odd that he had no better gift for pleasing the generality.

3. SCOTLAND AND IRELAND BEFORE THE BOYNE

D'Avaux was probably right in his belief that Melfort's dismissal came too late. In the following months the rapid decline of Jacobite fortunes was not stayed. The root of the trouble was that those who replaced Melfort were no more capable or farsighted than he had been.

With the change in the Irish secretaryship, for instance, the way was clear for acts of the Irish Parliament to inaugurate a new system in its own country. James had promised in a declaration

---

[46] Copies of these are bound in the Bodleian Library volume Antiq. C.E. 9.
[47] Carte MSS. 181, foll. 252–56.
[48] Carte MSS. 209, fol. 24.
[49] Carte MSS. 181, fol. 212.

dated May 18, 1689,[50] that he would institute a general toleration, leaving his Protestant subjects in quiet. His Parliament, however, curtailed the stipends of Protestant incumbents of livings in Catholic sections of Ireland, authorizing payment only in proportion to the Protestant population served by the clergymen concerned. Of course, in conditions of civil war, most of the Protestant clergy probably received no pay at all, making the act of no practical significance; on paper, nevertheless, English Protestants saw what they anticipated to be the future of the whole Anglican establishment.

In their anxiety to settle Ireland once and for all on a Catholic bottom, the extremists of Parliament did far too much. Abolishing order does not create stability. Whether or not it was just to revoke the Caroline Act of Settlement, and throw most titles to land into dispute — another ill-judged action of the time — it was unwise to do away with the principal taxpaying class, the landowners, at the moment when money was most necessary; and those who acquired land in one way or another as a result of the revocation had often no money to pay. The problematical permanence of any landholding in Ireland rendered unlikely the prompt and full payment of taxes in any case. Because of this and other mistakes, the financial straits of King James compelled him to coin base metals, and threw him into dependence upon the King of France for help.

Again, a far-reaching and comprehensive Bill of Attainder was passed, and had results which need not be weighed. Two thousand individuals of all ranks, from the Duke of Ormonde to the lowest members of society, were attainted, and their property confiscated, whether or not they presented themselves voluntarily for trial, as some of them, by the terms of the Act, were to be allowed to do. A great reinforcement of anti-Catholic feeling, which already existed in too formidable strength in England, was to be expected, and did in fact occur. James II is usually given credit for resisting these measures; it is only just to say that Louis XIV himself was much against them at the time.[51] But there was no way for the English to know this, and it did not avail to send agents to Eng-

---

[50] Clarke, II, 362–65.
[51] Louis XIV to d'Avaux, March 12, 1689, Hogan, 31.

land to reach understandings with former Revolutioners for the security of their lives and goods [52] when life and goods, it seemed plain to all, were unsafe in the only one of the three kingdoms still under Stuart rule.

In Great Britain, however, a semblance of a reaction did take place, in the shape of plotting. Some of the loyal (that is, Jacobite) lords and gentlemen of Scotland who had not taken the field under Dundee combined with an unscrupulous group of former supporters of the Revolution — known as "the Club" — with the purpose of leading the Scottish Parliament back to its old allegiance. The Club seems never to have been interested in any aspect of the proposed counterstroke except the establishment of a monopoly of places. Nevil Payne, an agent often encountered in the intrigues of the earliest years of Jacobitism, convinced Sir James Montgomery and Lords Annandale and Ross that he could "dispose of money, forces, and titles of honour as he pleased"; these men and the Earl of Arran, son of the Duchess of Hamilton and later Duke himself, professed devotion to the king in Ireland and to his queen (a devotion which might not have been expected from past conduct), who herself managed this affair from St.-Germain through Payne. Sincere supporters — Francis Turner, deprived Bishop of Ely, the Earls of Ailesbury [53] and Clarendon,[54] and a Mr. "As——," almost certainly Captain John Ashton, joined the Scottish group with misgivings. Ashton undertook to convey plans and instructions from England to France and back again.

The Club overreached itself by failing to distribute prospective rewards equitably among the other conspirators,[55] and by promising more that it could perform — a parliamentary restoration of James II. When sincere Jacobites learned the extent to which they were kept from knowledge of promises made and correspondence carried on in their names, "few of us desired to have more to do with Sir James [Montgomery]," said Lord Balcarres; they ceased to take part in Montgomery's parliamentary machina-

[52] *Ibid.*, 197–98.
[53] Thomas Bruce, Earl of Ailesbury (1656–1741).
[54] Henry Hyde, Earl of Clarendon (1638–1709).
[55] They offered nothing to Lords Dunmore, Linlithgow, and Breadalbane, the chief figures in the plot besides those named.

tions. Thereupon the three principal members of the Club posted off to London to betray the men whom they could no longer delude.[56] Their revelations led to a number of arrests in the summer of 1690,[57] but Payne's stubbornness under the torture inflicted in accord with Scottish law made convictions doubtful; the removal of James II from Ireland allowed the government to release the prisoners without danger to itself.[58]

Those in charge of Ireland were, perhaps, as unscrupulous, and certainly as incompetent as the Club. D'Avaux, Tyrconnel, and Nagle were the king's advisers at first, but the able French envoy was shortly recalled by a court faction at Versailles which took Melfort's side. Tyrconnel's character is well known: his intrigue with Louis XIV for supremacy in Ireland, even as a satrap of France,[59] revealed his essential lack of loyalty except to himself. Nagle, though a very honest man, as d'Avaux said,[60] had had no experience in political or military affairs at all. Talbot, Tyrconnel's nephew, appears to have been almost a cipher. The state of the army and of Irish politics therefore deteriorated rapidly in the last months of 1689, in spite of the arrival of Lauzun with French troops, exchanged for an equal number of untrained Irish sent to serve in France.[61] On William's side, Marshal Schomberg, with a Protestant army, also landed in Ireland in 1689 and commenced operations; Jacobite circles in London became aware in January 1690 that King William was expected to take the field,[62] but he did not depart until June.

The campaign leading up to the battle of the Boyne need not be described here. The kingdom of Ireland may be said to have changed hands by that battle; but it would be a mistake to forget

[56] Annandale's confession is printed in Sir John Dalrymple's *Memoirs of Great Britain and Ireland* (London, 1771–88), II, part 2, 101–106.

[57] Those sought were Lord Montgomery (not Sir James), Lords Clarendon, Yarmouth, Griffin, Castlemaine, Ailesbury, Lichfield, Preston, and Bellasis, Sir John Fenwick, Sir Edward Hales, Lords Hume and Oxenfoord of Scotland, and William Penn the Quaker.

[58] This account is drawn from Balcarres, 51–67; Dalrymple, I, part 2, 121–29; and Clarendon's "Diary, 1687–90," printed in *The Correspondence of Henry Hyde, Earl of Clarendon. . . ,* S. W. Singer, ed. (London, 1828), II, 300–25.

[59] Hogan, 87–88.

[60] *Ibid.,* 429. See also Berwick, I, 87.

[61] Hogan, 85–86, 284–86, 515.

[62] Clarendon, *Correspondence,* II, 300.

that the outcome had been predetermined to a great extent by the relative success of the two kings. Thus, if James had not been beaten at the Boyne, he would have been beaten elsewhere, because he had managed his resources so poorly — unless Louis XIV could have come to his aid with forces larger than could have been spared from the other theatres of the War of the League of Augsburg. After the battle, James fled to Dublin, and there may have considered his future. Although the situation in Ireland seemed hopeless, the fortunes of France were flourishing. Its army had met with an encouraging success at Fleurus, and its fleet, commanded by the comte de Tourville, had temporary control of the English Channel since the victory of Beachy Head. James had always sought an opportunity to cross into England or Scotland; here it seemed to be. The author of the latter part of James II's *Life* says that a message inviting the defeated king to head an expedition was sent by the marquis de Seignelay.[63] Be that as it may, James sailed as soon as he could, and disembarked at Brest on July 20, 1690. He left the Irish campaign behind him to die away in the hands of Tyrconnel and Lauzun and be terminated by the Treaty of Limerick. He believed the end of his troubles to be near, but he never saw any part of his dominions again.

Why nothing was done for him in 1690 is not clear. Tourville, while he controlled the sea, did not use his power to the best advantage; but whether it was because he was timid (an unlikely conjecture) or because he had no authority is of no importance to us. Berwick, James II's illegitimate son, attributed French inactivity to the hostility existing between Louvois, the French minister of war, and Seignelay, the minister of the navy.[64] Thomas Sheridan, who is, unfortunately, as dubious a source as he is an independent one, adds to the rather bare version of Berwick the detail that Louvois was unfriendly to James because the king had preferred Lauzun to Louvois' own son, for whom an early promotion was planned according to the nepotist principles of the day.[65]

[63] J. S. Clarke, ed., II, 407–409. The author of this part of the *Life* is not certainly known, but was probably William Dicconson, a prominent Jacobite with some independent knowledge of events. Berwick (I, 73–75) tells the same general story, omitting mention of the message.

[64] Berwick, I, 74–75.

[65] MS. "Political Reflexions," fol. 88.

Louvois had bred two sons to arms, the marquis de Courtenvaux and the marquis de Souvré.[66] There is no doubt that interference with their careers would make Louvois an enemy. On the other hand, almost any invasion of the minister's department would probably have had the same effect. The jealousy of the families of Le Tellier (Louvois) and Colbert (Seignelay) were also notorious: James II and his son alike were particularly close to members of the latter house over a period of many years. Out of these considerations, no doubt, arose the obstacle to an invasion of England, favored as it was by Seignelay. James's pleas were insistent, but vain. He returned to St.-Germain, and not long after commenced a time of unresigned quiet by his first retreat at La Trappe, the home of the austerities which he was to practise during the remaining years of his life.

4. LA HOGUE

In this melancholy state of mind, discredited by defeat in Ireland, impoverished by the cessation of all revenue except a French pension of 600,000 livres a year, and hurt by Louis XIV's refusal to help him further, at least for the present, James created a sort of court, in which Henry Browne,[67] Father Lewis Inese,[68] or Innes, and Sir Richard Nagle are said to have had the posts of Secretaries of State for England, Scotland, and Ireland, respectively. It should be noticed that the most important ministers of the exiled Stuarts henceforth hold the title of Secretary of State. John Caryll, secretary to the queen, and John Stafford, a former ambassador to Spain, are supposed to have been the other members of a council consulted on matters of state.[69] Melfort's favor was not

[66] E. Spanheim, *Relation de la cour de France*, Ch. Schefer, ed. (Paris, 1882), 199.

[67] Henry Browne (1641–1717) later made his peace with William III and became in 1708 the fifth Viscount Montagu.

[68] Lewis Inese, Rector of the Scots College at Paris, eldest of three brothers connected with that house. Cosmo, another of these, attained some fame as an ecclesiastical historian of Scotland.

[69] John Macky, *Memoirs of the Secret Services of John Macky, Esq.* (London, 1733), xxvii–xxviii. Macky has been formerly a principal source for St.-Germain in the early years, but his bias is obvious and his book lacks detail except where Macky himself is concerned.

disturbed by this development. He continued to give good and bad advice from Rome on all subjects, but particularly on Scotland. This "shadow court," or government in exile, had for its scope relations with other governments (that is, with the governments of France and its allies, the only ones which recognized James), the conduct of operations to rouse the spirits and confirm the faith of old Jacobites, and to make new ones, the direction of intelligence missions for the King of France, and making plans for the eventual overthrow of the Revolutionary regime.

The winter of 1690–1691 saw the detection of a more serious plot than that of the previous summer. A party of Protestant Jacobites, for the most part Anglicans who had opposed the Revolution, with a number of Revolutioners who thought that the Revolution had gone too far, had formed during the preceding months and found for themselves the name "Compounders," signifying that they desired to see the restoration of James II upon satisfactory terms.[70] Die-hards who favored the restoration of absolutism were called in contradistinction "non-Compounders." Some Compounders — Clarendon, Preston, and the deprived Bishop Turner — had been involved in the disclosures of the summer; others, like Ormonde and Lord Dartmouth, are mentioned as Jacobites now for the first time. They met secretly to mull over possible conditions under which they would work for a restoration, then dispatched Lord Preston and Captain Ashton from London to carry their proposals to France. Unhappily, the two were captured aboard ship on December 31/January 10, 1690/1, and their papers seized. Preston was frightened, and confessed: Clarendon, Turner, and William Penn,[71] he said, were members of the group, and Penn had told him that Ormonde, Dartmouth, the Earls of Devonshire, Macclesfield, and Dorset, with Macclesfield's son Lord Brandon, were also involved. Several Scotsmen — Lord Tarbat

---

[70] For the composition of this group see the *Calendar of State Papers, Domestic, 1690–91*, 282–83.

[71] A great deal of effort has been devoted to the exculpation of Penn. Preston knew, when he revealed his secrets, who Penn was, and had no motive, so far as I can see, for hurting him. If we are to believe that Preston lied, we must have evidence that he did so, or at least reasons why he might have done so which would not apply to all of those he accused. Acquittal of Penn on his general character alone will not do.

and the deprived Bishop of Glasgow among them — were implicated by the testimony of John Macky, a spy. Ashton confessed nothing, and once more there was too little evidence to shed noble blood, but Ashton was made a scapegoat and put to death. He was the first to suffer by judicial process, and was the cause of the first blood feud between the Jacobites and others, as we shall see.[72]

The purport of the messages was an important thing, and may well have alarmed the government by showing that a number of well-connected moderates were dissatisfied with the new settlement. It was precisely the moderate element that William and Mary had tried to cultivate in their reign so far. King James was not to return a conqueror, by these terms. If he brought foreign troops to England, he was to engage to send them away again as quickly as possible. He was to promise "to settle liberty of conscience by law," and to leave old grievances against him to the determination of a free Parliament. As immediate conciliatory steps, James was asked to be kind to Protestants at St.-Germain, to obtain permission for them to have their own religious services there, and not to allow casual correspondence from England to France — that is, to limit authority as the king's agents to chosen spokesmen of the compounding group.[73] This unpalatable advice James first received by the public prints, since the messages were quickly published, but, as a sign of disunion in the Revolution party, it must have been even more distressing to King William.[74] The plot being broken, the government took measures for its own safety, and an interval of quiet followed. The Compounders did not break up, however.

Perhaps some sign of a change in the disposition of the French court was responsible for the recall of Melfort from Rome in July 1691.[75] The earl took his leave of the Pope late in August,[76] and returned to France and to his functions as Secretary, for a draft

[72] I draw this account from the Life of James II (II, 441–43), Dalrymple (I, part 2, 169), and J. McCormick, ed., State Papers Addressed to William Carstares (Edinburgh, 1774), 128–30.

[73] Nicholas Tindal, Continuation of P. Rapin de Thoyras' History of England (London, 1745), III, 167n.

[74] Cf. Dalrymple, I, part 2, 162.

[75] James II to Innocent XII, St.-Germain, July 30, 1691. Carte MSS. 181, fol. 425. An English draft or translation is fol. 426.

[76] Carte MSS. 181, foll. 396–402v.

declaration and preamble written in mid-September [77] show his influence. The preamble defers "descending into particulars" until the meeting of a "free Parliament"; the declaration praises James's own "Princely Wisdome and Compassionate Care," and engages that he will "Sedately examine every thing where in the Subject hath thought himself agreived" in Parliament. James clearly meant to be judge of his own cause. Indeed, he seems not to have thought of his contention with the bulk of the nation as being between two equal parties. As it happens, these documents were not used, and it was just as well, for little good could have come of it.

At that time a man named Lunt, who testified in the trials at Manchester in 1694, was in Lancashire; he said later that he was employed in enlisting men for the Jacobites. If he was not a sincere Jacobite, he certainly made his living by pretending to be one. In November, he deposed at the later trial, he went over to France for instructions at the request of his Jacobite friends. He said that James told him "that he did not doubt but, the spring following, to be in a condition to come for England." With this word Lunt was in London, according to the deposition, in December 1691, while at the same time, or not long after, certain officers came over from France with commissions for themselves and others. In the following months there were meetings involving many of the most prominent Lancashire gentry.[78] At the trials referred to, Lunt's testimony was riddled by cross-examination, and the defendants on whom he had informed were acquitted, but there is evidence that at least a part, the most ridiculed at the time, was quite true.[79] Even if he did not come over in December 1691 with the news he said he carried, Sir Adam Blair, according to two sources, certainly did.[80] Colonel John Parker was also in London doing the sort of

[77] *Ibid.*, foll. 461, 463.

[78] "Information of John Lunt, gentleman," June 27, 1694, H.M.C. *Report* XIV, app. IV, 294–96.

[79] Tindal (III, 196) accepted this portion of Lunt's testimony. Two editors of accounts of the trials for the Chetham Society (W. Beamont, *Jacobite Trials at Manchester in 1694*, and A. Goss, *An Account of the Tryalls . . .* , printed at Manchester in 1853 and 1864 respectively) severely criticize in their introductions all the evidence given for the government, but particularly that of Lunt.

[80] "Adam Blair's Memorial, 1718," D. M. Thornton, *The Stuart Dynasty*

work which Lunt might have done, and was later lodged in the Tower for it. If Lunt lied, his lies represented the truth at least as a careful *pastiche*.

During the winter and spring, then, Melfort, having supplanted the former council completely,[81] prepared for the "entreprise infaillible," as it seemed to some.[82] A fleet of transports was equipped to carry an army to England; a powerful squadron to be commanded by Tourville was detailed to escort it; an army was embarked and ready. The English Jacobites heard of these preparations and were beside themselves with joy, according to Humphrey Prideaux: "Our Jacobites were come to that height of confidence to talk openly that all was their owne, and some of them suspended their payment of the taxes; and at the bishops visitation at Norwich, wch was the 3 latter days of Whitsun week, the Jacobite clergy would not own his jurisdiction [because he filled the place of William Lloyd, deprived for refusing allegiance to William III] and refused to appear. . . . I was with one of the deprived Bishops, who seemed as confident of goeing again very speedyly to his bishoprick as I was of goeing home again." [83]

A certain amount of preparation within England for the time of the invasion naturally took place now, at London and elsewhere. If Lunt brought no commissions to England in December, they were certainly issued, e.g. one dated March 10, 1692 to the Earl of Montgomery, eldest son of the Marquess of Powis, for a regiment of horse and the appointment of subordinate officers.[84] It is unlikely that an independent uprising would have attracted much support: "By what I find in all companies," an anonymous informant wrote to William Carstares, "there is not the least inclination in the English to an insurrectione; but all their hopes depend on a foreign force." [85]

(London, 1890), 333; Information of James Hunt, Richard Blackmore, *A True and Impartial History of the Conspiracy against the Person and Government of King William III*. . . (London, 1723), 148f.
[81] Sheridan, MS. "Political Reflexions," fol. 94.
[82] Melfort's Memorials, Carte MSS. 181, foll. 431–33b, 434–37, 438–44v, and 446–49.
[83] *Letters of Humphrey Prideaux to John Ellis*, E. M. Thompson, ed. (London, 1875), 151.
[84] H.M.C. *Stuart Papers*, I, 70.
[85] McCormick, 151.

To choose a time at which to carry over the troops safely, Tourville relied to some extent on intelligence of the English fleet —
its readiness, size, and position — sent from England. Melfort was
in charge of the English correspondence, and was later accused by
his vehement detractor, Sheridan, of having given inaccurate information, particularly that the English ships of the second rate
could not be ready to sail before June 10/21, leading the admiral
to misjudge the strength of the Maritime Powers at the Battle of
La Hogue in May.[86] Whatever Melfort may have told Tourville
or the Ministry of Marine, there is no sign that he relied upon the
information, since his own scouts were responsible for his intelligence and were active in reconnaissance before the battle; [87] on
the contrary, there is plenty of evidence that the French admiral
was aware of his inferiority, but was compelled to give battle by
royal orders, be the English "fort ou foible." [88]

By April 16, it was well known at Versailles that James was to
make a descent on England; he departed on April 21 for Nor-
mandy, by way of La Trappe.[89] He was at Quinéville, by the sea,
about April 28.[90] The exhilaration of the hungry before the feast
may well have pervaded the camp where the exiles gathered to
reclaim "their owne," on which their views were those of the
bishop cited by Prideaux. Before leaving St.-Germain, Melfort and
his master issued a declaration, which, when printed and sent over
to England, reflected the optimism of the exiled court.[91]

It begins well, with a promise to withdraw the French troops
when James should be settled in "the quiet and peacable possession of our Kingdoms," and to keep them in strict discipline
until that time, but what was quiet and peaceable possession?

---

[86] MS. "Political Reflexions," fol. 94; also the "Historical Account," H.M.C.
Stuart Papers, VI, 64. Fenwick's confession in 1696 attributes the information
to Admiral Russell and says that David Floyd (Lloyd) carried it to France.
See *Cal. S. P. Dom., 1696*, 492. But did Fenwick have first-hand knowledge?
[87] Forbin, *Mémoires* (Paris, 1829), II, 22. Ranke seems to have missed this
account in writing his own *History of England* (Oxford, 1875), V, 49.
[88] Sheridan himself mentions these orders. See also Dangeau, IV, 74, and St.-
Simon, I, 51. It should be mentioned that St.-Simon often uses Dangeau as a
unique source.
[89] Dangeau, IV, 61–62; N.-J. Foucault, *Mémoires* (Paris, 1862), 281.
[90] Foucault, *Mémoires*.
[91] Dated April 20, 1692, reprinted by Clarke, II, 479–88.

Absolute power, perhaps? I digress. There follows an apology for James II and an exposition of the Jacobite side of the Revolution and the War of the League of Augsburg. A warm prediction of future civil war if the country does not soon come to its senses leads to a promise of pardon, which, by its list of exceptions, is rather a proscription: [92] the Duke of Ormonde, the "Marques of Winchester," [93] the Earls of Sunderland and Danby, Viscount Cornbury, "John Lord Churchil," the Bishop of St. Asaph,[94] Bishop Burnet, Tillotson, Sir Stephen Fox, and other important political figures, but also the fishermen of Faversham who arrested James on his first flight, and the judges and others held responsible for the prosecution of Ashton and another Jacobite agent named Cross. It is odd that so many of the excepted were Tories: Cornbury, the eldest son of Lord Clarendon, a Jacobite; Lord Nottingham, chief now and later of the High Church party; Danby, whose Williamite title of Duke of Leeds was not recognized; Sir Stephen Fox, who had been present at the birth of the Prince of Wales; [95] and Ormonde, above all, by inheritance and pretension the voice of all Irish loyal churchmanship. Moreover, those who were pardoned were not absolutely so, but under the condition that their pardon should later pass the Great Seal, which might be, as it had been sometimes in the past, an occasion for extortion. Altogether, it had been more gracious to promise no pardon, but to refer the matter to Parliament. Every man who was excepted, or who might have been comprehended in the exceptions by inference, must have received a shock when he remembered little incidents of the Revolution and since in which he had exposed himself to the penalties, the full grisly penalties, of high treason. Naturally all their relations and friends, of whom Ormonde, Nottingham, and Cornbury had many who would otherwise have been Jacobites, were involved, and distressed, and finally repelled.

[92] "According to the report, it looks like the Irish Act of Attainder, which pardoned none." Sir Christopher Musgrave to Rober Harley, May 23, 1692, H.M.C. *Report* XIV, app. III, 492.

[93] Charles Powlett, ca. 1630–1698/9, had already been created Duke of Bolton by William III.

[94] William Lloyd, not to be confused with the deprived non-juring Bishop of Norwich of the same name.

[95] H.M.C. *Report* XIII, app. II, 53.

It did no good to follow this vindictive blunder with assurances of toleration, but there was a good passage intended to calm the fears of the Church of England while yet calling on Dissenters and Catholics for support: "that therefore men of all opinions in matter of Religion may be reconciled to the government and that they may no longer look upon it as their enemie, but may look upon themselves as equally concerned in its preservation with the rest of their fellow Subjects, because they are equally well treated by it, and being convinced in our judgment that libertie of conscience is most agreeable to the Laws and Spirit of the Christian Religion," and so forth, James ends with a promise that Parliament should decide the limits of a toleration which the king would heartily recommend to it. Good, but not good enough; the promise to maintain the Church of England was ungrammatical, and probably intended to confuse, but confused no one: "we will protect and mentain the Church of England as it is now by law established, in all *their* rights, priviledges, and possessions." The word italicized by me was underscored in the imaginations of contemporary Englishmen as well, for the possessive form used indicated that James regarded the Church of England as no church, but as a group of privileged individuals for convenience called a church. Not being thought of as a real body, its collective privileges and possessions were in doubt, however solemnly James might promise, for, as phrased here, it was possible that only the personal rights of members were assured. This is not an obscure, but an important, distinction, which was to leave its mark as late as the declaration issued by "James III" in 1715. Also, in view of the proscription of some of the most important Tory churchmen, as well as of the ecclesiastics Burnet, Tillotson, and the Bishop of St. Asaph, it is hard to imagine who would have been the leaders of any future resistance to oppression from within the Anglican communion, after the projected restoration. It was a very great mistake to issue such a statement, and the king soon had cause to rue it. A declaration to Scotland, of the same date, added another blunder to the total in the form of another list of exceptions; the arrogance of tone was more pronounced in this than in the other.[96]

Cynics may wonder that these two declarations were not filled

[96] A printed copy is Carte MSS. 181, fol. 476.

with promises meant to be broken. Although James II was no more trustworthy than most men of his time, he took a rigid stand on the royal word when directly pledged; hence his ambiguities. Melfort allowed this view in a "Plan of a descent" drawn up in January 1692,[97] recommending "that, if any of the protestant bishops and clergy come in, his Majesty shall use them extreamly well, and order all conveniences for their worship, where there are no churches: that all respect be paid to them: that fair words be given them by all concerned in the King's affairs: but no long audiences be given them, that they may not have the time to enter into particulars; a thing so dangerous, that it is by all means to be avoided by the King himself; whilst we his servants give them all opportunitys, and enter [into particulars] with them, if needfull since that is of less consequence to the King's service, than what he may say." In other words, James meant the Church of England no good, and must not be bound by detailed promises, which would necessarily interfere with his plans, because the royal word is infrangible. While this is not deliberate deception by lying words, it is yet deception, and deliberate.

James II's *Life* attributes these declarations to Lord Chancellor Herbert, an Irish Protestant at St.-Germain.[98] Sheridan contradicts this, it may be rightly, and would have the English one, at least, to be "Melfort's sole contrivance, without the privity of the King's Confessor, as father Warner himself assur'd Sher[idan]." [99] It is certain that the evasive phrasing tallies closely with the advice of Melfort in his "Plan" of January; besides, there is no other indication that Herbert had any voice in important matters after the abandonment of Ireland.

When the deposed king arrived at the seaside, he was kept waiting by the unfavorable winds which detained Tourville's squadron from its rendezvous with the transports. Finally, at La Hogue, this squadron was confronted with the combined English and Dutch fleets, but the French admiral was ordered to fight regardless of odds. Admiral Russell, commanding the Allies,

[97] Carte MSS. 181, foll. 451–58v. I follow the version given in James Macpherson's *Original Papers. . .* (London, 1775), I, 405.

[98] Clarke, II, 488.

[99] MS. "Historical Account," fol. 70; H.M.C. *Stuart Papers*, VI, 64.

was said to be a secret Jacobite, but used his numerical superiority and his great abilities relentlessly, to the undoing of the side he was supposed to favor. Tourville, although he did great deeds, was defeated; the next day the English fleet sailed close to shore and burned many of the surviving vessels. James watched the crushing of his hopes from the beach.[100] It may be that his inaction on this occasion, attested by Foucault, the *intendant* of Caen, in a letter of bitter complaint [101] (that he and the maréchal de Bellefonds "looked on there as at fireworks for the celebration of one of the king's conquests") might be more charitably attributed to shock than to indolence. If there was neglect, it was surely more the responsibility of Bellefonds and Tourville than that of James, whose tendency to melancholia is sufficient excuse. Everyone was agreed that Tourville was not at fault. "I am well satisfied with you, and with the whole fleet," was Louis XIV's assurance to him on his return to court in July.[102]

5. MIDDLETON AND THE COMPOSITION

James lingered on the coast, in chagrin or in lethargy, until late in June, when he returned to St.-Germain.[103] With his prospects, his aims must be lowered. "The Kings Declaration pleas'd none, & was turned into ridicule, burlesque Rimes in England," Sheridan said.[104] "None seemed to be more. . . [dissatisfied] than Admiral Russell," specifies the author of James II's *Life*.[105] Melfort himself saw that it was time for concessions. While James was at La Trappe in mid-autumn, the earl drew up a statement which he considered reasonable for a "Letter" from the king to the Parliament of England, dated November 2, 1692.[106] This letter would have left the Church of England to Parliamentary consideration, as well as the question of a toleration, and retrenched exceptions to pardon to an unnamed "few of the most

---

[100] Foucault, 285–86.
[101] To Pontchartrain, n.d., *ibid.*, 289–293.
[102] Dangeau, IV, 129.
[103] *Ibid.*, IV, 117.
[104] MS. "Historical Account," fol. 70; H.M.C. *Stuart Papers*, VI, 64.
[105] Clarke, II, 489.
[106] Carte MSS. 181, foll. 486–489v.

obnoxious"; in it the king promised to govern according to law and to choose as ministers "such as may be entirely trusted by my People; men of integrity and reputation." It seems harmless enough, but its implications were so unpleasant that Melfort's master refused to sign it, even if it would muster opposition sufficient to obstruct the passage of William III's Excise Bill, then pending action in Parliament.[107]

The French were anxious to bring their pensioner to reason: the marquis de Croissy submitted a draft of another such letter on November 23,[108] which contained an undertaking "to agree to any laws that shall be desired, at our hands, to secure the protestant religion, as now established by Law," and to "secure Liberty and property, not only from any maladministrations that may fall in, during our Reigne, but likeways against any invasion may be designed by our Posterity." These phrases were well chosen to make James furious. A softened version was submitted by Melfort on the same day,[109] but neither was sent.

One difficulty other than the king's own temperament was ignorance of the assurances desired by those who could be brought over by any assurances at all. A priest named Cary was sent over to discuss terms with Charles,[110] Earl of Middleton, former Secretary of State in England, who was now the most prominent Jacobite there, in spite of his Scottish origin, because of his known moderate sentiments, his discretion and his Protestantism. Unlike Melfort, he had also a good name in his own country, where he had been Secretary of State before the other.

Besides this advance, there was one to Russell, through David Lloyd. The admiral pledged continued loyalty (one is not sure what loyalty was to him) "upon condition that such a restriction were put upon the Regal power as to prevent for the future any

[107] Clarke, II, 506. See also the marquis de Sourches' *Mémoires sur le règne de Louis XIV*, ed. Cosnac and Pontal (Paris, 1882–93), IV, 157, for court talk about blocking this levy.

[108] Carte MSS. 181, fol. 505r and v.

[109] *Ibid.*, fol. 507r and v.

[110] The earl's Christian name is often confused with that of his father, the first earl (e.g. by K. G. Feiling, *History of the Tory Party*, 1640–1714, index, and Sir Richard Lodge in vol. VIII of the *Political History of England*, ed. Hunt and Poole). The second earl was born in 1650, and died at St. Germain in August 1719.

undue practices or the like steps as had been formerly made," and was promised by Lloyd that England should have "full satisfaction and security." [111] Shortly after this interview, Russell was removed, whatever his intention, and his usefulness was at an end. The same is true of Marlborough, with whom parallel negotiations had been going on.[112] Marlborough was imprisoned on his fall from favor, perhaps because of this or other double-dealing.

Middleton was not altogether at one with the demanding Russell, but sent Cary back to St.-Germain in January 1693 with an account of the desires of the Compounders, stated under eight heads, and a promise to come over himself if James would accept the conditions, with full instructions and authority from the group.[113] James decided to agree to all of the heads after consultation with the French king. A message to Middleton was dispatched on January 12; thereupon that lord sent over a declaration embodying the articles carried over by Cary, "and then follow'd it soon after himself." [114]

It is not certain when Middleton arrived in France, but it could not have been before March 20,[115] and was probably about three weeks later. He was presented to Louis XIV at Versailles on April 16,[116] and conferred with the two kings there. The urgency of such a conference suggests that it was held as shortly as possible after Middleton's arrival. The declaration earlier sent over was issued on April 17; as soon as it was printed it was distributed in England. Middleton took up correspondence on the 19th,[117] and was certainly known to be the first minister at St.-Germain by the 23rd.[118]

[111] Clarke, II, 499–500. Sir Winston Churchill and others have assailed Lloyd's or the *Life's* credibility. There is no room for argument here, but substantially, where the *Life* can be checked with other sources on the years of exile, it has been found to be correct. Ranke, vol. VI, in an appendix, distinguishes the trustworthy from the undependable sections. Lloyd had a reputation for honesty, whether or not deserved; that Russell might have been lying is very possible.

[112] Clarke, II, 446–448, 500.

[113] *Ibid.*, II, 501–02.

[114] *Ibid.*

[115] F. Ravaisson, ed., *Archives de la Bastille* (Paris, 1866–91), IX, 404.

[116] Dangeau, IV, 266.

[117] Middleton to ["Henry Brickley"] April 19, 1693, Carte MSS. 256, fol. 1.

[118] Dangeau, IV, 271.

It should be noticed that in the first of his preserved official letters, Middleton apologized to "Brickley," a pseudonymous agent, for not having as yet written to "Lord Churchill," but promised to do so soon.[119] This reference, under his older title, to Marlborough, has been previously overlooked by students of his Jacobite connections and activities, because it was couched in cipher, although a key to the cipher is bound in the same volume of the Carte Papers.[120] In the light of this and other evidence there is no doubt that Marlborough was one of Middleton's principals in his journey to France. To deny it would be to give away the truth to preserve the reputation of a great man in the face of every bit of contemporary matter with any bearing on the question. Few politicians of Marlborough's day pursued a consistently straight course; this fact should be remembered, and that by imposing our own standards on the past we only make room for distortion and misunderstanding. It happens that Marlborough was somewhat more shifty than many of his contemporaries, and that they knew him to be so. The Carte and Stuart Papers are records of these facts, and cannot be set aside as not fitting our preconceptions. I regret to say that I disagree with Sir Winston Churchill on this point.

Middleton, in comparison with Marlborough, was a man of high principle. He was a Protestant, and not at this time ready for conversion. A man of solid inherited fortune, he gave up, at least for the time, and as it turned out forever, everything he had. Nor did he take this step as a man of few family ties, like Bolingbroke, might do, for he had a wife and several children,[121] two of

---

[119] Carte MSS. 256, fol. 1. This volume is a book of copies of letters written by Middleton in his first years of office at St.-Germain.

[120] *Ibid.*, foll. 10r and v, 11.

[121] He wrote to Caryll, Oct. 9, 1694, "I have a wife and children at y[ou]r service s[i]r, if I had a small provision for them, I should have nothing left to wish for in the world.

Multa cupientibus, multa desunt: bene est cui obtulit deus
Parca, quod satis est, manu. . .

Thus you see, like hudibras in the Stockes,
I comfort myself with ends of Verse,
And sayings of Philosophers."

As for "plate, jewells, and pictures &c." the Earl quotes:
"Sunt qui non habeant, est qui non curat habere."
Carte MSS. 256, fol. 61r and v.

whom he offered for the Pretender in 1708. St.-Simon, among his hatreds, cherished one for the earl, and denounced him in his *Mémoires* for collecting his British revenues by arrangement with the Revolution Government. Middleton's way of life seems to point the other way. Even St.-Simon admitted that Middleton's wit made him acceptable in all quarters at Paris and Versailles.[122] Hoffman, the Emperor's envoy at London, wrote to Vienna on the occasion of his flight, "Middleton . . . has secretly left and gone to King James. He is a man of good understanding, acquainted exactly with conditions here," and suggested that this movement was a straw in the wind.[123] Now the mask was off, and Middleton could not return unless he brought James II with him.

His first tool for this was his new declaration, dated April 17, 1693, which the Compounders, including probably Russell, Marlborough, and the Princess Anne of Denmark,[124] younger sister of Queen Mary, had commissioned him to wring out of Anne's reluctant father. It was obtained with only one important difficulty — the acceptance of the guarantee of the Church of England by his confessors — which the whole court of St.-Germain was determined to surmount.

It was a sort of comedy: before the approval of the declaration — Sheridan says after, but why seek permission after? — the clause was submitted to Fathers Lewis Inese, Sanders, Betham, and Fenwick for their approval. Well acquainted with past publications, these divines insisted that where a promise was made to "protect and defend the Church of England" James should, upon peril of penalties after death, insert "the members of," to avoid promising to maintain a heresy and its institutions. This would weaken the declaration so that it would be no more satisfactory to the Compounders than the one of the previous year; indeed, it might be worse. Melfort, his own mind made up that the declaration must be issued, carried the clause without delay[125] to five French

[122] *Mémoires*, XV, 417–18.
[123] Onno Klopp, *Der Fall des Hauses Stuart und die Succession des Hauses Hannover in Gross-Britannien und Irland. . .* (Vienna, 1875–88), VI, 187.
[124] Middleton to Sackville, May 21, 1693, Carte MSS. 256, fol. 12r and v. I have deciphered this message by use of Sackville's cipher, *ibid.*, foll. 2–10. See also Middleton to Sackville, July 15, 1694, *ibid.*, fol. 39v.
[125] Sheridan assigns this part to Melfort. Middleton's intervention would probably have been regarded as improper.

priests — Sheridan says eight, but no matter — who approved it without change, having little knowledge of the issues in dispute; so little did they understand that they allowed James specifically to declare that he would not dispense from or violate the Test Act, which the other group refused altogether to permit. After the publication, the priests were compelled to withdraw their sanction; [126] Catholics, especially the Irish, were very much disappointed by it.[127] Nevertheless, it had to be so, and one may doubt that the French priests were so much in the dark as they have been said to be. The necessity did not preclude an attempt by cardinals of the Austrian faction to obtain a severe censure of James II in the next Consistory.[128] Their religion might not forbid their connivance at the loss of his throne, but stood clearly against his attempts to regain it, in convenient accord with the policy of the court of Vienna.

The full contents of the declaration were simple.

1. A promise of pardon under the Great Seal to all who would not oppose the coming attempt at restoration.

2. A promise to call a free Parliament for the redress of grievances.

3. An unambiguous promise to "protect and defend the Church of England," and its possession of all colleges and schools.

4. A promise to recommend establishment of liberty of conscience to Parliament.

5. Submission of the dispensing power to parliamentary limitation, coupled with a promise not to dispense with the Test.

6. A promise of assent to bills providing for frequent Parliaments, free elections, and the like.

7. A promise to reestablish the Caroline Settlement in Ireland.

8. A specific promise to abolish the hearth tax, which had already been done by Parliament since the Revolution.[129]

So sensible was this document that it was a pity that it had no

[126] Clarke, II, 507–10; Sheridan, MS. "Political Reflexions," 98–100.

[127] Ravaisson, IX, 419; Sheridan, 101–03.

[128] Bishop Philip Ellis to James II, Rome, July 13, 1694, Carte MSS. 209, foll. 114–17. Ellis, Bishop of Aureliopolis *in partibus*, was the Jacobite agent at Rome after Melfort's withdrawal and the death of Cardinal Howard.

[129] A printed copy is Carte MSS. 181, foll. 525 a and b.

better reception: the absolutists among the Protestants disliked
the partial destruction of prerogative, while the Catholic Jacobites added to this the religious aberration to two of the heads.[130]
A Whig rhymer within six weeks made available an "Explanation" of the declaration, in part as follows:

> And therefore by this Declaration,
> We promise pardon to the Nation,
> Excepting only whom We please,
> Whether they be on Land or Seas . . .
> As for the Church, we'll still defend it,
> Or if you please, the Pope shall mend it:
> Your Chappels, Colleges, and Schools,
> Shall be supply'd by your own Fools:
> But if we live another Summer
> We'll then relieve them from St. Omer . . .
> Next for a Liberty of Conscience,
> With which we bit the Nation long since,
> We'll settle it as firm and steady,
> Perhaps, as that you have already.
> We'll never violate the Test,
> Till t'is our Royal Interest,
> Or till We think it so at least,
> But there we must consult the Priest.

and so on.[131]

There is bite in this doggerel, and some truth. The key to the
declaration's failure, and to that of the Compounders, in fact, is
"perhaps as that you have already." There was nothing that
James promised England which she could not obtain more readily
from William. It was too late to promise these things, and James
would certainly give no more, thinking as he did that he had
already yielded too far. Besides, on what fulcrum was this lever
supposed to work? On Marlborough and Russell, who were only
Jacobites for purposes of insurance, and Princess Anne. Besides,
these were three persons who had no control over the course of
events in England, all being out of favor, and who had great expectations under the Revolution Settlement to set against the
merely contingent rewards to be expected from even the closest

---

[130] Clarke, II, 514; Sheridan, MS. "Political Reflexions," fol. 104.
[131] "The True and Genuine Explanation of one King James's Declaration,"
London, [June 8,] 1693, Carte MSS. 233, fol. 150.

coöperation with James and Middleton. Perhaps, believing that Middleton's mission would be a failure, they had sent him over regardless of that as a sop to the king, and were surprised to see their deliberately unacceptable offer accepted. For a year, therefore, nothing worth speaking of happened, although Jacobite agents went back and forth busily.[132]

6. THE FALL OF MELFORT

Melfort and Middleton were now both Secretaries of State. The *Memoirs* of John Macky assert that Melfort had always the advantage of Middleton in the confidence of the king, but this, like many of the spy's charges, is overstated, if not untrue.

It would be good to exonerate James II as far as is just from the imputations of such as Macky. It is true that Protestants and Catholics, other things being equal, were judged according to the king's religious preferences; it was natural that pensions, for instance, should be more numerous on the Catholic side of the fence. It should be remembered, however, that far more Catholics (including almost all the Irish at St.-Germain) were in exile than Protestants. Macky accuses the Catholics of letting Protestants starve, to force their conversion. He makes a point of the case of Sir James Montgomery, who ended his days at St.-Germain. Unfortunately for Macky, the betrayal of the Scots Plot of 1690, which was good reason to let Montgomery starve, had not kept the cunning hedger from being placed on the French pension rolls at the request of James's ministers shortly before his death.[133]

Another supposed sufferer from James II's discrimination was Denis Granville, deprived Dean of Durham, who had fled to France. Here again is direct evidence that James guaranteed at least one substantial loan to the Dean when he had no money of his own to give.[134] Also, Granville wrote in 1689 to his cousin the Earl of Bath, "common courtesy doth oblige me to acknowledge that I have met with as much curtesy now in France, from the

---

[132] Carte MSS. 209, foll. 94, 99; Carte MSS. 181, foll. 531–33.
[133] Middleton to Croissy, St.-Germain, Feb. 7, 1695, Carte MSS. 256, foll. 92v, 93.
[134] Carte MSS. 181, fol. 597v.

Roman Catholicks, as I have done heretofore among the Protestants . . . tho' I doe noways disown my religion." [135] In 1701, he wrote to a friend that he had been spared a retrenchment,[136] which implies some regular payments for his support.

As to Macky's charges regarding refusal of Christian burial to Lord Dunfermline and the forcible administration of the Catholic sacrament to Colonel Cannon, evidence is lacking. The first would not be a charge against James had it been true, but against French ecclesiastical authorities over whom he had no control. The second would certainly be very shocking to most Catholics, again, if true. Macky did not, however, need truth on his side, as I have shown.

The true cause of some insincere conversions was the establishment of the *tiers de l'économat,* set up before 1685 by Louis XIV to provide subsistence for Huguenots converted to Catholicism said to have been disinherited by their families, and continued after the Revocation of the Edict of Nantes, when, supposedly, all Huguenots were converted by decree. Because the deposed king of England had small funds to provide for his "poor workmen," [137] pensions on the *économat* offered a more certain source of income (dependent only on the collection of revenues of vacant bishoprics),[138] for which some few undoubtedly gave up their religious integrity; but not all of those who were converted, or even most, were such cases. If one wishes to account for conversions on a natural basis, it would be more appropriate to consider the force exerted on all foreigners in any country to conform to the national usages, and that mixed marriages, of which there were many, often led the Protestant partner to adopt the Catholicism of the spouse.

The two Secretaries were not friends, and must have had a good number of disagreements. In the end one must go. The English Jacobites insisted that it must be Melfort, and the King of France enforced their decision. In April 1694, Lord Griffin crossed from England with word that the Jacobites would have

[135] Granville, "Works and Letters," *Miscellanea* (Durham, 1860), 80.

[136] Granville, *Remains* (Durham, 1865), 199.

[137] Middleton to "Mr. Appleby" [Sackville?], July 15, 1694, Carte MSS. 256, fol. 39v.

[138] Sourches, II, 250.

no more of the senior secretary; this word was communicated to Louis XIV, who asked on May 26 that the minister be removed. This was done the next day.[139] John Caryll, later created Lord Durford, was appointed to fill the vacancy. Melfort left the court in early June and settled at Orléans in November.[140]

Melfort's harshness and lack of scruple in his efforts for the king left him few friends to lament his fall. One friend, Lord Ailesbury, asked James to dismiss the minister to show the impotence of his opponents.[141] That it did. Even more it showed the distrust the French felt in their dealings with Melfort since their discovery of a clandestine correspondence carried on by him with England.[142] This led them to exclude him henceforth from their confidence, and so far as they could from that of the court of St.-Germain; with what good reason time was to tell.

[139] *Ibid.*, IV, 332; Ravaisson, IX, 453–54; Dangeau, V, 17.
[140] Carte MSS. 209, foll. 200–74.
[141] Ailesbury to James, n.d., Ailesbury's *Memoirs* (London, 1890), I, 306–07.
[142] Ravaisson, IX, 426–27.

2

OLD KING AND NEW

(1 6 9 4 – 1 7 0 6)

1. JACOBITE CORRESPONDENCE WITH ENGLAND

The war between France and the Allies continued. Flanders and Italy remained the major theaters, while each side, as occasion served, planned diversions in this place or in that. Such a diversion, of course, was possibly the intention of Louis XIV in 1692: the restoration of his guest James would remove one from the list of his enemies at best; at worst, a civil war in England would keep English troops out of the theaters in which France was most directly concerned, at least for a time. Such motives worked in the minds of most kings and ministers, not only those of France — as shown in a later war when France's enemies gave aid (meager as it was) to the rebel Camisards in the Cevennes, or when Sweden and Russia chose different kings for Poland through the factions of her nobility.

England, during the time of the change of ministers in 1694, planned such a diversion, on a minor scale, to be sure, in the form of a descent at Brest, or one of the nearby ports, to be executed by General Tollemache at his discretion. In some way this intention came to be known to the French, who made such effective preparations that the landing failed, and Tollemache was mortally wounded.

What makes this of interest here is that Jacobite intelligence seems to have been used by the French, and that the Earl (later Duke) of Marlborough was probably one of the informants. Now, that Marlborough, a soldier's soldier, could have done such a thing as betray his country's military efforts is so shocking to our modern minds that a controversy has been made out of it which continues to this day. Let us look at it.

Preserved among the Nairne Papers, a portion of the great Carte collection in the Bodleian Library, are certain papers, some of which have already been cited in this study, which involve Marlborough in Jacobite correspondence. The most damaging of these is the "Camaret Bay Letter," named from the site of Tollemache's disaster, a translation of a message, presumably originally sent in cipher by Colonel Edward Sackville, who received it in turn from Marlborough, to Melfort, to whom it betrayed the destination of the expedition. If Marlborough's probity is to be maintained, this letter must be explained away, or its authenticity questioned. Mr. E. M. Lloyd marshalled the evidence available to him in 1894 to show that the information contained therein was already in the possession of the French authorities before the original could have been sent, deciphered, translated and relayed by Melfort, and that the preparations made by Vauban around Brest required weeks to carry out, and must have been begun before the date of the letter, written only shortly before the sailing of the fleet. Since at least two other sources of intelligence, Lords Godolphin and Arran, had previously sent the same word, the blame is not Marlborough's for "revealing" what was nearly common knowledge.[1] This is fair. Unfortunately for fairness, Colonel Arthur Parnell undertook in 1897 to attack the authenticity of all the papers which involve the prominent persons of the court of William, on various grounds, principally that they are not originals, but drafts or copies; that a certain Jacobite sympathizer, James Macpherson, in editing a selection of the papers[2] for publication had an opportunity to forge these documents and therefore did, being a person of such low moral character as would put Ossian's name to his own compositions; and that Marlborough's message, if it ever existed in the original, contained some contradictions.[3] These are all questionable judgments, and are wholly unacceptable in the light of other evidence,

[1] *English Historical Review*, IX, 130–33.

[2] J. Macpherson, *Original Papers, containing the secret history of Great Britain from the Restoration to the accession of the house of Hanover* (London, 1775).

[3] "James Macpherson and the Nairne Papers" *E.H.R.*, XII, 254–84.

independent of Carte and of Macpherson, which makes it clear (though not authenticating the Camaret Bay Letter) that these men, William's supporters at the Revolution, did correspond with James II, did supply him with information, and did receive pardons for their previous actions in return. Mr. Godfrey Davies made all this clear in 1920.[4] We can hardly forgive Sir Winston Churchill for using Colonel Parnell's article after it had been exploded, while mentioning Mr. Davies' work in a footnote only,[5] in the midst of a chapter on the subject.[6] This procedure leaves room for cynicism regarding Sir Winston's motives. Mr. Davies concludes that "Marlborough tried to purchase his pardon in the event of a Jacobite restoration by the most harmless acts of disloyalty which would achieve the end in view." It is at once a charitable and plausible conclusion. A worse one could be reached without grave injustice.

This is an example of the complexities of Jacobite intelligence which may not be forgotten when assessing the part of any individual in obtaining or transmitting it. Few original letters containing revelations have come down to us, precisely because it was to the Jacobite interest to destroy such originals after having deciphered and translated them for French use. Paris and the village of St.-Germain-en-Laye were full of spies, some of whom had convincing Jacobite records. Very early the French government had become aware of "leaks"; and also very early the English agents had become wary of disclosure of their identities. Therefore the Stuart Papers, now at Windsor, have many gaps in the series of original letters. The Nairne Papers, however, contain many copies and draft translations, made whenever a fair copy was to be sent to the French minister concerned. David Nairne, a Jacobite clerk, was trusted with these things, and made many of these translations himself. There also survive copies of messages in cipher sent into England by Middleton in the period April 1693–March 1695, kept as minutes for use by Nairne and Middleton, with keys to the ciphers used.[7]

---

[4] "Macpherson and the Nairne Papers," *E.H.R.*, XXXV, 367–76.
[5] Vol. I, 369 of the edition of 1947.
[6] Chapter 25.
[7] Carte MSS. 256. There is also a shorter sequence for a later period.

The type of information desired and sent was principally political, having to do with James's friends and enemies, and military and naval. Melfort had begun correspondence, for we hear of Marlborough's accounts to Sackville and Lloyd both of the army and the fleet in 1691,[8] but we know more of Middleton's time. In late 1693, perhaps November, there is a "Memoir on the State of England";[9] in December, Captain Williamson's advice to King James.[10] Middleton communicated a muster roll of William III's troops in Flanders to Barbezieux, the French minister of war, in late May 1694, of which only a copy of the covering letter survives.[11] Naval advices, including lists of the English fleet, were forwarded on July 6 and September 11, 1694,[12] on the latter occasion giving the valuable information that Russell's squadron was to winter in the Mediterranean. In December of that year, Middleton desired Sackville to bargain with one Sam. Atkins for advices to be paid for by the King of France;[13] there were also the naval advices for which, we later learn, Louis XIV paid 3,000 livres a year to Lloyd.[14] After more than two years of Middleton's management, the French found it profitable, evidently, to pay about £200 annually to one operative alone.

Plots are extremely difficult to disinter, particularly when they have been buried under a century or more of historical "debunking," but for an understanding of the other main object of Jacobite correspondence, it must be done. John Lunt, the supposed messenger of 1691, gave evidence in June 1694 of a conspiracy to rise and overthrow William's government, perhaps by assassination of the king. He involved in this plot a number of representatives of old Lancashire and Staffordshire families, who he said had held meetings at which he had been present, and had employed him to make journeys around the country and to St.-Germain and to enlist men in early 1691. In December 1693 he returned from one of his missions to St.-Germain and was engaged

---

[8] Clarke, II, 444–50.
[9] Carte MSS. 181, foll. 535–48.
[10] *Ibid.*, foll. 531–33.
[11] Carte MSS. 256, fol. 30v.
[12] *Ibid.*, foll. 36v, 52r and v.
[13] *Ibid.*, fol. 74. Deciphered by means of key, foll. 2–10.
[14] Carte MSS. 208, foll. 89v, 90, 93.

in such a conspiracy in London, but was led by qualms of conscience, he said, to betray it in the following spring. A good many arrests were made on this evidence, and some of the accused brought to trial at Manchester, where a local jury acquitted them all, when evidence was brought to show that Lunt's account of his movements was not chronologically possible, that he was a man of low character, and that he had deserted his wife and committed bigamy.[15] On the strength of these acquittals, editors of accounts of these trials have assumed that the affair was a fiction, concocted by Lunt and two or three friends. It was not entirely so. A list of commissions sent to England [16] in the early 1690's shows a striking similarity to the lists, given in Lunt's testimony, of commissions which he said that he had delivered: Thomas Tildesley, said by Lunt to have had a commission for a regiment of dragoons, actually had one; William Molyneux, son of Lord Molyneux, had the commission for a regiment of horse spoken of by Lunt; so did Townley of Townley. Sir Roland Stanley, William "Dickenson," and Sir William Gerrard he implicated as having junior commissions; they had them. Lord Salisbury, Lunt named on hearsay; even he is proved by the list to have been guilty. From all this, it appears that Lunt, although an unprincipled informer and possibly the fabricator of the plot, had at least a good deal of genuine information, perhaps obtained as a messenger or by acquaintance with messengers. Not knowing enough to make the stir, and obtain the rewards, which he desired, he seems to have made up falsely an assassination plot, of a kind which actually appeared only many months later. It was then for this reason that Middleton, who was certainly in touch with Townley within two months of the trial,[17] and probably was before it, wrote to the marquis de Croissy that the "Prince of Orange" wished to have honest people murdered by means of false witnesses.[18] The heaviest charge was false, although the minor ones were true.

The purpose of the correspondence which gave Lunt his open-

[15] H.M.C. *Report* XIV, app. IV, 309–17; Beamont, *The Jacobite Trials;* Goss, *An Account of the Tryalls.*
[16] Carte MSS. 181, foll. 559–62.
[17] Carte MSS. 256, fol. 71.
[18] Carte MSS. 209, fol. 147.

ing was to keep up a party of persons willing and able to bear arms, by encouragement, persuasion, a little intimidation, and constant communication. The commissions were a form of encouragement, and little more — some one pointed out that more regiments of horse would have been raised from Lancashire alone than England had ever had in the field. The dispersed printed matter was persuasion. In this, as in other communications, doubtful persons were reminded that loyalty and disloyalty would be remembered after the restoration; and awareness of the alertness and activity of the king over the water was cultivated by meetings, messages, traveling agents, and all other means, including Jacobite songs, toasts and other unimportant but noticeable nonsense.

However able he was in this sort of work, Middleton was unable to fulfil the promises authorized by his backers. Instead of a rising requiring the help of only a handful of French troops, he received proposals that the king invade with not less than 10,000 men.[19] In 1694 France had neither so many men to spare from her hard-pressed armies, nor the fleet necessary to escort so large a convoy. Seignelay had been succeeded by the comte de Pontchartrain,[20] a less active minister, and the state of the navy had declined sharply since the battle of La Hogue. There were plenty of reasons, therefore, to put off either invasion or rising in 1694 and 1695. All that could be done by Middleton during that time was to maintain relations with prominent Englishmen — Marlborough, Godolphin, and the Duke of Shrewsbury — and pass on whatever information could be of use to France. Jacobites in Parliament were instructed to block the passage of revenue bills, if possible, and, if not, to make them as "onnorous & clamorous and for as short a time as may be." [21] For the rest, leaders on the scene must decide for themselves on parliamentary tactics.[22] Middleton acknowledged his failure in dealing with Louis XIV and was willing to retire: he wrote to Caryll in September, "I should be very glad to be confind to Constantinople on condition

[19] Carte MSS. 181, fol. 577.
[20] Louis Phélypeaux, comte de Pontchartrain (1643–1727), was minister of marine from November 1690 until 1699.
[21] Carte MSS. 256, foll. 47v–50.
[22] *Ibid.*, fol. 88.

that Ld Melfort could carry our master home." [23] But there was little likelihood of that.

James II accommodated himself to his circumstances and devoted his time to religious exercises. Even at La Trappe his austerities provoked the admiration of the Abbot, Rancé,[24] who was by now an old friend. The author of his *Life* tells us "by contemplateing his own former failings as to his morral life, more than the indignities he had suffer'd in respect of his character, he was much more intent to doe penance for the one, then to be deliver'd from the other; this made him turn St.-Germains into a sort of Solitude, and not content with that, went to seek it at certain times where it was to be found in its greatest perfection." [25]

His followers adapted themselves to this life as best they could, the men of military age usually serving in the French armies, their wives and children and the older men remaining at St.-Germain, at Paris, or some religious house, living on small doles from James II, pensions on the *économat*, simple charity, or some soldier's tiny pay. Throughout these years a stream of "certificates of noblesse" attest the gentility of Irish and Englishmen who sought French commissions, or of their daughters who sought admission to convents of the higher class, for which such certificates were necessary.[26] The sum of 600,000 livres allowed to James annually by the King of France permitted few to be idle in his service at court. Those who could do so began to go home, as Henry Browne, a former Secretary, did in 1694.

2. THE PLAN FOR INVASION AND THE ASSASSINATION PLOT

In early 1695, the Earl of Arran made offers for himself and the Earl of Sunderland, and hinted that the Duke of Queensberry, Lord Breadalbane and Viscount Tarbat would be glad to have assurances of forgiveness.[27] Assured that bygones could be made bygones for a sufficient consideration, Arran, Sunderland, and a Scottish Catholic bishop, Leyburn, consulted, and urged an in-

[23] *Ibid.*, foll. 53v, 54.
[24] A. J. le B. de Rancé, *Lettres*, ed. B. Gonod (Paris, 1846), 385–86.
[25] Clarke, II, 528.
[26] H.M.C. *Stuart Papers*, I, *passim*.
[27] Only Caryll's answer, dated February 1695, survives. Carte MSS. 209, fol. 180r and v.

vasion as soon as possible with whatever forces could be got.[28] There were no forces. Could James trust Sunderland and Arran in any case?

An organization of die-hards sprang up at the end of the spring, when a number of non-Compounders met at a tavern for dinner, and agreed to send Captain Robert Charnock, formerly fellow of Magdalen College, Oxford, to France to recommend an invasion attempt, promising to bring out 2,000 horse to assist a French force, which should itself consist of 10,000 men — 8,000 foot, 1,000 dragoons, and 1,000 horse. Sir John Friend, Sir John Fenwick, Captain George Porter, Sir William Perkins, and one Peter Cooke were present at this meeting. Cardell Goodman joined the party after dinner. Lord Ailesbury, who had already once crossed to St.-Germain with advices from this section of the party, and Lord Montgomery were also there.[29] Charnock submitted these proposals to the king on June 17, assuring him that the mass of Revolutioners were now disaffected from William III, and that he might take advantage of this disposition if he were quick to act.[30]

During the summer no action was taken on the matter, because the campaign of Namur was in progress, and Louis XIV was hard put to it to keep his ordinary armies in the field, without creating new ones. In October, however, he was more amenable when Middleton approached him during the annual visit of the "English court" to Fontainebleau. "I assure you wee have earnestly press'd the performance of the match [invasion]," Middleton wrote into England, "to which we found him as well dispos'd as wee could wish, and deferres it only till he can raise the portion [money? army? fleet?]; I doe not Expect this will satisfie the empatience of a lover. . ." [31] Another correspondent was directed "to send ane exact account what fforces is now in England," probably to convince Louis XIV that the invasion would meet little resistance.[32]

[28] Arran to James II, March 13/23, 1694/5, ibid., foll. 178–79.
[29] Porter's confession, R. Blackmore, True and Impartial History of the Conspiracy. . . , 77–79.
[30] Carte MSS. 209, foll. 182–83.
[31] Carte MSS. 208, fol. 113.
[32] Ibid., fol. 114v. The key to the cipher is fol. 272.

At exactly what time the conspiracy for rebellion and invasion was joined to one for kidnapping and murdering King William is very difficult to say. At some point a commission was given to Sir George Barclay, a lieutenant-colonel of James's Horse Guards and agent in England for correspondence with the non-Compounders, to wage war on William III in his winter quarters.[33] Whether it was intended that he should use this as authority for an attack on his person is in doubt. Barclay came into England probably in January 1696.[34] With some recruits chosen from the English conspirators, of whom the best known is Fenwick, he obtained about twenty officers from among the English in France to bring their number up to the forty believed necessary for an attack on the royal coach as William returned from hunting. Among these officers, who came over secretly, were Lord Castlemaine, Colonel Parker, and Brigadier Rookwood.

While this plot was being organized, some of the conspirators, and many who knew only of the planned rebellion, were engaged in recruiting men who promised to rise to meet the invasion. Friend and Perkins had each a commission for a regiment of horse, as well as a part in the plot.[35] Goodman was to muster a troop;[36] and Mr. Tempest, of Durham, a regiment of dragoons. Probably only the higher ranks of these units were filled. A few persons who received commissions for the rising refused to assist in the murder, as did Bevil and Thomas Higgons, relations of the great Granville connection in the West Country.[37] Officers placed under Barclay's orders for other purposes, and paid (by Caryll) the expenses of a journey to England, were in some cases diverted to the assassination.[38]

The plans to land in England went forward rapidly, and at the turn of the year the best point of landing was debated. Pontchartrain seems to have suggested the region of Yarmouth, to which Middleton preferred Newcastle upon Tyne.[39] In early February,

[33] Porter's information, Blackmore, 80–81.
[34] James Hunt's information, *ibid.*, 154.
[35] *Ibid.*, 89.
[36] *Ibid.*, 138.
[37] *Ibid.*, 85.
[38] Harris's information, *ibid.*, 120, 127.
[39] Carte MSS. 208, foll. 226a v, 130v, 131.

preparations on the French side were so far advanced that the Duke of Berwick, now a lieutenant-general in the French army, was sent to England to arrange and command the rebellion to precede the landing.

His mission was the result of a misunderstanding between the French and English. It had never been the intention of the Jacobites to "come out" before an invasion — Sir John Friend told Brice Blair that "he would not meddle with raising his Regiment 'till he heard King *James* was landed" [40] — on the other hand, Louis XIV did not care for the risk of an unsupported campaign. Therefore he sent Berwick over with promises and authority to demand a reply. It was given out at court that the duke had gone to inspect the French battalions of Irish. Having arrived in England via the Romney marshes,[41] he found the English inflexible, and for good reasons.[42] Consider the possibilities which the Jacobites faced if they rose before a French army had crossed. Bad weather, bad faith, or bad planning could delay the landing until after the suppression of the rebellion. The Jacobites lacked proper arms — artillery, for instance — training, and popular confidence in their success. A small French corps could remedy all three of these defects. Without it, they would infallibly ruin the enterprise. Deciding that no rising was yet possible, and afraid of the implications of the assassination plot, of which he was apprised, Berwick left England within a week, passing no moral judgment on Barclay and his design, but only remarking, "le dessein me paroissoit difficile à exécuter." [43] He does not seem to have tried to stop it.

On February 15, 1696, the plot was to be carried out. Two informers, Captain Richard Fisher and Captain Pendergrass, gave separate warning of it, and William III did not hunt that day. When a third informer confirmed the word, Lord Portland pressed his sources to name their accomplices, which they had so far refrained from doing. Convinced that to secure the life which they had saved they must be definite, they yielded.

[40] Blackmore, 114.
[41] *Ibid.*, 154.
[42] Berwick, I, 144.
[43] *Ibid.*

William's hunting was deferred again the following week, and many arrests were made on the night of February 22/March 3.

In the confusion Barclay eluded capture, but many others — some 330 were lodged in London prisons alone [44] — were apprehended for their share in one or other of the two schemes. In Scotland a number were also confined.[45] The most deeply "dipped," as the expression was, gave much information. Fenwick implicated many highly placed persons, particularly Shrewsbury and Marlborough; Charnock, Porter, and the smuggler Hunt named the rank and file.

The punishment of the offenders was, on the whole, light. A handful were executed, including Fenwick, whose indiscreet accusations (however accurate) drove those implicated, in combination with less interested persons, to demand his death and silence. Some of those likely to have been condemned — Hungate and Richardson, officers of James II — luckily escaped. A few more — Bernardi, Blackburne, Cassills, Meldrum, and Chambers — were imprisoned for the duration of the reign by an Act of Parliament, renewed in 1702 and 1714, without trial. These unfortunates spent their lives in prison, frequently petitioning for their rights as Englishmen. They were denied the mercy of a royal pardon, although a fellow-prisoner, Counter, was released by Queen Anne.[46]

On the other side of the Channel, the expedition awaited the return of Berwick. It was thought that some statement was necessary, cautiously worded to avoid alienating friends; with this in mind, the proclamation of 1693 was completely rewritten and, with some omissions, was signed on February 28, 1696.[47] James considered that there was good excuse for an offer of less favorable conditions in the failure of the Compounders to restore him after the concessions of 1693, although he was influenced by Middleton to keep as much of his old assurances in it as possible. Fundamental disagreements being brought out by the debate

[44] For a list, see Rawl. MSS. A. 311, fol. 1.
[45] H.M.C. *Report*, XII, app. VIII, 51.
[46] John Bernardi, *A Short History of the Life of Major John Bernardi* (London, 1729); Bernardi, *The Most Sad and Deplorable Case of Robert Blackburne, John Bernardi, and Robert Cassills* (London, 1727).
[47] H.M.C. *Stuart Papers*, I, 110–12.

about the content proper to the occasion, it was determined not to disperse the new instrument until the landing was made.[48] And so it came to pass that James was criticized for issuing no declaration at this time, from which his enemies inferred that he intended to allow no concessions at all.[49] Since the proclamation was already printed and ready for issue, this was an unjust conclusion.

The religious clauses were less generous than those of 1693 by so much as the embodiment of the priestly objections must make them, omitting the promise not to dispense with the Test, as Ranke acutely noted.[50] The exceptions were enlarged to those who had informed against or betrayed the king, with a period of prescription of two years, to run from the landing, in all cases arising from this exception. A legal confirmation of all judicial proceedings since the Revolution, except the criminal prosecutions of Jacobites for Jacobitism, was also granted. Assurances of a free Parliament and the speedy withdrawal of French troops were linked to a promise to pay the arrears of William's troops — if they deserted to James. Considering the expectation that he would be restored by force of foreign arms, with assistance from his most devoted followers, one is surprised that so much was conceded. For this there were doubtless two reasons: the pleas of Middleton and the need of Louis XIV to have his troops back again. France could not face a protracted campaign overseas with her small navy, and with enemies on every side. If the invasion should not succeed before summer, it would not succeed at all. The twelve thousand men spared for this project could not possibly do the work if the whole country opposed them, and Louis could not send more.

It did not matter, as later became clear. The marquis d'Harcourt, who was to command the French under James, arrived at Calais late in February. The king himself left St.-Germain on February 28. At Calais he was to meet eighteen battalions of infantry and thirteen squadrons of cavalry.[51] The next day

[48] Clarke, II, 532–36.
[49] Tindal, III, 314.
[50] Ranke, V, 111.
[51] Dangeau, V, 372.

Berwick arrived at Versailles and reported to the King of France, having met his father on the way. On March 1 he was off again to join the force on the coast.[52] His message was a blow to the kings, but they did not give up hope; instead it appears that they awaited word of the assassination plot, which Berwick would have told them to expect. The first news of the arrests reached Versailles on February 29/March 10, followed quickly by Berwick,[53] who still pled for the invasion, but in vain. The scheme had plainly failed, although James II did not return from the coast until the first week of May, when Dangeau reported that "the King of England" was again at St. Germain.[54]

What are we to believe of the part of the two kings in the plot against the life of William III? Contemporaries were divided on this question, but the best informed of them were aware that some of those involved in the invasion plan — possibly even James and Louis — were ignorant of the planned murder. The prosecutor of Fenwick, Mr. Serjeant Gould, made the distinction; but he made the connection of the two plans seem closer by the omission of reference, in his summary, to the general nature of Barclay's authority, probably in order to make a more damaging attack on Fenwick, against whom a principal share in organizing the rebellion was the great charge.[55] Burnet assumed that James II was the planner of the plot, but Captain Knightly, a St.-Germain officer tried and condemned for his share in it, says otherwise. Knightly confessed that Barclay told him that "he [Barclay] had done the Business his Master sent him about, but that he had something put into his Head, by which he could do the King farther service," that is, the assassination, and that he desired to recruit a few "honest Fellows" to help.[56] Ranke writes, of the assumed participation, "All direct evidence is against it," but also that both Louis XIV and James II "would have been willing to pluck the fruit." [57] Hoffman, in his dispatch of 20/30 March, was unwilling to decide, although much evidence was then at hand, whether

[52] *Ibid.*, V, 373.
[53] *Ibid.*, V, 376–77; Sourches, V, 117–18.
[54] Dangeau, V, 405; Sourches, V, 137.
[55] Account of the proceedings against Fenwick, Rawl. MSS. A. 83, p. 29.
[56] Blackmore, 133.
[57] Ranke, V, 115.

James were guilty or no; Klopp, nearly two hundred years later, is no more sure than Hoffman.[58] Who may have put the idea into Barclay's head, as Knightly understood the matter, is therefore in doubt, the inference being that it was not James, who had sent his officers on other errands. Could it have been Louis the Great acting without his ally's knowledge? But whether the two kings, or one of them, did or did not incite Barclay to murder, they acted as accomplices after the fact by giving Barclay protection, though at a distance from Versailles or St.-Germain. In the following year Middleton received word of the safety of Hungate and Richardson "with incredible Joy. . . The King has ordered money to be sent to yow, and Cap[tai]n Hungate, to whom I desire yow to make my complements."[59] Middleton procured passes for the pair,[60] although they had been almost certainly involved in the murder scheme, to admit them to France. Moreover, Barclay received both his arrears of pay and a pension.[61] These rewards are not those of murderers, or of suspects, but of patriots. The only conclusion possible is that the two kings may not have ordered or "approved" the murder of William III, but that they were willing to profit by it and even to pay for it.

3. THE PEACE OF RYSWICK

Every motive of his own interest now inclined Louis XIV to make peace with his enemies. The war was unsuccessful, though not disastrous: the summer of 1696 was employed in a fairly fruitless campaign in Flanders; this costly futility was relieved by the Catalonian campaign, culminating in the capture of Barcelona, as well as the secession of Savoy from its alliance with England, Spain, and the Emperor, on favorable terms for itself; the truth was plain that now neither side could expect victory. Moreover, the question of the Spanish Succession had assumed such urgency that great efforts on both sides were willingly made to solve it, even at the expense of a truce between two bitterly

[58] Klopp, VII, 197–99.
[59] Middleton to Richardson, April 28, 1697, Carte MSS. 208, fol. 156v.
[60] Ibid., fol. 157.
[61] Ibid., fol. 161; Carte MSS. 210, fol. 358.

hostile camps, because neither could risk the permanent advantage which the undivided inheritance could confer upon the other. After less formal negotiations during the winter of 1696–97, a congress assembled at Ryswick for the conclusion of peace.

At this time James II, seeing the progress of the treating, and knowing that it could result only in his abandonment by his powerful friend, took care to issue a remonstrance against the proceedings of the congress,[62] and against any terms of the peace which ignored or derogated from his rights as *de jure* king of England. Since William III was a party to the negotiations, such terms were indispensable to the treaty. An attempt had been made at a compromise by reinstating the "pretended Prince of Wales" in the line of succession, in the first conversations on peace between La Haye and Velo, representatives of France and the Emperor, at Padua in late March 1696. France proposed that the Emperor persuade William III to settle the English succession question forever by acknowledging the son of James II as heir to the throne. The proposal was forwarded to the Emperor Leopold, who said that he did not know what to think of it. At any rate, it went no further.[63] This is probably the occasion of the proposal made by Louis XIV to James (related by Berwick and the *Life*) which James rejected, according to Berwick on the advice of his wife, as making the son accomplice to his father's robbery.[64] The *Life* goes too far in saying that the matter was already arranged with William.[65]

The treaty nevertheless contained a considerable alleviation of the poverty of the court, or of the financial troubles of Louis, who had, after all, to support its expenses. It was settled that the jointure of the former queen, set originally at £50,000 a year by Act of Parliament on her marriage, should be continued to her, for her own and her husband's maintenance,[66] relieving France of the burden of 600,000 livres annually allotted to them. No

---

[62] Declaration of June 8, 1697, Carte MSS. 181, fol. 670.

[63] Klopp, VII, 246–48, 509.

[64] Berwick, I, 172–73. He places the offer shortly after the peace, a mistake, Klopp believes, for shortly before it.

[65] Clarke, II, 574–75.

[66] H.M.C. *Stuart Papers*, I; Klopp, VII; P. Grimblot, *Letters of William III and Louis XIV* (London, 1848), I; and a few letters in Carte MSS. 208 and 200.

other source had ever provided any substantial amount for that purpose, since 1692, when the Pope had sent 55,000 scudi for the relief of poor refugees.[67]

It was expected that in return James II would remove to a place further from England, perhaps Blois or Avignon,[68] although no clause to that effect was included in the treaties concluded at Ryswick. The Court of Versailles was surprised to hear, four days after conclusion of peace, that the château at St.-Germain was to be the permanent residence of James II and Maria Beatrice.[69] The news of the signature of the treaties was carefully concealed from the pair, then the guests of the King of France at Fontainebleau; out of consideration for their feelings, Louis XIV "forbade the musicians to sing anything relating to the peace until the departure of the Court of England." [70] Thus there was no change in his respect for his friend. A few months later, "the King of England" took part in the wedding of the Dauphin's eldest son; [71] he continued to hunt with the French king's pack, and disappointed Portland, William's ambassador, of his sport; [72] and Barclay, Berwick, and other unpleasing persons remained in France, some of them even in the capital.[73] Portland warned the French authorities that if James remained where he was, the jointure would not be paid.[74] Middleton had predicted the use of this means to force a removal of a renunciation of his title. He had been very right. The jointure was not paid during the period of peace, 1697–1701, and in the following war was naturally not even considered.

Although he was allowed to stay near Versailles, with all the diversions then known open to his participation, the deprived king devoted himself still more to his former austerities, taking a lugubrious part in the festivities of Fontainebleau, to be sure, but a greater share in the rites and privations of La Trappe. Melfort

[67] Carte MSS. 209, fol. 70.
[68] Sourches, V, 343–44; Grimblot, I, p. 93.
[69] Sourches, V, 343–44.
[70] Dangeau, VI, 196–97; St.-Simon, IV, 239.
[71] Sourches, V, 367–68.
[72] Ibid., VI, 16; St.-Simon, V, 417.
[73] Grimblot, I, 168–172; Dangeau, VI, 297; Christian Cole, Memoirs of Affairs of State (London, 1733), passim.
[74] St.-Simon, V, 72.

was freed to return to Paris in November,[75] and saw his master occasionally. Middleton and Caryll, however, continued to conduct their correspondence with England,[76] without interference from him. Berwick, the most able of the younger men, retired into the country for most of the period of peace. The remainder of the court were old, in the main, and poor — so poor that some, like Sir John Maclean, would have gone home if the government had allowed them to do so.[77] Others went home by arrangement with the authorities or surreptitiously.[78]

Some of these *revenants,* and some visitors to France during the truce took care to ingratiate themselves with the government of the king *de facto:* Burnet, who let no gossip slip, wrote to Dr. Fall, Precentor at York, "Mr. Cunningham and Lord Lorn are come back, He saies the Court there is now as much despised and as openly as you and I knew it admired, but there is a spirit of open Impiety and unnatural lust raging there without any reserve." [79] As to the treatment of the court of St.-Germain in France, I think that it has been shown that this statement is untrue. As many sources as can be consulted on manners and morals there omit any reference to unnatural vice in so much as a single case. If an editorial mistake in printing this extract occurred, it might easily have referred to the French court, in which public confidence was waning; there also the habits of the duc d'Orléans and others were notorious. Of St.-Germain the evidence simply will not bear out Cunningham's remarks.

The state of the Jacobite party in England had deteriorated since Middleton's departure: Roger North, an outspoken opponent of the new regime, had retired to the country and taken up literary pursuits, and the Earl of Clarendon had abandoned politics years before. Fenwick and Preston were dead, having first forfeited confidence by betrayal. Ailesbury had been forced to

---

[75] Dangeau, VI, 228–29.

[76] According to Sheridan (*Political Reflexions,* 111) Middleton's post was saved for him by the King of France. James felt that he had no need for a Secretary of State.

[77] McCormick, 374–75.

[78] Cole, 130.

[79] H.M.C. *Report* IX, app. II, 463. Cunningham was the tutor of the eldest son of the Duke of Argyll.

leave England after the assassination plot, with many another. The clamor for the disbandment of William's army after the Peace of Ryswick was made, in part, by the Jacobites, led by those in Parliament. There was not much else that they could do. Those who could not stomach William were somewhat reconciled to the situation by the imminence of the succession of Anne, William having remained unmarried during the four years since the death of Mary. The death of the young Duke of Gloucester even made possible return to the senior line of the Stuarts on Anne's death, for no one expected her father to outlive her.

In Scotland disaffection continued for several reasons. The rigorous treatment of the Scots Episcopal clergy since the Revolution threw that party into the arms of the man who promised the restoration of the *status quo ante*.[80] There were also a number of Catholics of great birth and influence in Scotland, who were naturally in easier circumstances before the Revolution than after. The massacre of Glencoe, its stealthy preparation, and the royal collusion shown by the delay and lightness of punishment of the offenders provoked a feeling of hatred and suspicion which nothing but time could calm, and ten years had not yet passed. Some historians plead for William that "letters of fire and sword" were commonly issued in Scotland. They were, at all events, very uncommonly carried into effect. A more recent grievance, more important in the Lowlands, was the failure of the Darien Company, attributed to English jealousy armed with English influence, with more than enough reason to excite Scottish nationalists. Disturbances caused by this affair passed quite out of control in the summer of 1700.[81] That the Jacobites made good use of these irritations was known to the government.[82]

Ireland was not more submissive than her sister kingdoms, but more nearly impotent. The most loyal and able Jacobites had gone abroad to serve in the French army, if physically fit to do so. Those of greater age, and the infirm, who had disclosed their

---

[80] Charles Leslie, *The Rehearsal*, no. 23, Dec. 30, 1704; *The Case of the Present Afflicted Episcopal Clergy in Scotland* (London, 1690); and *A Short Account of the Grievances of the Episcopal Clergy in Scotland, Miscellany of the Spottiswoode Society* (1845), II.

[81] McCormick, 527–79.

[82] *Cal. S. P. Dom., 1699–1700*, 288.

feelings during the war in Ireland, sometimes found it unwise to remain, although clauses in the Treaty of Limerick, which brought that war to a close, should have protected them. Violations of that treaty deprived many Catholics and other loyalists of their estates and awarded them to William's generals and favorites, so that those who stayed were obliged to rely on friends and relations for support. The young, as they reached sufficient age to carry their education beyond the lower levels, went to the Continent to Catholic schools there or to the French army, often for life. Never in the history of Jacobitism, therefore, did a large body of wealthy and energetic men espouse the cause in Ireland after the capitulation of Limerick, although its religion, loyal sentiments, and political aspirations were such as to lead the nation to distinguish itself for James II.

4. THE LAST OF THE OLD KING

The Spanish Succession problem, which had dashed the Stuart designs, led slowly to their revival. Portland, during his mission to Paris in the winter of 1697–98, opened the discussion of a possible compromise. In the spring these were transferred to London, where the comte de Tallard was in direct contact with William III, and then to Loo in the Netherlands. The first treaty of partition was signed on October 2, 1698. The assumption on which this and a later treaty were based was that neither the Bourbon family of France nor the Habsburg branch of Austria could be allowed to inherit the whole dominions of Charles II of Spain, whose death without posterity was expected, without a dangerous disturbance of the balance of Europe. These two families possessed the strongest claims. A third, less objectionable, was that of the Electoral Prince of Bavaria, Joseph Ferdinand. The treaty of 1698, then, gave the bulk of the Spanish possessions to Joseph Ferdinand, but left large portions to the Dauphin and to the second son of the Emperor, Archduke Charles, the arrangement to be effective on the death of the reigning king.

Unfortunately for the prospects of peace, the Electoral Prince died in the following January. Another acceptable arrangement was sought, the basic assumption remaining unchallenged, and a treaty was drawn up in June 1699. The English representative signed this treaty, on his king's authority only, in February 1700; the Dutch followed in March. The Emperor, who desired a larger share for his son, although it was already enormous, held out, and did not approve the treaty. His obstinacy contributed to the French uneasiness on the treaty which, as we shall see, was to be the undoing of the labors of three years.

The Jacobites observed the negotiations impatiently. Peace would destroy their hopes, perhaps forever, since James II's health had declined rapidly, and his natural successor was only a boy. There were people in Scotland who encouraged Middleton with schemes, but without a foreign force how could Scotland hope to conquer England, or even act independently? France would not supply such a force at the cost of war and, if a permanent peace were once inaugurated, perhaps never would. Louis XIV was old, and might soon die, leaving an unsympathetic successor or an incompetent one.

His first aim now, at any rate, was to secure as much as possible of the Spanish power to himself, to the Dauphin, or to some other member of his family. He was successful. The King of Spain, Charles II, was angered at the division of his possessions before his death, and was led by indignation, and by the influence of Spanish traditionalists at his court, to make a will devising all of his dominions without exception to a younger son of the Dauphin, who if he refused to accept the undivided empire, must see it offered to the Austrian claimant, who, the Emperor having rejected the treaty, would be free to take it. This the King of France, regardless of his treaty obligations, could not bear. When the death of Charles II made the will public, Louis XIV accepted in the name of his grandson, the duc d'Anjou, who took the title of Philip V of Spain. The proclamation of the new ruler was peacefully carried out, to the consternation of the Emperor (whose obstinacy was to blame), England, and the United Provinces.

At first it seemed that they could do nothing — that the Spanish provinces in Italy and the Empire did not wish to be torn from their ancient union with peninsular Spain, as the treaty provided, and that powerful parties, in England at least, were so averse to war that the Maritime Powers could not enter the dispute except under grave handicaps. England's ministers had had no hand in making the treaty, and were not disposed to enforce it. William was embarrassed at his lack of support, but particularly by the attitude of the Tory party, on which his current ministry had to depend.[83] Besides, the English Succession was a problem in itself since the death of the Duke of Gloucester, the last survivor of Princess Anne's family, and, since Anne expected no more children, the last hope that no further regulation of the succession would be necessary.

Before he could devote his whole attention to the continent, William was forced to settle the succession beyond Anne. He had much too little faith in her judgment to leave it to her. Calling a new Parliament, he found it as Tory as the last, yet succeeded, before prorogation, in July 1701, in coaxing from it supplies for the army and navy, and in extending the right of succession beyond Anne to the Electress Sophia of Hanover and her Protestant descendants.

Louis XIV assisted him to some extent by beginning a series of measures frightening to the Maritime Powers. He recognized his grandson's eventual claim to the French throne, without requiring him to renounce the Spanish title in the event; he occupied the barrier fortresses, provided as a safeguard for Holland, with French troops; and he secured great and exclusive trading privileges for France in the Spanish colonies. Thus, when he entered into relations with England and the Low Countries for a continued peace, he was actually asking for time to make his power irresistible in any future war, and to introduce French commerce into the supposed preserves of other nations if peace should be his pleasure.

Fashions in history change, but Messrs. Lecky and Namier agree on the minute interest shown by England's aristocratic Parliament [84] in the bourgeois concerns of trade in the eighteenth

---

[83] K. G. Feiling, *A History of the Tory Party, 1640–1714* (Oxford, 1924), 335–40. See also Robert Walcott, Jr., "English Party Politics (1688–1714)," *Essays in Modern English History In Honor of Wilbur Cortez Abbot* (Cambridge, Mass., 1941), 105.

[84] However, Walcott ("English Party Politics," 86) finds fifty merchants in Parliament in 1702, including bankers.

century. Once convinced of danger to trade, Whigs and Tories would fight back to back. Their prompt action on the Settlement and the forces can be attributed, in part, to this, and in part to further assistance which William received from another unexpected quarter.

It will be recalled that Melfort had returned to Paris in 1697. By August or September of 1700 he was installed in a house in St.-Germain.[85] Here, for the next few months, was the center of Jacobite intrigue of the most irresponsible kind; a short time later Lord Manchester, the British Ambassador, complained of his insolent behavior in public places, which was beyond a diplomat's capacity for brushing aside.[86] In February 1701, Melfort wrote a letter to his brother, Perth, the governor of the Prince of Wales, discussing the possibility of an invasion of England by France in accordance with a plan said to have been already made, the reestablishment of the Catholic church, recent treasonable correspondence of the Duke of Hamilton with James II, and plausible reasons for dismissing Middleton. This letter, which need never have been written, since Melfort could easily have gone to see his brother, was placed by Melfort, or an accomplice, or a careless mail clerk, in the London mail bag. Detected, of course, in the London post office, it was sent to the ministers of William III, who on February 17/28 displayed it to Parliament. Under the circumstances, what could that body do but apply themselves with all haste "to consider the State of the Fleet"? [87]

The incident was well timed to provoke both parties, but especially the Tories. Nothing that the French Ambassador, the comte de Tallard, could say could help: he called Melfort "un fou et un extravagant," reminded Secretary Vernon that the man had no part in French counsels, and assured him that the plan of invasion was a fiction; to this Vernon coldly replied that he would be glad to think so.[88] Privately Vernon remarked, "It is plain by several accounts . . . that they are not willing to break with

[85] Cole, 206.
[86] Manchester to Vernon, Paris, Nov. 17, 1700, *ibid.*, 245.
[87] *Ibid.*, 319.
[88] *Ibid.*, 322.

us." [89] Torcy, the French foreign minister,[90] questioned Melfort, who admitted writing a letter, but not all of the things attributed to him; the French minister was certain that his aim was no less than to provoke war. When it was evident that Melfort had written the whole, Torcy consulted James II, then exiled the culprit to Angers.[91]

Perhaps as a result of the painful circumstances of this parting, James suffered a stroke which paralyzed one side of his body. When he was sufficiently recovered to travel, he went to take the waters at Bourbon, but he was never the same, after his return on June 7.[92]

Now that William was backed by parliamentary supplies, he could set about the forging of a new Grand Alliance. Holland and England could not agree with the Emperor that the Archduke Charles should receive the whole Spanish Empire by the terms of an ultimatum to be sent to France, but consented, without withdrawing their previous recognition of Philip V, to insist on a division, by which Naples, Sicily, the Spanish Netherlands, and Milan should fall to the archduke. This alliance, drafted in July, was signed at the Hague on September 7, 1701. A period of grace was left to Louis XIV for the acceptance of the terms, which might have been used for adjustment of the differences on both the Spanish and English successions, had not James II died on September 16. How far these terms might have reached may be judged by the question raised by William III and the Emperor of recognizing the Prince of Wales as heir to the throne.[93] There was no time for decision or discussion with France or James II, however, before the sentimental haste of Louis XIV had swept England and the rest of Europe into a war which would last a dozen years, and impoverish whole nations.

As James II sank into his decline, he was visited by his host of so many years, who assured him that his son would be recognized by France as King of England. This visit, on September 13, was

---

[89] *Ibid.*, 324.

[90] Jean-Baptiste Colbert, marquis de Torcy (1665–1746), Secretary of State for Foreign Affairs from 1696 to 1715.

[91] *Ibid.*, 330, 336.

[92] Sourches, VII, 31; St.-Simon, VIII, 100*n.*

[93] Klopp, VII, 248.

followed by James's death on the 16th; recognition by France and the Papal Nuncio came shortly after.[94] On November 23, the King of Spain's ambassador at Paris executed his orders to do the same.[95] Torcy desired that there should be no break with England, and insisted that he had opposed the recognition when it was suggested by the Dauphin and Mme. de Maintenon.[96] The English ambassador awaited instructions, and then returned to England without taking leave by the usual ceremonial call.[97]

In effect, the two countries were at war from that time. Imperial troops had already clashed, and this new development sent England pell-mell into the Imperial camp, where English public opinion could be counted upon to keep her. But William did not live to see the end of his life's work, for in March he was injured by a fall from his horse. He died on the 7/18th of that month.

5. THE FIRST OF THE NEW

The furor created in England by the recognition of the Prince of Wales was no greater than that at St.-Germain-en-Laye. The new titular king assumed the name of James III, by which for brevity I shall often refer to him.

He was thirteen years old, and an unhealthy boy. This unhealthiness showed itself in divers ways throughout his life — a serious case of measles at twenty, a nearly fatal attack of smallpox at twenty-three, a fistula at twenty-eight, and in the end a premature debility, which at fifty-five made him think himself too old for long journeys. His father was aware of the snares of Satan that an exiled prince might find in his way, for he had fallen into a good many in his own youth. He therefore watched his son and had him watched as, in his remorseful moments, he wished that he himself had been. The usual court conventions were observed in his education: the child was in the care of women until he was seven, when he was delivered to a male governor, the Earl of

[94] Cole, 418; Dangeau, VIII, 194; Clement XI to James III, Rome, Oct. 25, 1701, in Clement's *Opera Omnia* (Frankfurt, 1729), part 2 ("Epistolae et Brevia Selectiora") columns 87–88.

[95] Dangeau, VIII, 241–42, 244.

[96] Cole, 422; Père Léonard, "Mémoire historique" (printed in St.-Simon, IX, 433).

[97] Cole, 425; Dangeau, VIII, 206.

Perth,[98] who for his cares was raised to a titular dukedom,[99] and to two under-governors, William Dicconson and Dominick Sheldon, all Catholics.[100] The rules laid down for the supervision of the prince [101] were quite severe — it is only the beginning of them that he was never to be alone. No one was to whisper to him, to give him things to eat without permission, to show him books not previously shown to the governor or preceptor for approval, or to introduce other children to play with him except at certain times and under certain conditions. The boy was to be confined to his rooms except when the governor ordered otherwise, to hear Mass once a day, and to be instructed in his religion during regular school hours on Sunday. It was a careful plan, and produced a careful man. With some obvious differences, this plan was followed after his succession to the title, with the addition of his father's deathbed injunction, "Be a good Catholic, fear God, obey the queen your mother, and after God, be in an entire dependence on the King of France." [102]

He was in most respects, far more than his almost-sainted father, a good man. His Catholicism never wavered, in the most tempting circumstances, but had no taint of intolerance about it, as we shall come to see. Nor was he superstitious; he never believed that he could obtain his worldly ends by praying for them.

He was immeasurably loyal. Beginning life in conditions which called for unstinted generosity, with but meager resources, he had always to give assurances when money failed, assurances which would wear thin to his friends with their clothes; the money followed the assurances when it could be found, however, and some who begged deserved little. Even these were often not entirely overlooked. Let us forget, for once, the myth of "Stuart ingratitude" which has been used to explain so many improbable things by a few rather improbable authors. It was a rarer gift to know how to avoid letting the jealousy of one friend destroy his faith in another. On one occasion it took over two years to per-

[98] H.M.C. *Stuart Papers*, I, 119.
[99] Cole, 424.
[100] H.M.C., *Stuart Papers*, I, 151.
[101] *Ibid.*, 1. 114–17.
[102] St.-Simon, IX, 426.

suade him to dispense with the services of a man who would not be useful to him in any way, and who had probably betrayed his closest confidences. Even imperfect servants must feel his gratitude and his unwillingness to hear scandal, he believed, and so he told those whom he thought to be calumniators. He carried this quality to the point where it became a fault.

His bravery was acknowledged by all except pamphleteers. He served in three campaigns with the French army against Marlborough, risked assassination on two wild rides across France in 1715 during his attempts to reach Scotland, and underwent grave dangers there as his army slowly melted away; he outdid 1715 in a dash from Bologna to Lorraine in 1727.

His learning was of the kind called "polite." He spoke French well, and lost no facility in English, as all his letters show. Italian was his mother's language, learned in France and perfected in Italy. He had a taste for antique curiosities, not coupled with great knowledge, a feeling for good music which led him often to the opera, and a general appreciation for the works of erudition and for those who executed them. In Italy his associates considered him accomplished, which is an overstatement, courteous, which is true, and melancholy, which is a simplification.

On the side of action he was deficient, not through cowardice, but through inability. Had he succeeded peacefully to a settled throne, as George II did, he might have ruled; but the acquisition of power called for improvisation, daring of judgment, popular appeal, which he could never muster. He was a decent failure because his ineffectuality was never excused by unworthy recrimination, and because his failure did not lead him to abandon his friends with his hopes. This is not to say that they did not feel as if they had been deserted on some occasions, for his personality sometimes frustrated his efforts to help his followers; he kept his dignity to the last, and was cold to those who offended it; while this in itself is exasperating, James must also have been a good deal of a bore, to the detriment of his marriage and of his cause. And human weakness may have been beyond his grasp.

The court of St.-Germain continued in the path in which Middleton and James II had set it. The Earl, now given the English title of Earl of Monmouth, continued in office, because there was no one to take his place, and important business was in the air. The loyal non-juring element, which had separated from the rest of the Church of England rather than swear allegiance to William III after giving the same allegiance to James II, bestirred itself to show its continuing loyalty to the hereditary succession in the old line, by sending Dr. Charles Leslie, one of the ablest of Jacobites and non-jurors, to St.-Germain with their acknowledgment of James III's authority and a set of "Instructions" to which they wished him to give his assent.[103] It is to the queen's credit that she did not use her influence to prevent ratification. Without significant change it was signed on March 3, 1702, and dispersed in England among the Tories.[104]

The actions of this party require some explanation. Jacobites, and some who never earned that name, had sat uneasily under William, but were now able to accommodate themselves, in many cases, to the reign of Anne. George Granville, the later Lord Lansdowne, entered Parliament for the first time under Anne, a step which he had steadfastly refused to take since the Revolution, despite the pressure of the Granville connection.[105] Some of the non-jurors, feeling relieved of their oath to James II by his death, had returned to communion with the Church of England. Of course, the old ties remained strong, and the new subscribers to the Revolution Settlement were firmly opposed to the Hanoverian succession. Some Tories not Jacobites played with the notion of a regency of Anne for her half-brother, who would succeed her. Few now accepted the warming-pan myth. Lord Clarendon wrote to Dr. Turner of Oxford, when he heard that Dr. Wallis, Professor of Astronomy there, boasted of having seen proof that James III was no Stuart, "It is very strange, if Dr. Wallis know soe great a secrett, & soe useful an one, towards the quieting the Kingdome, that he would not divulge it in all this time, for wch he would

---

[103] A translation into the French of the original survives among the Stuart Papers; a retranslation of it is printed in H.M.C. *Stuart Papers*, IV, 3–4.

[104] A copy of the "Instructions" as issued is Carte MSS. 209, fol. 481r and v.

[105] F. E. Handasyde, *Granville the Polite* (Oxford, 1933), 76. Granville (1666–1735), grandson of a royalist of the Civil Wars, had for tutor William Ellis, later a prominent Jacobite, was nephew of Denis Granville, Dean of Durham, and cousin of the Higgons brothers, all Jacobites. For the Granville connection, of which the Earl of Bath was the head, see Walcott, 95–96, 98.

not have wanted thanks from those who could gratify him." [106] Indeed, there had been no investigation to justify William's suspicions for the good reason that no credible witnesses would deny that the delivery of Maria Beatrice was genuine, or that James III was the son borne by her. Since this was not disputed, the hereditary right remained in force, overriding in the many honest, intelligent men of all ranks [107] any Parliamentary claim whatsoever. For these the "Instructions" of March 1702 were designed.

The first instruction is that all Englishmen should know that James III offers to protect "all our subjects of the Church of England as it is established by law" — there it is again — in their legal rights and privileges, and in possession of their churches, universities and schools, and that he will carefully select for all posts in the church worthy men of the Anglican persuasion. The second provision is a promise that, if churchmen are sufficiently helpful in returning the country to its obedience to James, he will waive the right of nomination of Anglican bishops and other dignitaries, leaving that power to a committee of bishops headed by the Archbishop of Canterbury, during James's own life only. Also, for the first time, the first fruits and tenths paid by the clergy would be permanently remitted. Only clergymen who opposed the restoration "who by renouncing the principles of the Church of England [non-resistance] have no pretence to the benefit we intend her," are excepted. However James would not be obliged to persecute Catholics or Dissenters, and would refer the question of a toleration to a Parliament for settlement.

The third concession anticipates by some months the grant of "Queen Anne's Bounty," the use of first fruits and tenths paid by all beneficed clerics for the relief of the poorer of them, but does not pretend to such a redistribution as that, only to a remission to "loyal" clergymen. Still it is difficult to understand how it was that these instructions drew no more comment than they did. Ten years later Anglicans dickering with James anxiously desired promises already given in this instrument, and

[106] Rawlinson MSS. (Bodleian Library), Letters 92, fol. 67. Dr. Turner was brother to the deprived Bishop of Ely.

[107] For a statement on Parliamentary sentiment by Sir John Bolles, see *Cal. S. P. Dom., 1700–1702*, 499, 501, 505.

publication of its terms is the *raison d'être* of some clauses of declarations issued in 1715. Bishop Burnct lamented that his own share in Queen Anne's grant was not well known, and that the effects of her donation were overlooked while at another time "those who promoted it would have been looked upon as the truest friends of the church." Burnet would perhaps have been surprised, if that reaction had occurred. At any rate the two grants passed relatively quietly, and James's was forgotten.

6. LOVAT AND HOOKE

The years of the minority of the young king were occupied in waiting for an opportunity of invasion during the war now being waged, and in correspondence with Scottish and English notables — more Scottish than English, be it said, because of the conversion of Lord Middleton. During James II's last days, he exhorted his Protestant ministers and officers to renounce their error and return to the true Church.[108] Middleton was directly addressed, but took no immediate action. In March he countersigned the "Instructions," and did other business in the following months, but in August 1702 he retired, and became a Catholic. Some said, in a spirit of mockery, that he claimed to have had a vision. The Earl does not mention this in his "Reasons," written on his withdrawal, of which the original draft survives.[109] Among these reasons he repeated his desire to be free of office, an old idea of his. He had always held himself free to resign, he said, and not being an Englishman, or the owner of large English estates, has felt that it might be well for such a person to hold his office. Now that he has become a Catholic, and incurred the detestation reserved by Englishmen for the convert, the reasons for his retirement have become overwhelming. He denied worldly views, and asserted that he wished most to be free from the temptations of the court. Toward the end the clerk's handwriting breaks off, and

[108] Dangeau, VIII, 480; St.-Simon, IX, 426–27.
[109] Carte MSS. 209, foll. 194–96. These "reasons" became "The Earl of Middleton's Letter to his Lady," printed 1702. A copy is in the Bodleian Library volume R.I. 19. Jur. The Catalogue of the Bodleian and the Index of H.M.C. *Report* I assign this paper to the first Earl of Middleton, who died in 1674 and was never a Catholic.

Middleton's own takes up, less legible than in any other holograph of his. He was evidently emotionally disturbed. If one sides
with St.-Simon, one can attribute this to anger, or fear, or haste,
but it is possible to believe that his conversion was sincere, and
therefore disturbing. The evidence is as much on that side as on
the other. But one must not accept St.-Simon's assignment of
Melfort's renewal of strength in the party as a cause.[110] It did
not occur until 1704, two years after Middleton's conversion.

His retirement did not last. Within a year he was back at his
post. The reasons for his retirement were still valid, but no more
acceptable person could be found to execute the very necessary
business of the king. Thenceforth he was the complete master of
the court, the confidant of the queen, the king's admired friend,
and director of the fate of the British and Irish "colony," as we
should say nowadays. Only the Drummond faction headed by
Perth remained independent, and kept up its own large Scottish
connection.

The affair which brought Middleton back into employment was
the growing discontent in Scotland, which first showed itself in
the sending over of one James Murray in January 1702–03 for the
purpose of forming a project of insurrection or descent.[111] Simon
Fraser, a contender for the Barony of Lovat in Scotland, and a
man of unsavory antecedents, also brought a scheme of invasion
by a body of 5,000 men, which he represented as necessary for a
rebellion of 12,000 Scotsmen already promised. Not seeming to
have as much authority for his proposals as the French desired,
he was sent back, in the company of another Murray named John,
to obtain a picture of the state of parties in Scotland, and the
desires or needs of the loyal chiefs and gentlemen, with other
details.[112] James Murray, as an envoy of Middleton, had already
gone over again, with warnings of Lovat's mission.

[110] As Mr. W. C. Mackenzie (*Simon Fraser, Lord Lovat, His Life and Times*,
London, 1908, 80n) has done.

[111] Murray's instructions, Carte MSS. 209, foll. 418–21; Colin Campbell's
declaration, *A Collection of Original Papers about the Scots Plot* (London,
1704), 21–22.

[112] Instructions to John Murray and Lovat, Carte MSS. 180, foll. 355, 371–
72. Mr. W. C. Mackenzie makes a different interpretation of these documents
(available to him only through Macpherson), *Simon Fraser, Lord Lovat*, 98–
100, 110.

These messengers were given credential letters, including at least one unaddressed, to Jacobites in that country. On his return to Edinburgh, Lovat went as quickly as possible to the Duke of Queensberry, by this time well tied to the Revolution by office and habit, and told what he knew of the plot, then passed into the Highlands to enlist or entrap the nobility and chiefs of clans in his scheme, with the unwitting assistance of John Murray. After another visit to Queensberry, when he betrayed an unaddressed letter to which he had set the name of the Marquess of Atholl,[113] he left Scotland again for France. The betrayal had strong motives behind it. Atholl had driven Lovat out of Scotland by prosecution for Lovat's rape of the marquess' sister, and was an enemy of Queensberry for both political and family reasons. Lovat could thus both strike at his enemy and gain Queensberry's influence for the reversal of the outlawry under which he had lain since his crime. The flimsy evidence of Atholl's relations with St.-Germain was reported to Anne,[114] and measures might have been taken against the marquess, had he not been informed by Robert Ferguson, "the plotter," in time to make a personal appeal to the queen for justice.[115] He obtained it, because nothing could be proved against him. Lovat's revelations resulted only in the arrest of Sir John MacLean, David Lindsay, and a man named Keith, who were in England without passes (it was pretended in order to ask for pardon). MacLean, the chief of his clan, informed on the others after his arrest, or they might have gone unnoticed. James Murray had a narrow escape; the Earl Marischal of Scotland and the Earl of Hume, besides the Duke of Hamilton, were revealed to have made treasonable commitments,[116] but were too highly placed to be prosecuted without more evidence.

The disclosures eventually caused a quarrel between the two Houses of Parliament in England: the Whig Lords desired to proceed against some of the Tories implicated by MacLean — Marlborough and his friend Godolphin — and to harass Lord Nottingham, the interrogator of MacLean, for not having reported

[113] Nairne's note on a copy of the letter, Carte MSS. 180, foll. 446v, 447.
[114] Queensberry to Anne, Sept. 25 [O.S.], 1703, *A Collection. . . about the Scots Plot*, 7.
[115] Atholl's Memorial, *ibid.*, 8–13.
[116] Lovat's Information, Aug. 11 [O.S.], 1703, *ibid.*, 5.

this part of MacLean's testimony to that house. The Commons, on the other hand, were predominantly Tory, and objected to that proceeding. Quarrels between the Houses usually ended in a heated stalemate. So it was in this case, since the Whigs were not strong enough to initiate action against the ministry, of which Marlborough and Godolphin were now the leaders, even in the House of Lords.

It is certain that many of the Scottish lords, not yet (before the Union) members of that chamber, were of loyal, or Jacobite, tendencies,[117] that some of them had long been in correspondence with the court of St.-Germain, that the government was unwilling to proceed to extremes against them, and that Lovat was a great rogue. This time, being in France when the "Scots plot" was published, he paid the penalty. He was immediately suspected, and finally arrested, by the French government, at the request of the Jacobites. His first explanations were almost as unconvincing as the later ones to which he was driven by the questions of Lord Middleton.[118] The Secretary made the most of the visits to Queensberry, and mocked the pretense that the duke protected Lovat for old times' sake. Middleton exclaimed at Lovat's story, that Queensberry and his friends, known to act only in their own interests, "will act against these same interests, to the point of exposing themselves to quartering, and having their possessions confiscated, and their posterity degraded from the nobility, and all that from pure friendship!" Lovat was imprisoned at Angoulême, and was lucky to get off so lightly. For years he remained there, imploring help from everybody, feigning a conversion which he easily forgot afterwards, and which deceived none, and alleging a gigantic misunderstanding.[119] Everyone understood him all too well.

At that time the French would probably have lent no troops for Jacobite uses, but a few months later Lord John Drummond,

[117] *Ibid.*, 22–23.

[118] Middleton to Torcy, June 16, 1704, Carte MSS. 238, fol. 54r and v; "Interrogatoires pour Milord Lovat," *ibid.,* fol. 59; "Extrait des Reponses de Milord Lovat. . . " [Feb. 1704], Carte MSS. 180, foll. 428–29; "Remarques sur les Reponses. . . " *ibid.,* foll. 430–35.

[119] W. D. Macray, ed., *Correspondence of Nathaniel Hooke, 1703–1707* (London, 1870), I, 107; II, 146–49.

a son of the "Duke" of Perth, whose family maintained its ties in Scotland by birth and marriage as anchors both there and abroad, came to the French with a more serious project of an expedition to Scotland, which was considered, and unwillingly rejected, by the marquis de Torcy and others in June, 1704.[120] One of the difficulties of the French in making any decision was lack of proper intelligence.

The next year, when it seemed that the release of troops for Scotland was possible, Nathaniel Hooke was sent by Torcy to Scotland. Hooke was an Irish officer, a former nonconformist minister in Monmouth's rebellion, then a Catholic and a Jacobite, and now a half-pay colonel in the French service. He was a thorough opportunist, and had now attached himself rather more to France than to England. He opposed Middleton's caution in deferring a rising until it could be decisive through proper foreign support, and chose to believe the contrary advice received through the Drummonds. When his mission was proposed, Hooke asked to be foremost an agent of Louis XIV, and requested that St.-Germain should be kept in the dark,[121] but Middleton and Queen Maria both came to know, in spite of that. Proper credentials were provided by Louis XIV and the Queen Mother, including letters from the former to the Dukes of Hamilton and Gordon, the Marquess of Montrose, the Earl of Errol and the Earl Marischal, and Lord Drummond,[122] and sent to Scotland in August 1705, with the first fair winds.[123] While there he saw Gordon, Errol, and Marischal, and had word from Hamilton and most of the others. Hamilton met Hooke in the dark, so as to be able to swear that he had not seen him.[124] Hooke returned to France with letters from the former Bishop of Edinburgh, General Buchan, and others whom he had been sent to see,[125] landing at Dunkirk on September 25. He was received at Fontainebleau with a long memorial on the condition of Scotland about three weeks later.[126]

---

[120] Add. MSS. (British Museum) 20, 318, fol. 112.
[121] Macray, I, 167-71.
[122] Ibid., I, 208-22.
[123] Ibid., I, 238, 263.
[124] Ibid., I, 268-71, 275, and 277-78.
[125] Ibid., I, 291-303.
[126] Ibid., I, 372-428.

The substance of his account was that Hamilton, the natural leader, protested loyalty, but refused to deal with Middleton or his colleague Caryll, and that he was suspected of seeking an opportunity to take the throne for himself. Hooke was not alone in his opinion, for the most active Jacobite in Scotland, George Lockhart of Carnwath, shared it, and was stronger in his suspicion of the duke.[127]

This is Hooke's account. Lockhart supplements it with depreciation of the agent's understanding, and a fear that Louis XIV intended to make a diversion in Scotland and ruin the Jacobites who would come out and be massacred or hanged, for no reason but the recall of English troops from the continent.[128] The queen was satisfied with his conduct and his information.[129] Belief in the division of the Jacobites — Atholl against Hamilton, Perth against Middleton — caused the matter to be dropped, in spite of the constant stream of pet schemes submitted from all loyal quarters.[130]

The English court was aware of Hooke's motions. Captain John Ogilvie, a former soldier of James II in the French service who had returned to Scotland, was admitted to the secret, saw much of the correspondence, and betrayed it all.[131]

This betrayal and other considerations justify Middleton's caution, but it was not alone sufficient to attain the desired end. The majority of James III, reached on his eighteenth birthday, introduced a new factor, the personality of the monarch, as important to the course of events as that of his father. He must have set to work at once on the vast correspondence which spanned the continent, inspired thousands to passive loyalty or rebellion, and now lies almost unread in the archives of Windsor Castle, for Middleton wrote shortly after this momentous White Rose Day "Le Roy mon maitre s'applique au travail presentem[en]t avec l'habileté d'un maître ouvrier." [132] He would have been a master work-

---

[127] Lockhart, The Lockhart Papers (London, 1817), I, passim. W. C. Mackenzie treats Hamilton as a "Middleton" man, without naming a source (Simon Fraser, 122). I believe this to be an error.

[128] Lockhart, I, 148.

[129] Add. MSS. 20,293, fol. 40.

[130] E.g. Add. MSS. 20, 311, foll. 70–71, 72, 74, 75–76, 68–69; Macray, II, 7.

[131] H.M.C. Report XV, app. IV, 276–77. For Ogilvie's career, see p. 160 of that volume.

[132] Middleton to Torcy, June 28, Carte MSS. 238, fol. 16.

man indeed, if his letters could have got him three kingdoms. The coming of age of the young king nevertheless transformed the policy of the aging Middleton into a vigorous one; and it was not long before he took up other tools than the pen.

3

PROMISE

(1 7 0 6 – 1 7 1 4)

1. SCOTTISH JACOBITES AND THE UNION

The period which followed was the most active and hopeful in the history of Jacobitism. It is true that there was little immediate change. Life at St.-Germain went on in much the same way. It was because of Jacobite conduct in the Scottish Parliament that the Union of England and Scotland became such a pressing matter, however, second to no other. Two acts of that Parliament, that "anent Peace and War," and that "of Security," made conceivable a movement to place James III and VIII on the throne of an independent Scotland, even if England submitted to the Hanoverian Succession. The first was a limitation on the power of Anne's successor to make war or peace; the second provided that Anne's successor in Scotland should be of the royal line of Scotland, but *not* the same person as should succeed her in England. The Jacobite succession in Scotland would be such a danger to the Hanoverian rulers of England that it could not be permitted, although Scotland itself mattered little to the insular and more wealthy English Government.

If Union alone could extinguish this possibility, there must be a Union, and quickly — such a Union as would set up a Parliament which would have the authority to revoke the acts objected to and would, through secure control by England, be kept from passing any more such acts. The Jacobites, who in Scotland called themselves "Cavaliers," opposed a Union in the Parliament at Edinburgh because they shared with the Whigs the expectation that it would preclude a restoration in Scotland, as well as for the

genuinely patriotic reason that the Union, if not concluded originally on unfavorable terms for Scotland, was likely to be altered
to her disadvantage after the destruction of the separate Scottish
state. Considering the alteration of the Scottish law of treason
made at the desire of George I and his ministers, were they not
wise? The Presbyterians shared this fear, more especially with
regard to their Established Church, which differed radically from
the English one.

Therefore it is not surprising that a rising was concerted in
Scotland during 1706, when the debates on taking the first steps
toward a Treaty of Union had excited popular feeling in all
parties.

The Dukes of Atholl and Hamilton, George Lockhart of Carnwath, members of the Gordon family, the Earl of Errol, and representatives of the Cameronian sect in the western Lowlands had
set the day; the point of assembly was to be Hamilton, and Edinburgh was to be seized. According to Lockhart and John Ker of
Kersland, a Cameronian spokesman, Hamilton withdrew from the
conspiracy for a private reason, which Ker thinks was his desire
to be king himself.[1] Ker, at any rate, was acting in what he thought
to be his own interest, and had a large share in entraining the
Cameronians through his hereditary influence in their councils,
pointing out that the Union would bind them to recognition of a
prelatical church in England, at the expense of their nonconformist coreligionists. And so, "the Presbyterians and Cameronians
were willing to pass over the objection of his [James's] being
Papist; for, said they (according to their predestinating principles), God may convert him, or he may have Protestant children,
but the Union can never be good." [2] But there was no rebellion,
Hamilton having withdrawn.

Hamilton was, strangely enough, the leader of the Jacobite
party in the Scottish Parliament, and used it for his own ends.
The Jacobites, if they were to advance their own cause, would
have to present a united front against the proponents of the
Union, as several of the leaders recognized, and agreed to do. Had
they used their numbers in Parliament to secure commissioners

<hr />

[1] Lockhart, I, 197–200; Ker's *Memoirs* (London, 1727), I, 28–30, 36.

of their own beliefs for the negotiation of the Treaty of Union,
these representatives could have demanded such terms as England would not grant. As is well known, Hamilton broke the
Jacobite opposition to pieces, rising unexpectedly late in an evening's sitting to propose that Parliament should leave to Queen
Anne, and thus to her English ministers, the nomination of the
Scottish commissioners. Since the Godolphin ministry would thus
control both sides of the table, the question was practically settled
when the Jacobites wavered, some being absent, and divided their
vote on the motion. Hamilton's motives are not clearly known:
Lockhart believes that the Duke of Argyll, Queen Anne's Com-
missioner for Scotland, had promised him a place as a Scottish
representative. Hamilton was not named, and it was said that
Argyll refused to serve himself because he was kept from honoring
his promise to Hamilton. This seems very easy, and disguises the
probability that Hamilton would insist, if he sold himself, on a
higher price. Argyll may well have been excluded by his official
position.

Be that as it may, the Jacobites were represented on the commission by Lockhart of Carnwath, Viscount Duplin, and the
Laird of Grant. The Earl of Mar was claimed by them as a
sympathizer,[3] but it is hard to believe that he could have been
an earnest one in 1706, when he had more to expect from the
Whigs, having been made Secretary of State in the last months
of 1705. At this very time he wrote to the Earl of Marchmont of
the "intear union" which he desired: "Certainly it is the solid
fundation for putting the two nations on one bottome to all
posterity, for sattling our present jealousies and humours and to
prevent all fears we may have of dangers to our present constitution."[4] Mar's "great talent" after all, as Lockhart said, "lay in
the cunning management of his designs and projects, in which it
was hard to find him out, when he desired to be *incognito*; and
thus he shewed himself to be a man of good sense, but bad
morals."[5]

Hamilton did not retain the Jacobite confidence, such as it

[3] List of Commissioners given to Torcy, April 27, 1706, in Macray, II, 51–52.
[4] H.M.C. *Report*, XIV, app. III, 158.
[5] Lockhart, I, 114.

was, after this betrayal or stupidity. When, in July 1706, another Scottish agent was sent to France with the usual desires for assistance and plans for a revolt, it was Captain Harry Stratton or Straiton who was chosen, a member of the Lockhart group, which was more willing to rely on the Duke of Atholl, who was at least a man of honor, though vacillating in politics. Atholl was thoroughly estranged from the English ministry; he considered that he had been personally injured by the Lovat plot, and became more deeply "dipped" than he had been before.[6] He had been opposed to Hamilton in personal rivalry and family disagreements [7] before the fiasco of the Union commission occurred. After it he had the added objection of political disgust. It is odd that Atholl, who in his actions at least had formerly been a supporter of the Protestant Succession, should have allied himself with the reactionary Drummond family, led by the titular Duke of Perth, the recognized Catholic leader at St.-Germain. Perhaps Middleton's conversion was influential in forming this relationship, but Perth had also been converted, in 1685, and had kept in high favor with James II in so doing — a change of mind similar to Middleton's. Scotland's aristocracy was close-knit by marriage, however, and the answer may lie there to some extent. Perth was the second husband of the widow of Atholl's cousin, and also uncle (by marriage) of Atholl's first wife.[8] There was always some means of maintaining correspondence with relations, however distant, in those days, and this channel was the one which Atholl used. That Atholl had taken Perth as his friend at the court was probably enough to lead Middleton to remain on good terms with Hamilton.

Then, in the following year, when Hooke, once more rather the agent of Louis XIV than of James III, was chosen to explore Scotland, he was particularly careful to see Atholl first, because Middleton was suspicious of Hooke's intent, and Perth was not. Middleton's caution had reduced the confidence reposed in him by the French ministry, but caution was his first duty, both to

[6] G. M. Trevelyan, *England under Queen Anne* (London, 1930–34), II, 238–39.

[7] He and Hamilton were brothers-in-law by his first marriage.

[8] G. E. Cokayne, ed., *Complete Peerage*, articles "Atholl," "Hamilton," "Perth," and "Tullibardine."

James and to his friends, who were liable to be butchered to get the French army out of its increasing difficulties.

The Earl left no room for misunderstanding. In February, when Hooke was preparing to leave France, Middleton wrote to Chamillart, the French minister of finance:

. . . . you may be assured beforehand that one will find nothing there but well-disposed men, grain, meat, things to drink, and a certain number of swords and muskets, although not enough for such an extraordinary and important occasion. The queen has also observed that the help which the Scots can expect from the king is not indicated. . .[9]

Hooke later accused Middleton of directing Nairne to write a letter to the Scots with whom he was in relations, telling them that France would not help them, and that they would be ruined if they believed Hooke.[10] That there is no such letter extant is no proof that there was none, but Hooke's failure may have misled him in believing that Nairne wrote one.

The agent left Dunkirk on April 17, 1707, and landed at Slains Castle, the seat of the Earl of Errol, on April 10/21.[11] He bore letters to Atholl, the Earl Marischal, the Earls of Kincardine, Errol, Glencairn, and Buchan; to Hamilton he brought a promise of the Garter, and promises of suitable promotions to many others.[12] The Duchess of Gordon was found to be bargaining with Ker of Kersland, the "Honest Cameronian," for his help in a rising unsupported by France,[13] the thing most agreeable to Hooke and to Louis XIV. Atholl and Hamilton (the latter does not appear to have seen the emissary) were less confident.[14] Military advices from the Marquess of Drummond were despondent: "We have only very few arms. . . There are no cannon. . . There are neither powder, nor cannon balls, nor grenades, nor gunners, nor bombardiers, nor sappers. . ."[15]

Hamilton, Marischal, Viscount Kilsyth, Captain Straiton, and Lockhart of Carnwath were very reserved in their communications

[9] Macray, II, 122–23.
[10] Ibid., II, 128n.
[11] Ibid., II, 202, 205.
[12] Ibid., II, 130–41, 150–52.
[13] Ibid., II, 206–07.
[14] Ibid., II, 211.
[15] Ibid., II, 232–34.

with Hooke, and those of this group who saw him had little to say. If they dealt with anyone, they meant it to be Middleton, through the usual channels. Nevertheless, Hooke brought back letters from a good number,[16] and a Memorial signed by several,[17] promising thirty thousand men if Louis XIV could furnish eight thousand regulars, arms for the new levies, and a general of rank and quality. James III must come in person. Among his new adherents, another statement asserts, would be the Cameronians and some other Presbyterians, thirteen thousand strong.[18] Hooke returned to France with all these advices and made his report in late July.[19] The French ministry found it encouraging, in the aftermath of defeats in Flanders and elsewhere, but could not at that time act upon it; it is probable that the decision was made almost at once to take advantage of the discontent shown, by sending a small expedition in the following year.

2. THE ATTEMPT OF 1708; THE PRETENDER IN THE FIELD

For ten years Middleton had been compelled by circumstances to restrict his activities to procurement of intelligence, intrigue with whatever persons offered themselves as supporters of the cause in Great Britain, and cautious advice to the French ministers to avoid ruining the Jacobites at home with a feeble or premature effort. In 1708 Louis offered six thousand men, arms for thousands of recruits, and some money; the Pope offered more money provided that there were a successful landing.[20] The Scottish Jacobites had recklessly promised to bring out a force which would have been certainly as great as, if not greater than, any ever dreamed of from them. It was not, however, through Middleton, but through Hooke and his agent Ogilvie that word reached Scotland at the turn of the year that an expedition would be sent in the following March.[21] Charles Fleming was employed to prepare

---

[16] *Ibid.*, II, 262–78.
[17] *Ibid.*, II, 256–62.
[18] Strachan's recital, May 23/June 3, 1707, *ibid.*, II, 308–10.
[19] Hooke's narrative, July 29, 1707, *Secret History of Colonel Hooke's Negociations in Scotland in 1707* (Edinburgh, 1760), 5f.
[20] James to Clement XI, May [10], 1708, H.M.C. *Stuart Papers*, I, 224.
[21] Macray, II, 534.

the loyalists of Lothian and the counties north of the Forth for the arrival of a French squadron in that region. Fleming left St.-Germain on February 29, and arrived at Slains on March 13. His warning was given, and the Jacobites began preparations to serve, as they thought, under the Duke of Berwick.[22] The victor of Almanza had another assignment; the comte de Gacé, created for this mission maréchal de Matignon,[23] was given charge of the troops, and the comte de Forbin, an able sea commander, was to transport the troops to Scotland, much against his will.[24]

The English government lacked not eyes to see in this affair. John Ogilvie, the spy of Harley, was so deep in the secret that he had written the essential details of the matter in the middle of November from Edinburgh; he was mistaken only on the number of men promised, saying ten thousand instead of six, but this may have been a misrepresentation by Hooke.[25]

The fleet — 21 privateers, two men of war converted into transports, and an escort of five men of war — was to carry 5,100 troops, instead of the 6,000 promised. There were to be 12,000 arms, but no saddles for Scottish cavalry. The equipment of the fleet was explained as preparation for privateering forays of little account separately.[26] Only on February 29 was the generality of the court at Versailles, represented in this case by the marquis de Dangeau, aware that these armaments were designed for use against England.[27] The English resident at the Hague, Dayrolle, had informed Boyle, an English Secretary of State, more than two weeks earlier. Even with this tentative information, the English could not be certain of the destination, so fearful were the Dutch of a raid on their coasts,[28] until the beginning of March, when the Duke of Lorraine's courier confirmed the news to Dayrolle in an independent betrayal.[29]

Before James III left St.-Germain to join the troops now as-

[22] Fleming's narrative, Hooke's Negociations, 151–54; Lockhart, I, 240.
[23] Charles-Auguste de Matignon, comte de Gacé (1647–1739).
[24] Forbin, Mémoires, II, 239, 248–49.
[25] H.M.C. Report XV, app. IV, 460, 464–66.
[26] J. H. Owen, War at Sea under Queen Anne, 1702–1708 (Cambridge, 1938), 239.
[27] Dangeau, XII, 88.
[28] Owen, 240.
[29] H.M.C. Lords MSS., VII, 567.

sembling at Dunkirk, he drew up a Declaration, the first of his reign, to Scotland, dated March 1, 1708.[30] He repeated the pardon provision of 1696, with its two year prescription period for espionage or betrayal in France since the Revolution. The settlement of the Church of Scotland he left to a Scottish Parliament; the Protestants were to remain in control of universities, schools, and churches in any case. Parliament would be advised to confirm post-Revolutionary judicial proceedings, with the exception of those against Jacobites for actions ordered by James III or his father. Thoughtfully, James promised to pay the arrears of officers and soldiers who deserted from the other side to join him. The most significant provision, a counter to the threats of Anne's government was this:

> We do hereby promise that the Vassals of such who obstinately persist in their rebellion, shall be deliver'd from all servitude they were formerly bound to, and shall have Grants of their Lands to be held immediately of the Crown; Provided that upon our Landing they declare for Us and come in to Our Service.

On March 7 James III took his leave of St.-Germain, he hoped for the last time, King Louis bade him goodbye with what von Noorden calls the "Wunsche auf Nimmerwiedersehen." [31] Unfortunately, the Pretender had contracted measles from his sister, Princess Louise Marie, who had just recovered from it, and was prostrated at Dunkirk almost immediately after he had joined Middleton and Perth there on the 9th.[32] "Imagine a man in despair, who wanted to be wrapped up in bedclothes and carried to the ship. The doctors cried out that it would certainly kill him," wrote St.-Simon, who loved a dramatic picture.[33] On the day that James arrived, an English squadron under Admiral Byng anchored off Gravelines.[34]

On receipt of the news Louis XIV vaccillated. It is possible, and is suggested by two independent sources, that Pontchartrain,

[30] H.M.C. *Stuart Papers*, I, 218–21.
[31] Carl von Noorden, *Europäische Geschichte im achtzehnten Jahrhundert* (Leipzig, 1870–82), III, 233.
[32] Forbin, II, 251; Dangeau, XII, 96.
[33] *Mémoires*, XV, 422. Cf. Dangeau, XII, 97.
[34] Owen, 245.

the French minister of marine, had taken a dislike to the project from the beginning, and used administrative delay to prevent its execution.[35] Forbin was nevertheless ordered to obey the Chevalier, who wished to sail at the first opportunity.[36] This he did, after a hasty embarcation, on March 17. It was a rough passage, and three ships, bearing 800 of the precious 5,100 troops, were forced to turn back.[37] James conducted himself well, although his officers and those of the French troops "all vomited to the point of tears." [38]

The French pilots overshot the Forth and a coasting trip of six leagues, according to Forbin, but more likely of fifty miles, was necessary, before the squadron anchored off the mouth of the Firth on the night of March 23.[39] Forbin received no reply to his signals, and in the morning, when the English squadron eluded in the Narrow Seas was seen to come up, he resolved to run past it for home without disembarking the troops.[40] The reason for failure to answer the signals was probably the expectation of the Jacobites that he would come to the southern shore, near Leith, where *Protée*, a frigate strayed from the main body, made land and was boarded by a Mr. Malcolm, a pilot provided by Fleming's associates.[41] Several times the Chevalier de St.-Georges, as the Pretender now called himself, begged to go ashore on the coast of Fife, even alone, but was refused, at last, very bluntly.[42] The expedition, much the worse for rough weather, and with one ship of war, *Salisbury*, missing, returned to Dunkirk on April 7, 1708. The troops crowded below decks must have suffered many losses from cold, hunger, and cramped quarters. "While we lay on board," an English soldier wrote of his voyage from Flanders in one of the ten battalions of foot sent to Scotland to meet the danger of French invasion, "we had continual Distruction in ye foretop; ye Pox above board; ye Pleague between Decks: hell in

[35] *Sheridan, Political Reflexions*, 119; Dangeau, XII, 97n.
[36] Forbin, II, 252–53.
[37] Hooke, *Negociations*, 139; Forbin, II, 255.
[38] *Ibid.*
[39] Hooke, *Negociations*, 140–41; Owen, 253–54.
[40] Forbin, II, 256.
[41] Hooke, *Negociations*, 152; Owen, 253–54.
[42] St.-Simon, XV, 430; Forbin, II, 258–60.

ye forecastle, and ye Devil att ye Helm." [43] The French must have had the same, if not worse conditions.

In Scotland the lords and lairds who had been notified by Fleming were in consternation when the news of the failure arrived, for they had had no notice from James that he was turning back, no messenger having been landed from the French main body. They dispersed to their homes as quietly as possible. A good number of gentlemen were summoned to appear before the Privy Council, which they were very quick to do.[44] Some might have suffered, it was said, had not Hamilton, who was arrested with the rest, made terms for the Jacobites to join the opposition to Godolphin and Marlborough, for there was no lack of information to hang them with, from Ker of Kersland, who acted as a common informer or worse,[45] or John Ogilvie.

The fall of the Tory clique from the coalition ministry in February 1708 had created Hamilton's opportunity. Robert Harley's intrigue to obtain the principal posts of government for himself and other Tories resulted in a dissolution of the coalition and a Tory eclipse until 1710, when the Whigs were to take their turn of political exclusion. Just now Whig measures prevailed: battalions were recalled from Flanders; Habeas Corpus was suspended; a universal oath of abjuration of the Pretender ("James III's" official name) was imposed. The funds and the Bank of England suffered from the needless panic, it being the usual expectation that the Jacobites would repudiate most of the national debt and seize the resources of the Bank for their own purposes. An effective landing might actually have destroyed paper credit.[46] The many Scottish arrests [47] were not followed by harsh punishment because of an approaching election (in which Whig severity would be trumpeted by the Tories), the influence of some of those detained on the Whig side, and the natural moderation of a Whig

[43] J. M. Deane, *A Journal of the Campaign in Flanders, MDCCVIII* (privately printed, 1846), 6.

[44] Fleming's narrative, Hooke, 155-57; Lockhart, I, 247-48.

[45] Lockhart, I, 249, 294, 302-07.

[46] Tindal, IV, 61.

[47] Hamilton, the Marquess of Huntly, the former Bishop of Edinburgh, the Earls of Errol, Seaforth, Aberdeen, and Nithsdale, Fletcher of Saltoun, the chiefs of Lochiel, Appin, and Struan, and the Earl Marischal were among them. *Ibid.*, IV, 65.

government headed by two Court Tories, Godolphin and Marlborough.

The Pretender, or Chevalier, or James III, was now humiliatingly free of occupation at the age of twenty, and felt his obscurity in the world oppressive. Two grandsons of France, the duc de Berry and the duc de Bourgogne, were to make their first appearance as soldiers with the army in Flanders, which Bourgogne, with the "assistance" of his cousin, the duc de Vendôme, was to command. It was thought that James had an excellent opportunity to make a name for himself, in the company of these illustrious, if inexperienced, figures. The court of Versailles knew of the plan on April 9, 1708,[48] before the Chevalier had returned to St.-Germain, where he spent the short time before the commencement of operations.[49] Then, *incognito*, he took his place as a volunteer, with the suite and equipage usual for a nobleman of high rank.[50] Having no particular duties, he went where he liked in the camp, which happened to be with the troops recruited from his own dominions.[51] His behavior was very good, or had the reputation of being so,[52] unlike that of the duc du Maine, the natural son of King Louis, on a similar occasion. At the battle of Oudenarde he was attached to the French princes, traditionally a safe place to be, whether or not by his own choice is not clear. It was said that the princes treated him with scandalous neglect (it is St.-Simon who speaks),[53] but he was freed from dependence on them at the end of the campaign. As simply as the young king had lived, by French royal standards, this first campaign was very costly; and the second had to be one of retrenchment, both at camp and at home,[54] where the charities among the exiles were much curtailed.

In 1709 the commander in the field was the very able maréchal de Villars; both James and Berry were volunteers.[55] There can be

[48] Dangeau, XII, 114.
[49] *Ibid.*, 121, 140.
[50] St.-Simon, XVI, 132.
[51] *Ibid.*
[52] Mme. de Maintenon to the princesse des Ursins, July 1, 1708, St.-Simon, XVI, 200n.
[53] *Mémoires*, XVI, 477–78.
[54] H.M.C. *Stuart Papers*, I, 227–28, 233–34.
[55] St.-Simon, XVII, 173.

no question that the Chevalier's courage was remarkable, especially at the great battle of Malplaquet. It was said that the English opposing the *maison du roi,* with which he charged six times,[56]
recognized him by his Garter; also that Marlborough spoke of his
conduct with high praise to a captured Jacobite officer.[57] It was
recalled that he had been ill of a fever before the battle, and had
only reached the army just in time to take his place.[58] This was
true, but we need not accept as gospel that he took his quinine
during the action.[59] The duc de Bourgogne (who was not there)
wrote to King Philip V, "He showed in the last battle the courage
proper to such a prince as he is." [60] He was, in short, a legend.

The third of his campaigns was less spectacular than the second,
but still very spirited. A sort of demon would almost seem to have
taken possession of him, a desire to show the world what he was
made of. Is this to be attributed to the praise he received for his
former conduct? Many of the letters of his aide-de-camp, Charles
Booth, speak of his carelessness of his own life in the warfare in
Flanders during the summer of 1710. He left St.-Germain in the
second week of May; [61] already on May 31 his aide complains of
his reckless exposure to danger. Booth asked Berwick to speak to
his half-brother about it; the duke "looked blancke shook his
head and said nothing." [62] James would bear no admonition,
because it had become an established maxim that when action,
however slight, took place, "we loose 3 kingdomes, if we have not
our share." [63] In the middle of September the Pretender relieved
the officer's anxiety by withdrawing from camp after the fall of
Béthune, giving ill-health as his reason.

[56] F. E. de Vault, *Mémoires militaires relatifs à la succession d'Espagne sous Louis XIV* (Paris, 1835–62), IX, 352.
[57] The marquise d'Huxelles to the marquis de la Garde, Dangeau, XIII, 40.
[58] St.-Simon, XVIII, 158.
[59] Sourches, XII, 67 and note.
[60] Bourgogne, *Lettres,* A. Baudrillart and L. Lecestre ed. (Paris, 1912–16), II, 37. See also Vault, IX, 347, and the *Mémoires du chevalier de Quincy* (Paris, 1899–1901), II, 378.
[61] Dangeau, XIII, 153.
[62] Booth to Middleton, Arlieu, May 31, 1710, Carte MSS. 210, foll. 132–34v; Booth to Middleton, June 1, *ibid.,* fol. 135.
[63] Booth to Middleton, Haucourt, June 28, *ibid.,* foll. 185–90v.

While the king was campaigning, the minister was at work. In the spring of 1709, Middleton shared the general expectation that France, staggering under her successive defeats at the hands of Marlborough at Blenheim, Ramillies, and Oudenarde, would make peace on almost any terms, and took measures to secure for James and his mother any advantages possible. The English government informed Torcy that the Pretender should remove from France to some other place,[64] any he liked (but of course several countries were bound to England by treaty not to receive him), and that they would provide for him if he went.[65] Middleton was sure that acceptance of a pension from Anne would be construed as a renunciation of James's rights. Moreover, the government, after having made the Pretender a dependent, could discontinue payment.[66] Luckily for both king and minister, the Gertruydenberg negotiations were rendered futile by the high demands of the allies, and the need for peace was not met for three years, a fortunate breathing-space.

Before the year 1709 was out there was a revival of the Scottish descent plan, when Colonel Wauchope, captured on *Salisbury* in 1708, returned with a report on the state of Great Britain. This report found some credence in the council of state, with Mme. de Maintenon, and some others.[67] Louis XIV had the most sanguine expectations of precipitating a great rebellion with a tiny force of regulars, which Torcy and some others thought impossible.[68] Estimates and plans were called for. Louis hoped to find eight battalions of foot, three regiments of cavalry, two of dragoons, and twelve to fifteen thousand arms.[69] During January 1710, there was much more talk of the kind, but at the end of the month the project was cancelled.[70]

[64] Middleton to Torcy, St.-Germain, April 30, 1709, Carte MSS. 180, fol. 233r and v.

[65] Beauvillier to Middleton, Paris, May 27, 1709, Carte MSS. 210, fol. 86r and v.

[66] Middleton to Beauvillier, St.-Germain, May 27, 1709, *ibid.*, fol. 84r and v.

[67] Torcy, *Journal inédit . . . pendant les années 1709, 1710 et 1711,* ed. F. Masson (Paris, 1884), 54–56, 62, 64–65.

[68] *Ibid.,* 66–67, 81.

[69] *Ibid.,* 93–94.

[70] *Ibid.,* 128–29.

3. TORY ADVANCES TO JAMES III

In July 1710, the anxieties of the French were much relieved by news of public affairs in England. Queen Anne, prevailed upon by Mrs. Masham, her favorite, to dismiss the ministry of which Marlborough and Godolphin were the leaders, was strengthened in her decision by the unpopular Sacheverell persecution and by the general disapproval of the failure of the Gertruydenberg peace attempt.[71] On June 14, the Earl of Sunderland, the minister most obnoxious to the queen, was dismissed, and in the succeeding months the others were also removed. Godolphin was replaced by Robert Harley on August 8. Marlborough continued to command uneasily in the Low Countries, knowing that the immediate object of the new chiefs of the ministry, Harley, the Chancellor of the Exchequer, and Henry St. John, a Secretary of State, was to bring to an end the war in which the duke had served so brilliantly, though inconclusively. Louis and Torcy pondered an invasion while these divisions prevailed,[72] but in the autumn found a better way to work. Before the end of August the Earl of Jersey, St. John's colleague as Secretary of State, was in touch with the abbé Gaultier, a French priest of obscure origins but high acquaintance, and the negotiations for the Peace of Utrecht had begun.[73]

The general course of the communications which passed between the two governments has no place here. Early, in October 1710, the Pretender was mentioned in Gaultier's conferences with Jersey, with a suggestion that an agreement with the new ministry on the terms of a restoration was possible "if he thought as they did."[74] At the beginning of 1711 Gaultier was sent to France by Harley, Jersey, and the Duke of Shrewsbury with a request that peace conferences be resumed for the first time since

---

[71] Walcott, who should know, tells us (p. 109) that the overthrow was the result of a coalition of all dissatisfied groups — Tories, courtiers, the "Country" party, and dissident Whigs.

[72] Torcy, 225–27, 253–54.

[73] Gaultier to Torcy, Aug. 1 N.S., 1710, G. M. Trevelyan, "The 'Jersey' Period of the Negotiation leading to the Peace of Utrecht," *E.H.R.*, XLIX (January 1934), 101.

[74] Gaultier to Torcy, Oct. 7 N.S., *ibid.*, 102.

1709, and with a secret mission of conferring with Berwick.[75] St. John did not know of the steps being taken until April.[76] Since Louis XIV refused to confer with Holland, the Tory ministry decided to abandon her, and to obtain a separate peace. France was determined that Philip V should remain king of Spain, although she had in 1709 conceded the Habsburg claim of the Archduke Charles. In a brusque reversal of previous policy, England, as Mr. Trevelyan says, gave France the cue to hold out to get Spain for Philip in the approaching treaty.[77] The country desired peace, and was willing to pay for it, since Spain was no possession of England. The loss of Brihuega was "one comfortable loss in Spain" to the Tory Swift, but it made the terms of peace even more disappointing than ministerial complaisance had done.

The Parliament elected in 1708 was considered insufficiently Tory in composition for the accomplishment of the great work of peace, Whigs having a different view of acceptable conditions; it was dissolved, and a new election held, which was a great victory for the Tories. Not all of the Tories, of course, were Jacobites, but a large group of Jacobites and others was formed, called the October Club, from the supposed favorite drink of its country squire members. The naïveté of the faction can be, and has been, overestimated, as the list of its members — Sir William Wyndham, William Shippen, George Lockhart and Sir Thomas Hanmer are among them — shows.[78] When Parliament met, in November 1710, the October Club became identified with Henry St. John, the second man in the government.

St. John and Harley, although they had left the government together in 1708 and had come in together two years later, differed in temperament and in policy. The secretary and his followers favored radical therapy. The dismissal of the Duchess of Marlborough in January 1711 and the replacement of the duke by the Duke of Ormonde at the end of the year did not content them. The Jacobites, especially, meant the army to be officered from top to bottom by their own friends, as a step to the seizure

[75] *Ibid.*, 104; Berwick, *Mémoires*, II, 196–97; Torcy, *Journal inédit. . . ,* 348–49, 352, 426.
[76] *E.H.R.*, XLIX, 100.
[77] *Ibid.*, 105.
[78] A more complete list is to be found in Tindal, IV, 235.

of power. Harley, on the other hand, desired a more moderate solution, which the actions of his own party and of suspicious Whigs made impossible. The necessities of the negotiation of the peace also made his way perilous; in direct proportion as the rapprochement with France advanced, the gulf between England and her allies grew wider, and dangerous to the Tories because one of these allies was the heir to the throne, George of Hanover. In displeasing the Elector by concluding peace in such a way, the Tory party drew to itself much of the odium which kept its members out of power in the period 1714–44, and alienated the royal family from them until even later.

It is not surprising that Harley was slow in ending the war, was friendly to the Jacobites in the hope of substituting a favorable king for a hostile one when Anne should die, and was criticized for his hesitation by everyone.

When Gaultier was in Paris in early 1711, he saw only Berwick, not James or his mother, and the conference was kept secret from them and from Middleton until June, when it was found necessary to inform the Pretender, though not the others.[79] On the English side, St. John assumed charge of the intrigue on Jersey's death in August,[80] an event which may account for the failure of the ministry to send over a plan of operations to Berwick and James at the former's camp in Dauphiné, as Gaultier had promised earlier.[81] Through the summer of 1711 the Chevalier waited there, incurring suspicion of his "tour of France" by his long stay,[82] and received no word before the time of his return in early November.[83]

Gaultier was again in Paris in the winter, and saw Berwick there, putting off a definite agreement until the English army had been reformed and peace had been obtained. Neither the French ministers nor the English put the Pretender before the peace.[84] For the following twelvemonth the matter lagged; only Gaultier

---

[79] H. N. Fieldhouse, "Bolingbroke's Share in the Jacobite Intrigue of 1710–14," *E.H.R.* LII (July 1937), 444.

[80] Trevelyan, *E.H.R.*, XLIX, 100.

[81] Berwick, II, 198.

[82] Dangeau, XIII, 424, 429, 436, 444; St. Simon, XX, 335.

[83] Berwick, II, 198; Sourches, XIII, 231.

[84] *E.H.R.*, LII, 444–45.

was used as an intermediary, and a worse one could hardly have been chosen. It was a discouraging endeavor at best, as Middleton had written to an agent in England in 1710: "It is the life of a dog, to be allways hunting in a cold scent. Sometimes, like enchanted ground, we have a view of it, & when we draw near it vanishes." [85] Middleton did not show his discouragement by letting tentative offers from Marlborough drop, although while the duke commanded there seemed little hope of his support;[86] on the contrary, he exhorted the general in touching terms to return to his duty, reinforcing his moral argument with appeals to worldly motives: "You cannot be safe, but by being Just, nor great but by being good," were the words he put into the mouth of the queen mother.[87] When Marlborough had fallen, he was more willing to make promises, which Middleton received coldly: "He had it in his power to have been good & great . . . and now can only pretend to the humble meritt of a postboy, who brings good news, to which he has not contributed.[88] He also had the French plenipotentiaries to the coming peace conferences instructed to take care of his master's interests,[89] although he was not as yet informed of the work being done, as was supposed, by the Tories in England, but only of a vaguely favorable inclination in Queen Anne and her parliament.[90] Either with or without Middleton's knowledge the possibility of secret correspondence with Anne herself was pondered,[91] and promises made to the Church of England were copied out and sent over.[92] The assurances were, in the main, those of the 1702 "Instructions," and of no interest except as a sign of their permanence as Jacobite statements of policy.

St. John, now created Viscount Bolingbroke, visited Paris in August 1712, staying with Torcy, and visiting Fontainebleau on a

---

[85] Middleton to "Knox," Oct. 9, 1710, Carte MSS. 212, foll. 12v, 13.
[86] Middleton to Torcy, Chaillot, July 6, 1710, Carte MSS. 238, fol. 206.
[87] "Heads of a letter to Gournay" [July, 1710], Carte MSS. 238, fol. 208r and v. "Gournay" was Marlborough. See ciphers printed in the introduction to H.M.C. *Stuart Papers,* I.
[88] Middleton to Tunstall, Nov. 18, 1711, *ibid.,* fol. 226.
[89] Carte MSS. 180, foll. 277, 281, 309–16.
[90] "Mémoire du Sieur Lamb [Charles Leslie]," April 1711, *ibid.,* fol. 291.
[91] Drafts of such a letter are *ibid.,* foll. 301–02 and 305–07v.
[92] "Abstract" of such a letter, Carte MSS. 210, fol. 409.

courtesy call to the king of France. Before his departure from Paris, he and the Pretender regarded each other and the opera from separate boxes, but probably did not meet.[93] Had the ministry succeeded in its earlier (were they nominal?) efforts to remove the exiled court from France, there would not have been any encounter; the Pretender's departure was requested in August 1711, by Prior, the English diplomat, and urged as essential to peace in January 1712, although many already knew that some arrangement between Anne and James was hoped for.[94] James left Paris in September for Châlons-sur-Marne, which was not far enough for public opinion in England. When the Duke of Lorraine offered him the castle at Bar, he accepted, and established himself there, outside Louis XIV's dominions, in late February 1713. No sooner was he there than he sent for Charles Leslie, an old servant, to hold services for his Protestant followers; [95] he had asked permission of his former host for such a step, but had been refused it. He also rid himself of his Jesuit confessor, Father Thomas Eyre.[96] Leslie arrived in August, and was cordially received, as his English friends soon heard.[97]

Harley's sincerity in the scheme began to be suspect at the same time that he asked for Middleton's dismissal, while James was still at Châlons. Had Middleton resolved to hold his place regardless of trouble, he might well have done it, for the queen mother found the prospect of parting very painful. She wrote on January 28, 1713, that if her own opinion were followed, he would never be replaced, "but alas i am grown so insignificant, and so useless to my friends that all i can do is to pray for them." [98] The insistence of the ministry was assisted by Viscount Galmoy (titular Earl of Newcastle and an officer in the French service),[99] saying

[93] Dangeau, XIV, 209–15; Sourches, XIII, 477–78, 480–81, 486.
[94] Fieldhouse, "Oxford, Bolingbroke, and the Pretender's Place of Residence, 1711–14," E.H.R., LII (April 1937), 290; "John Scrimgeour" to James III, Feb. 26 [O.S.], 1711 [–12], Carte MSS. 211, foll. 11–13.
[95] Middleton to "Lamb" [Leslie], March 21, 1713, Carte MSS. 212, fol. 51r and v; H.M.C. Stuart Papers, I, 260.
[96] Eyre to Gualterio, St.-Germain, May 22, 1712, Add. MSS. 20,310, fol. 55.
[97] Nairne to "Abram" [John Menzies] and to "Berry," Aug. 26, 1713, Carte MSS. 212, foll. 58v and 59, and 59r and v.
[98] Carte MSS. 211, fol. 186r and v.
[99] Piers Butler, 3rd Viscount Galmoy (1651/2–1740).

that the Protestant Jacobites had once held Middleton "in very good esteeme . . . but that sense he changd his religion, they had not soe good an opinion of him." [100] Still, there was no need to dismiss him yet, since Harley, now Earl of Oxford, would promise nothing before the conclusion of the peace, even if he were sincere. During the next few months doubt of Oxford's good intentions grew; a promise to Gaultier of help for the cause rekindled hope for a time, but his unwillingness to take the only effective step and recall James to England damped it quickly.[101] Payment of Queen Maria Beatrice's jointure was provided for under the terms of the Treaty of Utrecht, confirming that clause of the agreement of Ryswick,[102] but no action was taken to secure the Pretender's position in England before the death of Queen Anne, although it was urged many times.[103] On the eve of the opening of Parliament in 1713, it was again proposed by Berwick that the Chevalier go to England and appear with Anne as her heir on that occasion, to be accepted by the "concurrence" of both houses, Berwick hoped.[104]

Bolingbroke had corresponded separately with Berwick since returning to England in the autumn of 1712.[105] Moreover, Ormonde, the English general, sent indirect word to Berwick that he was open to advances from the Pretender in October 1713, and Marlborough was said to offer himself if the charges raised against him since his fall by the Tories should be dropped.[106] The Earl of Mar, a weathercock, tendered his services through Mrs. Jean Murray in the spring of 1712.[107] Simon Harcourt, son of the Tory

[100] Galmoy to Middleton, St.-Germain, Jan. 29, 1713, Carte MSS. 211, foll. 211–14v.
[101] Fieldhouse, *E.H.R.*, LII, 444; James III to Torcy, Bar-le-duc, April 18, 1713, L. G. W. Legg, "Jacobite Correspondence, 1712–1714," *E.H.R.*, XXX (July 1915), 504. Mr. Trevelyan (*England under Queen Anne*, III, 249) sees the plan for a *coup d'etat* in this letter as a sign of absolutist tendencies. Would this apply to William III's *coup* in 1688? I hope that the analysis of James' letters in this study will balance Mr. Trevelyan's opinion, highly respected as it must be.
[102] H.M.C. *Stuart Papers*, I, 264.
[103] *Ibid.*, 266.
[104] Berwick to James, St.-Germain, Aug. 18, 1713, *ibid.*, 273.
[105] Berwick to James, St.-Germain, Oct. 26, 1712, *ibid.*, 248.
[106] *Ibid.*, 277–78.
[107] Letters of April 22 [O.S.] and May 9 [O.S.], 1712, Carte MSS. 211, foll. 28–29, 67–68.

Lord Chancellor, needed to be cautioned about his sentiments; [108] and when the peace was proclaimed fifty or sixty merchants and gentlemen gathered to celebrate, drank "to the new Convert & disappointment to the Hannovers," and sang "the K[ing] shall enjoy his own again." [109] That James was on the verge of conversion to Anglicanism was rumored in England.

It may be wondered what could have made so many devoted friends where at best lukewarm ones had been before. The ministry was by this time known by many to be in relations of some sort with the Pretender; of these a good number believed that a Restoration could hardly be prevented in the near future. Gaultier was not above using the name of one great man to bring in another. Again, there had been almost unbridled publication of Jacobite pamphlets and sheets in the previous years.

Charles Leslie's newspaper, the *Rehearsal*, published from 1705 to 1708 is an example. Regularly every week it purveyed Filmerian political theory to anyone who wanted it, however many or few. "And after *Nebuchadnezzar* had been turn'd to a *Beast* for *Seven* Years, when his *Reason* Return'd to him, *his Lords* and *his Counsellors sought unto him, and he was Establish'd in his Kingdom*. Dan. iv, 36. The *Line* of *Succession* was not Broke . . ." [110] is a fair sample of style and content — Scriptural quotations strung together to justify the doctrine of non-resistance, the hereditary succession, and irresponsible monarchy. The *Rehearsal* collapsed, probably for lack of money, but in 1711 Leslie returned to the attack with the simpler, more readable *Finishing Stroke*, a pamphlet written in answer to Hoadly's *Original and Institution of Civil Government*. Simpler, but yet intolerably heavy. Leslie quotes Cicero, Aristotle, Quintilian, and Bodin, as well as the Scriptures, to prove that the family authority vested in Adam,[111] divided among the descendants of Noah,[112] devolved in each nation in the hereditary line from its founder to the rulers of the seventeenth century. There was never a state

[108] Galmoy to Middleton, Paris, June 10, 1713, *ibid.*, foll. 234–35.
[109] Dr. Clinch to Middleton, May 24 [O.S.], 1713, *ibid.*, foll. 121–22v.
[110] *Rehearsal*, No. 24 (January 6 to 13, 1704/5). Italics are Leslie's.
[111] *Finishing Stroke* (London, 1711), 7–10.
[112] *Ibid.*, 43–44.

of nature, and no contract between king and people was possible.[113] Of course exceptions to the rule of succession are mentioned in the Old Testament, each carefully explained as acts of God, who can dispense with any law.[114] Woe unto the peoples who usurp God's right to make kings: "They have set up Kings but not by Me, they have made Princes, and I knew it not." The fate of Israel must serve as a warning to England.[115] There is no excuse for deposing a king, or "disinherison" of the first-born, for forfeiture would not be to the people, inferior to the king, but to God, the only superior.[116] If it should be objected that the pagan historians were unaware of the authority by which their kings reigned, the answer is that they were not divinely inspired, having no Bible to guide them.[117] It is very neat, and was convincing to many, including a good number of highly educated clergymen.

There were other such pamphlets: *Jus Sacrum*,[118] which cited the Bible and Civil and Common Law to the same effect as Leslie; the *Loyal Catechism*,[119] the author of which by leading questions taught that man was "to be subject not only for Wrath, but for Conscience Sake," that "there is no Power but of God," that one must "next unto God, obey your King and Queen. . . . knowing that they be ministers appointed by God to rule and govern you. . . . they that resist shall receive unto themselves Damnation"; and also "A Letter from Mr. Leslie to a Member of Parliament," [120] which related Leslie's comfortable reception at Bar, repeated the promises to the Church of England made in 1702, and spoke of unsuccessful efforts made by James at St.-Germain to obtain freedom of worship for his Protestant servants. The most bitter controversy about this welter of papers (and not one tenth of their names are mentioned here) was provoked by

[113] *Ibid.*, 14.
[114] *Ibid.*, 58.
[115] *Ibid.*, 75, 83–84.
[116] *Ibid.*, 86.
[117] *Ibid.*, 91–92.
[118] *Jus Sacrum, or a Discourse wherein it is . . . prov'd . . . that No Prince ought to be Depriv'd of his Natural Right . . .* (London, 1712).
[119] *The Loyal Catechism* (London, 1713).
[120] First printed 1714; reprinted in *Somers' Tracts*, XVI, 213–23.

George Harbin's *Hereditary Right*,[121] for which Hilkiah Bedford was mistakenly sentenced to stand in the pillory after the succession of George I. There was a rumor that the book was especially licensed for the printer by William Bromley, a member of the October Club and Bolingbroke's colleague as Secretary of State. Thus, as Tindal remarks,[122] concealment seemed to be abandoned by the Jacobites, as if some great victory had already been achieved.

4. THE RELIGIOUS OBSTACLE

Until the autumn of 1713 Middleton held his post at Bar; then, when Torcy advised James strongly to send him away, James unwillingly did so, on December 2.[123] The earl retired to St.-Germain. Sir Thomas Higgons, a titular knight of the important West Country family, closely related to the Granvilles [124] and others, but little qualified for high office, succeeded him within two weeks. It was hoped that this sacrifice would bring Oxford to be frank, but it did not.

The most important reason on James's part was that he would not change his religion. He never meant to change when he offered to hear the reasoning of Anglican divines on the subject when he should be restored; when Leslie said, "If to hear implies Conversion, then he has promis'd to be converted," [125] he must have known that the implication did not follow, for his first attempt to speak to James, before any restoration, had been entirely useless.[126] James certainly did not mean it to be taken for granted, for he repeated in successive letters his wish to choose his religion for himself, and his claim to toleration if he remained a Catholic: "They must not take it ill if I use the same liberty, I

[121] *The Hereditary Right of the Crown of England Asserted* (London, 1713).

[122] Tindal IV, pp. 333–34.

[123] Fieldhouse, *E.H.R.*, LII, 447; James to Torcy, Bar-le-duc, Dec. 2, 1713, app. to F. Salomon's *Geschichte des letzten Ministeriums Königin Annas von England, 1710–1714* (Gotha, 1894), 332.

[124] Warrant No. 207, Dec. 14, 1713, Warrant Book M 19, W.S.P.

[125] *Somers' Tracts*, XVI, 218.

[126] Berwick to James, Aug. 23, 1713, Mahon, *History of England from the Peace of Utrecht to the Peace of Aix-la-Chapelle* (London, 1836–54) I, vii (appendix).

allow to others, and adhere to the religion which I in my conscience think the best." [127] Gaultier and Torcy tempted him as
few have been tempted; he was a young man, and of small experience in these matters, but he clung to his religion for all that,
retaining his good will toward his Protestant friends, which was
itself to cost him great and bitter things in the future. Gaultier
wrote to Torcy on January 26, 1714:

> To be King of England one must profess the established religion of
> the country; if one is out of England, one must not think to return to it
> by conquest, because the English will never allow themselves to be con-
> quered . . . one must not have them as enemies; on the contrary, one
> must lead them, and promise them adroitly more than one intends to
> give them.[128]

Again he wrote on February 6/17:

> It is absolutely necessary that you disguise your religion or change it
> entirely, to adopt that established by the laws of your country. It is not I
> who gives you this counsel . . . it is for you to think it over and ask
> the Lord to let you know the part you ought to play, and what you
> should do for His greater glory, and to save a nation which without
> you would never be able to be happy or tranquil. . . .[129]

Any who tell James that restoration is possible on other terms,
Gaultier says to Torcy on February 19, are deceiving him while
bargaining with Hanover.[130]

Before this it was plain that only "amusement" was to be
expected of Harley; the Chevalier wrote to Gaultier on February
1 complaining of his treatment during the past three years, when
he had sacrificed liberty of action; his "advocates," he said, pressed
him to renew his "litigation," and he had resolved to do so if
within three months he had not received clear proof of the sincerity of Oxford and Queen Anne.[131] He did not expect this
proof, for he wrote again two days later, "We must count on
these gentlemen no longer, but try to address ourselves to another
quarter." [132]

[127] "Abstract of a letter," May 2, 1711, Carte MSS. 210, fol. 409.
[128] Legg, *E.H.R.*, XXX, 508.
[129] *Ibid.*, 508–09.
[130] *Ibid.*, 511.
[131] *Ibid.*, 334–35.
[132] *Ibid.*

What other resources had he? Bolingbroke had already expressed his thoughts to d'Iberville, the French Ambassador, on February 5: while James remained a Catholic there was no hope of a restoration, even if he married a Protestant princess,[133] which he was unlikely to do. By the end of the month it was clear that the Pretender had to choose. Invitation by a faction of one party did not mean an offer to rule unopposed, but it was a good chance which he let pass, so good a one as he was never to have again. He wrote to Torcy declining to change his religion, and included a stinging answer to Gaultier's suggestion of February 1: "Thank God I understand my religion better than to have the effrontery to ask the Lord whether it is for his glory to abandon him." [134] He later wrote a conciliatory reply to Oxford, but persisted in his refusal to change.[135] The English stood fast with an assurance to Gaultier that the Grand Turk would have a better chance than the Pretender while the latter remained a Catholic.[136] James complained to Cardinal Gualterio,[137] Protector of the English Nation at Rome:

. . . . the abbé Gaultier behaves in a terrible fashion, for he has not only advised me to abandon the Catholic religion, but has pushed effrontery so far as to write me that I must write the Pope that since my interest obliges me to pretend to quit the Catholics I would not be the less attached at heart to the Catholic religion and to the Pope for that.[138]

The Tory ministers did not cease to speak of their attachment; April saw them reassuring Gaultier that they would serve no successor of Anne but her brother.[139] No action to change the established succession followed, however, nor was any payment made of Queen Mary's dower.[140]

These men, or most of them — Oxford, Bolingbroke, Mar,

[133] Legg, *E.H.R.*, XXX, 508; Fieldhouse, *E.H.R.*, LII, 457.
[134] *E.H.R.*, XXX, 513.
[135] *Ibid.*, 515. See also "Abstract," March 13, 1714, Carte MSS. 210, foll. 409v, 410.
[136] *E.H.R.*, XXX, 517; *E.H.R.*, LII, 458–59.
[137] Filippo Antonio, Cardinal Gualterio (1660–1728) Nuncio to France from 1700 to 1706, a French partisan at Rome. For a character sketch see St.-Simon, XIII, 109–10.
[138] Extract by Gualterio from James' letter, April 23, 1714, Add. MSS. 20,292, fol. 64.
[139] *E.H.R.*, XXX, 517.
[140] H.M.C. *Stuart Papers*, I, lv–lviii.

Ormonde, Lansdowne, and others — were now thoroughly "dipped," but had received no reward for it, having given nothing but words. They had arrived at a stalemate on James' religion, and were divided among themselves. The Lord Treasurer's almost fabulous vagueness and some personal slights had completely estranged Bolingbroke, and the Secretary of State took advantage of Lady Masham's favor with the queen to work against his fellow-minister. As it became certain that Oxford was unwilling to help them, the Jacobites turned to his rival; moreover Queen Anne, outraged by the demand of the Electoral Prince for a summons to the House of Lords, made without consulting her, seemed to favor them. Ormonde was reported to have spoken frankly to her in the spring of 1714,[141] and Masham gave Bolingbroke the benefit of her advice and influence in the closet. Lockhart of Carnwath drew his Jacobite friends into support of Bolingbroke in return for a vague engagement that the Secretary would arrange for the Pretender's recognition as heir as soon as Oxford and his friends should be dismissed.[142] To the French ambassador, d'Iberville, Bolingbroke confided that he was prepared to face civil war.[143]

Oxford had neglected to fill the army with "honest men," [144] despite the recommendations of his followers.[145] He was negligent of business, slighted the October Club, and seemed to be drinking heavily, as the queen complained. Bolingbroke rose in favor through his handling of the Schism Act in June, but Gaultier was still uncertain enough of him to doubt the wisdom of informing him of Oxford's communications with the Chevalier. Parliament was prorogued on July 9/20. A violent quarrel in Anne's presence between the two ministers at a Cabinet meeting on July 27/ August 7 precipitated Oxford's dismissal, and left the Secretary free to form his own cabinet, composed mostly of Jacobites.[146]

[141] Mahon, I, viii (app.).
[142] Lockhart, I, 476–78.
[143] Salomon, 308–09.
[144] Ibid., I, 441; Carte MSS. 231, fol. 40v.
[145] Orrery to Harley [c. Sept. 1710], H.M.C. Report XV, app. IV, 605.
[146] Wyndham was to head a Treasury Commission, Harcourt to be Lord Chancellor, Ormonde to command the Army, and Francis Atterbury, Bishop of Rochester, was to hold the Privy Seal. Trevelyan, England under Queen Anne, III, 295.

Time was short, and his cabinet was still incomplete when Anne fell into her last illness; while Bolingbroke reversed his course and bargained with Whigs [147] for support after her expected demise, a Privy Council meeting was called for July 30. Two un-summoned Whig dukes there appeared and claimed their seats. Afterwards this pair, Argyll and Somerset, carried measures to vest control in the Duke of Shrewsbury, who had withstood Jacobite temptation,[148] and to secure the country for the Elector of Hanover. This was done before Queen Anne died, on August 1/12, 1714, in the early morning. The greatest Jacobite oppor-tunity was past.

[147] Carte's interview with Lansdowne, 1724, Carte MSS. 231, fol. 40v.

[148] Galmoy ("Newcastle") to Middleton, Paris, Jan. 24, 1713, Carte MSS. 211, foll. 208–09.

4

FAILURE

(1 7 1 4 – 1 7 1 6)

1. THE FLIGHT OF BOLINGBROKE

Anne's death aroused Maria Beatrice, at St.-Germain, and her son at Bar-le-duc to a high pitch of excitement, while their more sober counselors were absent — Middleton sent away and Berwick, whose influence had been great since the appointment of Higgons, besieging Barcelona for Philip V of Spain. Not waiting for advice which would have taken weeks to arrive, James left Bar *incognito* [1] and arrived at Paris with plans for an embarcation and pleas for assistance. He was premature, Torcy told him; Louis XIV advised him to leave France immediately, for his passage to England would not be allowed.[2] France had lost its taste for war. The Chevalier therefore departed for the "eaux savonneuses" of Plombières in Lorraine, where he issued a declaration of his claims on August 29.[3]

Addressed to "all Kings, Princes, and Potentates," it is really directed to the people of England, assuring them of the author's sympathy for his subjects and his fear that they might fall prey to arbitrary government under the Elector of Hanover, now George I. "He his [sic] a foreigner, a powerful Prince, & absolute in his own Country, where he has never met with the least contradiction from his Subjects: He is ignorant of our Laws, Man-

[1] James to Torcy, Tuesday [Aug. 21, 1714], app. to St.-Simon, XXIV, 477.
[2] Berwick, II, 208–09. Cf. Louis XIV to d'Iberville, Versailles, Aug. 22, 1714, St.-Simon, XXIV, 477–78. Bolingbroke's assertion that this journey was "a farce acted by concert" is thus disproved. *Letter to Sir William Windham* (London, 1753), 78.
[3] Printed by D. G. Forbes, *Culloden Papers* (London, 1815), 30.

ners, Customs, & Language. . ." It is easy for us now to see that James was wrong, and to conclude that he was insincere, but could he know that the very strangeness of England was to be a factor in relaxation of royal control? He goes on to remind the people that the government would find "no rest 'till it return'd again to it's true Center." He repeats his former promises briefly, narrates his attempt to reach England on Anne's death, and re-asserts his claims, "which do, & shall remain in their full force & vigour."

Resuming, though cautiously, his correspondence with the Tories, he found that all hope was not yet abandoned, despite the exclusion of Bolingbroke, Oxford, Ormonde, and Lansdowne from office. Bolingbroke reaffirmed his friendship for Louis XIV and d'Iberville before Queen Anne was long dead.[4] The former rivals in the cabinet were beyond possibility of reconciliation in opposition to the new Whig government of George I, more be-cause of Oxford's virulence than anything else: the earl actually projected an attack on his enemy in the House of Lords; when, later, he relented, and proposed a junction of forces, Bolingbroke recalled irresponsible statements attributed to Oxford, and re-fused.[5] But some others were willing to be friends with both — Lord Lansdowne and Bishop Atterbury took this part — and gave hope for the future in England.

In France, with the best will in the world, Louis the Great could not dream of commencing war with England at that mo-ment, even for an adopted son. If anything else were to be done, it must be with James's own resources at first; after a good begin-ning, substantial but unofficial help in the shape of half-pay French officers, arms, and Irish "volunteers" might follow.

Berwick returned from Spain in November, and found that the correspondence now spoke of a reaction in England against the division of official spoils among the Whigs and the exclusion from places of all the principal Tories. It seemed worth money to cultivate officers dismissed in the reduction of the army after Utrecht, and to treat with undecided persons to make them

[4] Bolingbroke to Torcy, 19/30 Aug., 1714, St.-Simon, XXV, 476.
[5] Fieldhouse, "Bolingbroke and the d'Iberville Correspondence," E.H.R., LII (April 1937), 673–74.

Jacobites. Ormonde and Mar sent reports of plans for rebellion in the western counties, where Ormonde, Wyndham, and Lansdowne had great estates and interest, and in Scotland, if James should land. Berwick suggested completion of the scheme for a rising, and on November 28 advised the Pretender to go to Scotland "as soon as possibly he can," and offered to accompany him.[6] By all means James must act quickly to avoid being crushed in the early stages of recruitment and organization by Dutch or German troops. All pretended friends must be conciliated: Marlborough was a deceitful wretch, and Oxford a trouble-maker of doubtful loyalty, but they must be kept neutral at least, although no positive good could be expected from them. Bolingbroke was the mainstay of the plans of this time.[7] A cloudy scheme to bring the Mediterranean fleet into the Pretender's service was not discouraged. Plans for England, however, were made with disturbing slowness,[8] the chief Tories being in terror of impeachment, and anxious for decisive action before Parliament should find time and cause to turn upon them. "Upon the whole," Berwick wrote on February 23, 1715, "I believe your Majesty will find that nothing is yet in reddiness, nor can be soon." [9]

Berwick found it convenient to apply at Paris and Versailles for money and supplies. Higgons' uselessness as a correspondent (for he had not a proper command of French) necessitated in March the recall of Middleton to Bar from St.-Germain, where he had been placed with Maria Beatrice, in the guise of a visitor to Lorraine, a cumbersome and transparent device. Once more with James, he was used for the most confidential work, including the drafting of Ormonde's commission as Captain-General.[10] Bolingbroke objected to the recall, but was induced to withdraw his objection, for the time being, in April.[11] Success in relations

---

[6] Berwick's memorandum, Percy Thornton, *The Stuart Dynasty* (London, 1890), 345; Berwick, II, 210–11.

[7] Thornton, 347–48; H.M.C. *Stuart Papers*, I, 335. Marlborough offered and paid £2000 in August 1715 for the use of the Pretender. H.M.C. *Stuart Papers*, I, 401, 407; Carte MSS. 211, foll. 323–24.

[8] Berwick's letters of Feb. 3 and 8, 1715, Thornton, 349.

[9] *Ibid.*, 351.

[10] H.M.C. *Stuart Papers*, I, 353–54, 357.

[11] *Ibid.*, 359.

with the French was made difficult by the employment of Lord Stair as ambassador of George I at Paris, where he quickly organized an efficient, but by no means omniscient, system of espionage,[12] and reported all he could learn of the Pretender's activities to his government. Nor were the preparations of the Highlanders unobserved.[13]

D'Iberville, who was apprised of some of these things, informed Torcy in October 1714 that Bolingbroke wished to go to France after the next parliament; this intention was confirmed in March 1715 by threats of impeachment based on Matthew Prior's revelations.[14] During the night of April 4th he told d'Iberville that he was fleeing. He arrived in Paris at some time before the 14th, when Berwick sent news to James III of his presence.[15] At first Bolingbroke stood clear of the Jacobites in public, and pretended to have no understanding with them or the Court of France, but went south for a time.[16] Appearances having been safeguarded, he offered suggestions and advice to Berwick secretly,[17] while writing renunciations of politics to the circle of the notorious *intrigante*, Mme. de Tencin.

Les brouilleries en Angleterre seront heureusement terminées par rapport à moy, pourveu qu'elles me laissent passer la vie dans une douce oysiveté. Mon ambition est eteinte quant la Reine est morte; elle a fait place a d'autres passions; et j'aime mieux estre des parties qui se font dans une certaine petite maison a Paris que de remplir les premieres charges du gouvernement. . .[18]

That such parties and passions were not strange to him is attested by d'Iberville's report a year earlier that the then Secretary of State suffered from "the effects of neglected venereal disease." [19] This letter gives some support to the charges that

[12] See a list of Stair's expenses, June–September, 1716, J. M. Graham, *Annals and Correspondence of the Viscount and the first and second Earls of Stair* (Edinburgh and London, 1875), I, 391.
[13] Montrose to Stair, February 1715, *ibid.*, 275.
[14] Fieldhouse, *E.H.R.*, LII, 678.
[15] Thornton, 353.
[16] Fieldhouse, *E.H.R.*, LII, 679; Berwick, II, 213.
[17] Thornton, 357; H.M.C. *Stuart Papers*, I, 359, 362.
[18] Bolingbroke to Mme. de Ferriol, June 26, 1715, Bodleian Library MS. French d. 18, fol. 5r and v. For her reputation, see Maurice Boutry, *Intrigues et missions du Cardinal de Tencin* (Paris, 1902), 12.
[19] D'Iberville to Torcy, May 11, 1714, *E.H.R.*, LII, 677.

Bolingbroke was far too fond of female company of the worst sort, for Mesdames de Tencin and Ferriol were known members of a political clique, and Mme. de Tencin's relationships with the abbe Dubois and others for the advancement of the fortunes of her brother, Pierre Guérin de Tencin, could not have recommended her to the society of anyone whose interests conflicted with her own. Mme. de Ferriol, at least, did not at this time have his full confidence.

Perforce Bolingbroke's flight left English affairs in the hands of the Duke of Ormonde, whose wealth, rank, and connections [20] placed him before all but the most able, but whose mediocrity should have subjected him to many quite unintelligent persons; for if, as Bolingbroke advised Berwick, Ormonde needed Lansdowne's wisdom, he must have had little of his own.[21] In addition to his intellectual limitations, Ormonde had the difficulty of succeeding the runaway viscount: he was watched, and had not the skill to conceal his actions. Bolingbroke scorned Ormonde for his removal from England in midsummer of 1715,[22] but can scarcely have ignored the effect of his own, which he did not mention, on all those left behind. His means of attack, a posthumous publication, is suited to his method, innuendo.

It is essential that Bolingbroke's misrepresentations be discarded, as his biographers have not so far done. The *Letter to Sir William Windham,* his justification of this period of his life, is full of distortions of the characters of his associates, and some rank untruth — for instance, the date of entering the Pretender's service is set back several months — so that, unchecked with other material, it is useless for history. Of all the periods of his life this was the most discreditable, although he had earlier helped to wreck the Tory party by divisions between himself and Harley, and later he was to taint the constitutional Opposition with his presence in its ranks; even his "philosophical" writings are as

[20] Ormonde was married successively to daughters of the 1st Earl of Rochester and the 1st Duke of Beaufort; a brother-in-law was Earl of Grantham, a niece Lady Ashburnham, a brother Earl of Arran in Ireland. These are only the closer relations.

[21] Berwick to James, May 1, 1715, Thornton, 357. Marshal Keith appraises Ormonde's character in his *Fragment of a Memoir* (Edinburgh, 1843), 3.

[22] *Letter to Sir William Windham* (London, 1753), 136–37.

shallow as a brook while as sounding as the sea. Nevertheless, it is this period that he devoted his life to explaining; his Jacobite enemies are those whom he attacks most virulently: it is his behaviour at this time of which he was most ashamed. Of what particular actions will be seen.

2. BOLINGBROKE IN FRANCE

Bolingbroke's suggestions to Berwick, which the Duke forwarded to James, seem to have given no radical turn to a draft declaration of April 22,[23] which was then being considered. It is almost entirely a repetition of previous utterances: general pardon except to those who resist the Restoration; a frequently repeated promise "to make the Laws of the Land the inviolable Rule of Our Government" and to "protect secure and maintain Our Subjects of the Church of England by Law established in the full enjoyment of all their Legall Rights" and so forth; and confirmation under the Great Seal of the Instructions of 1702, with the significant change that the grant of first fruits and tenths shall be perpetual. As usual by this time, there are promises to establish a toleration and to pay naval and military arrears to deserters from the enemy, and a charge to all subjects to return to their duty. This may have been the Declaration which was shown to Bolingbroke in May;[24] we have no record of his disapproval. On the contrary, Berwick wrote that he was "violent for the prerogative, and never said a word of religion," in their earliest conferences.

Bolingbroke, at any rate, was removed from the scene during his stay in the south, and did not return until July, when according to his own story a person authorized by the English Tories came to him and told him that they expected him to take sides with the Pretender. Thereupon he went to Commercy to meet James, and accepted the seals as his Secretary of State. He pleads as his excuses the Act of Attainder[25] against him, which was not actually passed until afterward, and the call of the party, loyalty

[23] Carte MSS. 180, foll. 334–39.
[24] Berwick to James, St.-Germain, May 1, 1715, H.M.C. *Stuart Papers,* I, 362.
[25] *Letter to Windham,* 103, 110.

to which overrode dynastic considerations.[26] After an interview
which he describes as unsatisfactory — quickly reported to Lord
Stair, by the way [27] — he nevertheless went on to Paris to handle
the work of obtaining help from Louis XIV.

He found himself obliged to advise delay as soon as he was
acquainted with the difficulties of his position,[28] but he took care
to treat with contempt those who had every title to respect; what
wonder that "the whole tribe of irish and other papists were ready
to seize the first opportunity of venting their spleen against a
man, who had constantly avoided all intimacy with them," [29]
when he might have wooed them for his own good and his
master's? Bolingbroke was behaving as a fool or a madman to
believe that he, and perhaps Berwick, could take England by
themselves. Most of the Jacobites abroad were Catholics; it is
probable that a majority were Irish; yet to him the Irishman and
the Catholic were objects of scorn, even when he could not work
without them. "Care and hope sat on every busy Irish face," [30]
was his summary of their efforts, not distinguishing the valuable
from the worthless. That he did not trouble to distinguish is
shown by his casual reference to "Mr. Dillon." [31] Who was he? He
was General Arthur Dillon, "homme de grande réputation," an
officer who had distinguished himself in Dauphiné in 1707, and
at the capture of Kaiserslautern in 1713, when he commanded
only a small force;[32] altogether he had behind him in 1715 a
military career of at least twenty-seven years, and had been a
lieutenant-general in the French service since 1706. But for the
termination of the war he might have attained the distinction of
Berwick himself, and in any rising in the British Isles he would
have been the leader that the Jacobites had never had. Bolingbroke dismisses him as a mere political adventurer. Among others

[26] *Ibid.,* 110–111.
[27] Hardwicke, *The Hardwicke State Papers* (London, 1778), II, 534.
[28] Letter to James, July 23, 1715, quoted in T. Macknight's *Life of Bolingbroke* (London, 1863), 459–60.
[29] Bolingbroke, 8–9.
[30] *Ibid.,* 124.
[31] *Ibid.,* 240.
[32] Dangeau, XI, 329; XII, 99. He was born at Roscommon in 1670, and died
at St.-Germain in 1733 (C. E. Lart, *Parochial Registers of St.-Germain-en-
Laye,* II, 162*n.*).

not named by him, but summarized as "Irish," were Generals Lee, Dorington, and Sheldon. Bolingbroke despised these men at a time when any friend who was not hopelessly indiscreet could be of assistance, if not vitally necessary, for he no longer had at his call a governmental machinery, with clerks, treasurers, ambassadors, and soldiers to execute his decisions. He must be all these for himself, or find what help he could.

Now that he was committed he was impeached, and not before, as Bolingbroke would have us believe.[33] This was in August; on September 10 the Act of Attainder took effect; it was followed by the erasure of his name from the roll of peers.

Although a great deal of time had now passed, the English Jacobites were no more ready for a rebellion than they had been at Anne's death, and Berwick advised delay to await the formulation of some definite scheme. In the meantime France was to be importuned, but in this Bolingbroke's failure was certain, France having no help to give. She had escaped from the recent war by a peculiar combination of circumstances at Gertruydenberg, followed by the fall of the Whigs, but with absolutely empty coffers. The arms left in her hands after the reduction of her army could be very useful to the Jacobites, but there was no way to let them have them without provoking another war, since Stair's spy service seemed to make a secret transfer impossible.

If the French needed more to make them shy, Ormonde's arrival in Paris on August 7 [34] should have been sufficient, although the Duke explained his flight as a measure for his personal safety, not as the collapse of his plans. For them he asked a large sum of Louis XIV, which was in the end obtained from the king of Spain — 428,520 French livres,[35] or about £30,390 at the rate of exchange then prevailing. More money was obtained from a fabulously wealthy banker, Antoine Crozat, the proprietor of Louisiana, for a promise of a title.[36] This brought in 50,000 écus

---

[33] *Letter to Windham*, 111–12.

[34] Dangeau, XVI, 9; Thornton, 372.

[35] "An Account . . . ," March 1716, Carte MSS. 211, foll. 323–24. Marshal Keith had heard that 1,000,000 livres were obtained from Spain (*Fragment*, 8). An additional sum of 400,000 écus, about £70,000, was promised, but not obtained in time to be of use in the rising. H.M.C. *Stuart Papers*, i, 414.

[36] Berwick to James, Marly, June 18, 1715, H.M.C. *Stuart Papers*, I, 368.

(of the 100,000 promised), amounting to £9,346. The Pope contributed over £20,000 between March 1714 and January 1716; Marlborough had given £2000 under his cant name "the Lawyer," [37] and a mysterious "D:N" — the Duke of Norfolk? — sent a like amount by the hands of a Father Southcoat. Roger Kenyon, called "Mr. Johnson," [38] contributed or collected £5000 in England for his master. These sums, 25,000 louis d'or from the Duke of Lorraine, and some minor contributions were all that could be got outside of Scotland. Whether so much could have been had without the influence of Louis XIV is an open question; in any case, his nephew the Regent is not known to have given a penny from the time of the death of his uncle on September 1, 1715, until after the rising of 1715 was over, although he promised continuance of favor.[39]

On the other side of the Channel, Ormonde's departure left the initiative to the Scots, for the leaderless English could do no more than riot.[40] John, Earl of Mar, had once been a Whig, but had associated himself with Oxford and Bolingbroke during Anne's last years, so that the accession of George I drove him from office and placed him very oddly at the head of the Jacobites in Scotland. When a first plan of embarcation was abandoned on the advice of Berwick and Bolingbroke,[41] a messenger named Charles Kinnaird had already left England on July 7/18 with instructions framed by Ormonde and dictated by Mar, which arrived before July 26.[42] They were demanding, and therefore discouraging: Louis XIV must find arms for 20,000 men, a train of artillery, a large sum of money, and 500 officers, besides a large body of troops. There seemed, just then, to be a possibility of

---

[37] That Marlborough is "the lawyer" is plain from the ciphers in the introduction to H.M.C. *Stuart Papers*, I.

[38] For this identification see Carte 210, foll. 381–82.

[39] James to the Duke of Lorraine, September 1715, Carte MSS, 211, fol. 349.

[40] Berwick, II, 223; Hardwicke, II, 536; H.M.C. *Report* XI, app. IV, 158–59. Sir Charles Petrie's "Jacobite Activities in South and West England in the Summer of 1715" (*Transactions of the Royal Historical Society*, 18: 85–106) amounts to a list of riots and arrests compiled from newspapers. To the best of my belief, Sir Charles exaggerates Jacobite strength.

[41] James to Bolingbroke, July 18, 1715, Thornton, 366–67; Bolingbroke to James, July 23, Mahon, I, app. xi; Berwick, II, 220–22; James to Louis XIV, July 1715, Carte MSS. 211, fol. 347r and v.

[42] Bolingbroke, 130–32; Berwick, II, 222; H.M.C. *Stuart Papers*, I, 377–79.

getting help from Sweden,[43] which could have supplied the arms
and troops; but artillery and money, beyond the limits of the
enumeration just given, were out of the question, as James confessed to Bolingbroke.[44]

On close application to Torcy, however, the viscount discovered
a readiness to assist far beyond his hopes. "Ralph (Duke of
Berwick) is sent for again, and, till he comes, they will not speak
more plainly. In the meanwhile Talon [Torcy] is of opinion
that you may please to drop, even to those about you, such short
and general things, as may make those imagine there is no thought
of an immediate undertaking. I shall do the same to those busy
flies which buzz all day about me, and he will throw out words
to the like effect." [45] A courier was sent to Spain to get promises
of more money and arms from Philip V, Pontchartrain undertook
to have ships ready by the end of August, and advances were made
to the duc d'Orléans as insurance against the death of Louis XIV,
which would make him Regent of the child Louis XV. News of
the development was sent to England.[46] But evidently the French
were not to furnish troops, for James wrote to Bolingbroke at the
end of August, "This last will surely convince our friends that
they must now act on their own bottom." [47]

3. THE FIFTEEN

This the Scots had already done. Mar left London secretly, in
company with General George Hamilton, arriving in Scotland
about August 1,[48] having been urged by the English Jacobites to
take matters into his own hands when it was learned that warrants
for many arrests had already been made out.[49] On August 6/17
Mar sent word to friends at Edinburgh that he intended to set
up his standard, and called a meeting by a letter dated August

[43] Berwick, II, 226.
[44] H.M.C. *Stuart Papers*, I, 380.
[45] Bolingbroke to James, Paris [Aug. 7], 1715, *ibid.*, I, 387.
[46] *Ibid.*, I, 388; Bolingbroke, 149–50.
[47] H.M.C. *Stuart Papers*, I, 397.
[48] Tindal, IV, 436; H.M.C. *Stuart Papers*, I, 525. Marshal Keith (p. 10)
dates the arrival at the beginning of July, when we know that he was still in
London.
[49] Lockhart, I, 486.

19/30, which duly took place at Braemar on August 26/September 6, 1715.[50] It is therefore unlikely that Mar rose on receiving a letter written by James without Berwick's knowledge, as Berwick says, delivered in September,[51] since the decision had been "ruminated, plotted, and set down" as long as six weeks before the standard was raised. In fact, the commission sent to Mar was dated September 7 New Style, and could not have reached him in less than two weeks, but more likely three. It is apparent from James Murray's letter of September 3 to the Pretender that the first news of Mar's action did not come to France until about that time, and that it was through Bolingbroke, and not disregarding him, that he dealt with the king. Mar asked for a commission as James's general,[52] which was immediately dispatched. If Bolingbroke and Berwick did not advise sending it, an alternative cannot be imagined, since by the time of its arrival the Scots were in arms, and the commission only gave authority for what was already done. Withholding it would have left room for disputes within the little army of rebels, and might even have led to bloody defeat.

Berwick was already beginning to grow suspect to the party. His unwillingness to forfeit all he had gained in France — his marshal's baton, his rank, his estate at FitzJames-Warty, and other good things — was opposed, after the death of Louis XIV and the end of his tacit support of James III, to Berwick's desire and duty to lead the army of his half-brother in England or Scotland: "Your Majesty knows where the difficulty lies," he wrote on October 7, "and that I am not my own master." [53] A few days later his brother spoke of withdrawing confidence from the duke.[54]

Ormonde's West Country scheme had really been broken up, but the unknowing Jacobites abroad arranged for Ormonde and the Pretender to embark at St.-Malo for England; Ormonde was

[50] Peter Rae, *A History of the Late Rebellion* [Dumfries, 1718], 187f; Keith, 10–11; Allen Cameron's Account, H.M.C. *Stuart Papers*, III, 558; Lord Provost of Edinburgh to Secretary Stanhope, Aug. 23, and to the same, Aug. 26 [Old Style], W. K. Dickson and M. Wood, ed., *The Warrender Letters* (Edinburgh, 1935), 75–76, 79.

[51] Berwick, II, 246.

[52] H.M.C. *Stuart Papers*, I, 415.

[53] *Ibid.*, I, 430.

[54] *Ibid.*, I, 434; James to Berwick, Oct. 14, 1715, Carte MSS. 211, fol. 329.

to go first, and James to follow when there was news of a safe landing. Ormonde left Paris on the evening of October 24,[55] when James was still at Commercy in Lorraine.

In Scotland, Mar had met with better success than his precipitancy deserved. He had brought out many of the nobility and gentry who had been involved in the 1708 affair, and were barred forever from Hanoverian favor. Of these, the Earl Marischal and his brother James Keith, the Murray family, represented by the Marquess of Tullibardine, eldest son of Atholl, and a younger son, Lord George, and the chiefs of loyal clans — Seaforth, Lochiel, Glengarry, and others — were out with all the men they could bring. James Murray, son of Viscount Stormont, was sent to Scotland as Secretary of State for that country, on October 25,[56] but was captured by the Austrian authorities in Flanders on the way.[57] Perth was seized for the Pretender early in the rising by Colonel John Hay, but no vigorous action was commenced either to conquer Scotland or to destroy the Hanoverian troops in that country. Six thousand foot and eight hundred horse had joined Mar in November, but a few were already secretly treating for pardon from George I.[58] Thus Lords Huntly and Seaforth excused themselves from the army to defend their own lands, and did not return.

French aid was naturally expected, and its failure to arrive was bitterly bewailed and blamed on Bolingbroke, who was accused of negligence and treachery.[59] By his own account and that of Berwick, the Secretary at Paris was unjustly accused; [60] still, the only effectual preparation to send stores to Scotland was made by the Count of Castelblanco,[61] an immensely wealthy man, and a son-in-law of Melfort, "who under that title set up for a medler in english business," without the assistance of Bolingbroke, and even against his will.[62]

[55] H.M.C. *Stuart Papers*, I, 446–47.
[56] Tindal (IV, 448) notwithstanding. H.M.C. *Stuart Papers*, I, 443.
[57] *Ibid.*, I, 459.
[58] Keith, 16, 23.
[59] *Ibid.*, 12–13.
[60] Bolingbroke, 199–206; Berwick, II, 275.
[61] Don Jose de Roxas, Count of Castelblanco. See Torcy, *Journal inédit* . . . , 293.
[62] Bolingbroke, 206–08.

Ormonde was off to St.-Malo, and English agents were sent over with a warning to members of his party: one Campion to Cornwall, a Courtney to Devonshire, and Kenyon to the North.[63] A declaration was signed on October 25,[64] at Commercy, the countryhouse of the prince de Vaudémont, on Bolingbroke's representation that some such paper was necessary.[65] Several letters to the magistrates of London, the universities at Oxford and Cambridge, and the army and navy were also prepared, with assurances of respect for those vested interests.[66] On October 28 James left Commercy for Paris, where he lodged secretly with Lauzun,[67] who had brought him from England in 1688, and after a short stay moved on to St.-Malo. At Nonancourt, near Dreux, he was awaited by a bravo named Douglas, and others, who were supposed to "stop" him, on orders from Lord Stair. Exactly what methods were to be used by these unofficial constables one cannot say, but one suspects the worst, eighteenth century morality not having quite that horror of political assassination which historians of the nineteenth century would have liked. The postmistress suspected them of designs upon some traveler, and had them arrested before James' arrival. Stair obtained their freedom from the Regent, thus avowing that they were his agents.[68] James was aware that the roads were dangerous for him; Bolingbroke had written on October 20, "Stair has some jealousy that you . . . are in motion. . . He has people on most of the roads." [69]

From the port, when he reached it, he had hoped to go directly to England, but he found that Ormonde had already returned from the English coast, where he had made the prearranged signals and had no response. This is not strange; Wyndham, Lans-

---

[63] Thornton, 393–94.
[64] Carte MSS. 180, foll. 340–41.
[65] Bolingbroke to James, Oct. 18, 1715, Thornton, 395.
[66] H.M.C. *Stuart Papers*, I, 438.
[67] Dangeau, XVI, 238n.
[68] St.-Simon, XXIX, 275–81. J. M. Graham (I, 297n) refused to consider St.-Simon's account without confirmation. This is to be found in documents printed by P. E. Lémontey in his *Histoire de la régence* (Paris, 1832), II, 371–83; and also in the *Mémoires* of the maréchal de Villars, ed. the marquis de Voguë (Paris, 1884–1904), IV, 90.
[69] H.M.C. *Stuart Papers*, I, 440–41.

downe, Sir Richard Vyvyan, and many others had been arrested before Ormonde sailed. Plans to seize Bristol and Plymouth were frustrated. Only a handful of diehards proclaimed "the King" at St. Columb in Cornwall.[70]

James stayed at St.-Malo for a few days, watching Ormonde as he prepared for another attempt to reach England. "I am in pain for him," he wrote to Bolingbroke in late November, "as the surest game they may be waiting for him on the western coast." [71] At some time after November 28, he left St.-Malo and recrossed northern France to Dunkirk, arriving in the middle of December, Old Style. There, it may be by deliberate oversight of the Regent,[72] he was allowed to embark for Scotland, probably on December 16/27.[73] So secretly did he move, and so quickly, that for weeks the French court, at least, was ignorant of his whereabouts.[74]

There is no need or room to pursue the course of the rebellion in detail here: chapters are usually devoted to it in any general history of Great Britain in the period. The Pretender's landing at Peterhead, on December 22 Old Style, was too late to revive the spirits of the insurgents; already parts of their army had melted away. A detachment which had ventured south as far as Lancashire was trapped with its English recruits at Preston, and desertion had reduced the strength of the main body to three thousand foot and seven or eight hundred horse.[75] A council of war decided to take the army away from Perth, a step, it was acknowledged by Mar, in bringing the rebellion to a close with a minimum of bloodshed.[76] The English Jacobites were dispersed or imprisoned; French help, of which Ormonde had secured from the Regent a promise unknown to Bolingbroke,[77] was not forth-

---

[70] Tindal, IV, 443.

[71] Letter of Nov. 24 and 28, H.M.C. *Stuart Papers*, I, 469. I do not accept Professor Wolfgang Michael's interpretation of this letter (based on selective quotation) as contemptuous of Ormonde and therefore ungrateful.

[72] St.-Simon, XXIX, 273–74.

[73] H.M.C. *Stuart Papers*, I, 479; Dangeau, XVI, 287.

[74] Dangeau, entries for Nov. 24 and Dec. 5, XVI, 243, 257.

[75] Keith, 25–26.

[76] John Sinclair, *A True Account of the Proceedings at Perth* (London, 1716, reprinted at Edinburgh, 1845 in *Spottiswoode Miscellany*, II), 459.

[77] Ormonde to Mar, Morlaix, Dec. 27, 1715, and Ormonde to James, Oct. 21,

coming; and the Scottish army could not do without it. The pleas of the Earl Marischal and others notwithstanding,[78] it was decided after the retreat from Perth to disband the army and get the leaders out of the country as quickly as possible. Lord Drummond, General Sheldon, and Mar, now a titular duke, went on board ship with James on the night of February 4/15, 1716, to sail for France, leaving General Gordon in command. Various other officers were brought off in the following months. Those who were not were captured, and the most important suffered for high treason.

A charge of cowardice has been made against the Pretender for "deserting" his troops in Scotland, but his presence was anything but a blessing to them; had he remained, as his son was to do in 1746, he would have brought a thorough search upon the Highlands, after the inevitable scattering of his army. This search would have turned up not only noblemen and officers for punishment, but a great crowd of "private men," who might not all have been executed, but who would certainly have been imprisoned for months, and perhaps transported in the end. Some were punished in this way as it was. Also, although it is romantic to read of the risks taken to conceal a defeated prince, there would be a great deal of real danger to all who fed, sheltered, or clothed him, whether he finally escaped or not. There was good reason for him to leave Scotland when he did. Aside from that, it was a bold feat to be in Scotland at all; James III had risked ambush at Nonancourt and every other hamlet on his path from Paris to St.-Malo and from there to Dunkirk, and travelled the whole length of the North Sea when the English fleet was alert and overwhelming in strength. Under the charge there lies a feeling of dissatisfaction that James was not butchered to make a Hanoverian holiday.

James and Mar arrived at Gravelines on February 10/21, 1716. A week before, Ormonde had returned to Paris from Brittany, confessing his failure, and alleging betrayal.[79] It was soon known

---

H.M.C. *Stuart Papers*, I, 480, 442. The news of Preston may have deterred the Regent from complying with his promise. Hardwicke, II, 550.

[78] Keith, 27–28.

[79] Dangeau, XVI, 321.

that Maclean, his former secretary, was responsible.[80] The duke went to meet the Chevalier on the road from Gravelines, and together they were rumored to be in the vicinity of Paris about February 26.[81] Less than two weeks later he was at Commercy, before taking his way to Avignon.[82] As a token of his disapproval of the rebellion, the Regent of France put on half-pay the officers in the French service who had followed James to Scotland. Even the Earl of Tynemouth, son of the exemplary Berwick, lost his regiment,[83] at the demand of the English Secretary of State, Stanhope, that France should fulfill her obligations under the treaty of Utrecht.[84]

4. THE GREAT DISMISSAL

At some time during his stay of not more than ten days at Paris, the Pretender dismissed Bolingbroke.[85] The latter relates [86] that when James arrived he lodged at St.-Germain, that there he received Bolingbroke "with open arms," and that the minister urged him to go to Lorraine before he was forbidden to stop there, and the Duke of Lorraine warned not to permit him to do so. This the Pretender did not desire to do; he asked Bolingbroke to obtain for him an interview with the Regent. The Regent refused, and the Pretender, Bolingbroke says, made a pretence of leaving on the morning of Sunday or Monday, March 1 or 2. Then, still according to Bolingbroke, he moved to a house in the Bois de Boulogne, and on the following Thursday, March 5, Ormonde came to the minister with a holograph letter demanding his papers, dated Tuesday, March 3. The meantime, Bolingbroke says, James spent in company with "his female ministers," "lurking," and "pleasing himself with the air of mystery and business." He saw the Spanish and Swedish ambassadors at Paris,

[80] H.M.C. *Stuart Papers*, I, 452; Berwick, II, 257–58.
[81] Dangeau, XVI, 326–27.
[82] *Ibid.*, XVI, 337.
[83] *Ibid.*, XVI, 344.
[84] Graham, I, 309.
[85] M. Jean Dureng (*Le duc de Bourbon et l'Angleterre, 1723–1726*, Toulouse, 1911, 352) has somewhere acquired the erroneous notion that Bolingbroke quit the Pretender's service of his own volition.
[86] Bolingbroke, 209–19.

and possibly the Regent. The "cabal" of the Bois de Boulogne, it is said in the *Letter to Sir William Windham,* brought about Bolingbroke's fall, by putting forward certain aspersions of his character and conduct which the "victim" proceeds to refute. Alas! that these are not the reasons (which Bolingbroke certainly knew) seriously advanced for the dismissal, for he refutes them so convincingly.

The other side of the story must be told. Mar was chosen to receive James III's correspondence for him on March 1,[87] so that if the Chevalier deceived his Secretary of State in moving to the house in the Bois, he had already withdrawn his confidence from him. Ormonde had sought and obtained a promise of arms from Orléans in October, concealing it from Bolingbroke at the Regent's request,[88] so that it is evident that the viscount was not a man the French wished to deal with. No minister of James could long hold office under those circumstances. The Irish and other Catholics had been slighted by the Secretary, and the Scots were furious at his supposed neglect of the war. In any case the stay in the Bois de Boulogne had little or nothing to do with the decision to remove Bolingbroke.

What was alleged was formulated into "Articles," a copy of which Tindal obtained and printed; [89] other copies still exist, so that it must have been fairly widely known. "I. Lord Bolingbroke was never to be found by those who came to him about business. . . II. The Earl of *Mar,* by six different messengers . . . acquainted Lord *Bolingbroke* . . . of his being in distress for want of arms and ammunition, and prayed for a speedy relief; and though the things demanded were in my Lord's power, there was not so much as one pound of powder sent in any of the ships, which by his Lordship's direction parted from *France.*" Article III was that General George Hamilton was sent to him to be introduced to the French ministers, an introduction which Boling-

---

[87] Thornton, 430.

[88] H.M.C. *Stuart Papers,* I, 480, 482; Bolingbroke, 182–87; Sherlock's interview with Carte, Carte MSS. 231, fol. 49. I incline to Ormonde's account in the first reference.

[89] Tindal, IV, 475–76. A MS. copy of these charges is preserved in Rawlinson MSS. (Bodleian Library) A. 311, fol. 15. A summary of another is printed in H.M.C. *Report* X, app. I, 181–182.

broke failed to make, although Hamilton obtained an interview with the Regent by other means. Article IV was that Bolingbroke deferred giving directions to Castelblanco about sending stores in his possession to Scotland until too late. Article V was a statement of the suspicion of many Jacobites that Bolingbroke was both indiscreet and dishonest. Article VI charged that the minister bungled the secret sending of arms by asking, and being formally refused, public permission to transport them of the French authorities.

We possess Bolingbroke's defense, nominally written by his secretary, Brinsden, against these, the real charges.[90] To the first he replies that he never refused to see or was inaccessible to authorized persons, but disregarded useless people. He knew nothing of a shortage of arms until the arrival of General Hamilton (in early February),[91] but had Mar and James remained in Scotland a few days longer, they would have had 10,000 arms and 30,000 pounds of powder, which the ships sent earlier were not large enough to transport. Of Castelblanco he says nothing except that he meddled in English affairs, but does not explain his failure to send directions for shipping the munitions. He excuses not introducing General Hamilton to the French ministers by saying that they would not grant the general a *public* audience. The suspicions of the Jacobites he strikes at with raillery against "Men Women, & Children, people for the most part of no name in the world, or else of very bad characters," "a whole tribe of Jesuits," and such terms. He ends by defending himself against the charge, not raised in the articles, of correspondence with the English government.

An anonymous answer [92] to this defense, one backed by the evidence we have, rips it to shreds. "His Ldspps Letters are not calculated so much to clear himself, as to weaken the K--gs interest in England, & to discourage all correspondence with him . . . an innocent Man with his Ldsps pen could have made a more plausible Defence." The author gives Bolingbroke the lie

[90] Rawlinson MSS. A. 315, foll. 15–17v. Another copy is printed in extract in H.M.C. *Report* X, app. I, 182–83.
[91] Dangeau, XVI, 316.
[92] Rawl. MSS. A. 311, foll. 18–21v. An abstract of another copy is printed in H.M.C. *Report* X, app. I, 183.

in the matter of the shortage of powder, of which he asserts that
the viscount was well informed, to the knowledge of Ormonde
and Mar, and gives the current prices of muskets in France, which
were very low. He points out that Bolingbroke did not answer
the sixth charge, relating to a public permission, and assures his
readers that the French port officials would have connived at
private shipment of arms. Moreover, the ships previously sent to
Scotland were large enough for small loads of arms and powder,
if not for great ones. A hint that Ormonde was responsible for
the delay is answered sharply. Those arms which would have
arrived in February were procured, not by Bolingbroke, but by a
private gentleman on his own credit; Ormonde had also obtained
a large number of arms by his own devices. Hamilton's mission
remains mishandled by Bolingbroke's account, the answerer says,
because Ormonde and Queen Maria had no notice of Hamilton's
arrival. Bolingbroke had disappointed Ormonde of business conferences on two occasions, appearing days late when speed was
important; "instead of discoursing about business he drank to
excess & early on the 2d day after returned to Paris without saying
anything to the purpose," the author says of one such meeting;
of another, "at length he came, when dinner was on the Table.
before dinner was half done, he rose up hastily & pretended
urgent business to call him away." Bolingbroke had offered to
rely on Berwick's judgment of his case, and was answered, "I
believe that D.[uke] will for the same reasons appeal to his
Ldspp to clear himself," and is charged with communicating,
together with Berwick, with Marlborough. As to "want of
Secrecy; I can assure you that in the midst of his Wine, he discovered Secrets of the greatest importance to some of the very
persons, whom he now represents in such black Characters; & that
they expressed a concern at his imprudence." Besides, of the
"Jesuits," "his Ldspp cannot be ignorant that no person of that
order was ever employed in business by the K - - - or Q - - - -." His
Lordship had attacked the queen for ruining him; the author
closes by saying that Ormonde and the other Jacobites were unani-
mously for the steps, while the queen had no hand in it.

Those are the charges and countercharges. On some points
there is confirmation of the anonymous author's reply. Six letters

sent by Mar during the rebellion were received by Bolingbroke, surely not all so delayed as to leave him in ignorance until February.[93] General Hamilton's letter of February 13 tells us that General Dillon had carried his report to the Regent when Bolingbroke did not, and that he was well received, with the question addressed to Dillon, "Why didn't you bring him [Hamilton]? You knew the road"; and Castelblanco had complained to him of a countermanding of the shipment of arms.[94] Mar mentions the unanimity of the Jacobites on the dismissal in a letter of March 25,[95] but he was an interested party.

In view of these facts, although Bolingbroke had some right on his side, he had to go. He had alienated every friend in the party, even the English,[96] and all factions agreed that he was useless, to say the least. The key to his behavior is the part played by Ormonde; if Bolingbroke's conduct had not been strange, the duke would not have taken the lead in his dismissal; and certainly he would never lead a Catholic reaction against Bolingbroke's Protestant beliefs. After all, it was not Ormonde who gained by his friend's fall, but Mar, who took his place, and testimony on the character of the duke, although it does not emphasize "parts," always gives him credit both for integrity and loyalty to Protestantism. Only one important Jacobite, Berwick, stood by Bolingbroke, and his refusal to go to Scotland as general cut him off from confidence forever. It was unfortunate that better care was not taken to keep Bolingbroke neutral, but James probably lost his temper; still, this is a tactical, not a moral issue.

Before leaving this unpleasant subject, the countercharge of Bolingbroke in the *Letter to Sir William Windham* concerning the Declarations issued during his ascendancy must be considered, to clear up the contemporary political views of the Pretender, which have been much obscured by them. Two Declarations for

[93] They are listed in H.M.C. *Stuart Papers*, IV, 69–70, as having been handed over to Brinsden, Bolingbroke's secretary, in September 1716, with other papers. Their dates are given as Oct. 21, Nov. 3, 19, and 30, and Dec. 6 and 8, 1715.

[94] H.M.C. *Stuart Papers*, I, 502–03.

[95] *Ibid.*, II, 3.

[96] James III to the duc d'Orléans, March 6, 1716, *ibid.*, II, 5. If this seems improbable, the quarrel with Oxford may explain it.

Scotland and England were signed at Bar on July 20,[97] then were printed and dispersed. In August another for Scotland was drawn up, but not issued.[98] Finally, when Ormonde and James were about to leave France, Bolingbroke drew up Declarations which were somewhat altered by James and signed at Commercy, October 25, 1715.[99]

These alterations unquestionably left Bolingbroke unsatisfied: he wrote to James on November 2 that the Declaration for England, then being printed with the changes made, gave only ambiguous security to the Church of England, and none at all for that of Ireland.[100] There the matter dropped for a time. Both of the Commercy Declarations were reprinted at Perth during the rising,[101] and copies were distributed far and wide. When Bolingbroke had been dismissed at least a year, and possibly many years later, during the long period of time in which he occasionally worked on the *Letter to Sir William Windham,* he reflected on the alterations and used them to attack his former master and to ingratiate himself with George I.

"I cannot say that he sent them [the declarations] to the queen to be corrected by her confessor and the rest of her council: but I firmly believe it," he says, and again, "the whole tenor of the amendments was one continued instance of the grossest bigotry; and the most material passages were turned with all the jesuitical prevarication imaginable." [102] It is true that the changes show a desire to satisfy the ever-present claims of conscience. There are eight material alterations in the original draft, made in the hand of Nairne the clerk; [103] with one exception, a deletion of a promise to secure the Church of Ireland, the changes of meaning are only such as to absolve the Pretender of adherence to two churches at once. If this be bigotry, Bolingbroke is justified. To reduce Queen Anne's memory from "glorious and blessed" to

[97] Carte MSS. 180, fol. 2 (for Scotland) and fol. 3 (for England).
[98] *Ibid.,* foll. 328–333.
[99] *Ibid.,* foll. 340–41 (for England); Tindal, IV, 453–54*n.* (for Scotland); H.M.C. *Stuart Papers,* I, 449 (for England); *Somers' Tracts,* XVI, 190–93 (for Scotland).
[100] Mahon, I, app., xxix–xxx.
[101] H.M.C. *Stuart Papers,* I, 448–49.
[102] Bolingbroke, 277–78.
[103] H.M.C. *Stuart Papers,* I, 449.

merely "glorious" is impiety in his eyes; her "eminent justice and exemplary piety," a formal phrase, as he admits, was shocking when changed to "inclinations to Justice." [104]

The other comments are of much the same nature: the longest is that upon a reference to the Declaration for England of July 20 inserted into the one of October 25 by the Pretender. The passage as altered reads, "to such a Parliament [a free one] let it belong to make effectual provision not only for the security and re-establishment of all those Rights, Priviledges, immunities and Possessions which belong to the Church of England, and wherein We have already promised by Our late Declaration of the 20 July to secure all the members thereof, but also for the better maintenance of those who serve at their Altars, if any further provision of this kind shall be found necessary." This, Bolingbroke says, limits his promise to the things already promised in the earlier document,[105] which reading shows that it does not, since James promises also to increase clerical stipends if Parliament so chooses. Even so, his next thought on the subject is a further misrepresentation: "what does that [the Declaration of July 20] promise? Security and protection to the members of this church in the enjoyment of their property," which, Bolingbroke thinks, is no security to the Church of England itself.

The relevant passage is not as narrow as that. "And in particular, we likewise Promise, upon Our Royal Word, to protect and secure Our Subjects of the Church of England, by law Established, in the full injoyment of all their legal Rights, Priviledges, and Immunities, and in the sole possession of all their Churches, Universities, Colledges and Schools." Clearly these last items are not the property of the members, but of the Church of England. Thus it is impossible to accept the contention that evasion is the object of the reference; probably James spoke the truth when he wrote, "it is of consequence that such papers should be all of a piece and not in the least clash with one another." [106] Bolingbroke relied, in making his assertion, on the blurred memories of those who had seen the declarations, to make contradiction difficult. One

[104] Bolingbroke, 280.
[105] *Ibid.*, 287.
[106] James to Bolingbroke, Commercy, Oct. 21, 1715, H.M.C. *Stuart Papers*, I, 443.

conclusion is firmly established: James would promise nothing he could not do, and his promises, read for what they are, with the proper meaning given to each word, were sufficient to anyone except people who either had a deep-rooted aversion to his Catholicism alone, or believed that some of James's political views must be anachronistic, regardless of religion.

This is what Bolingbroke would not accept. "He has all the superstition of a capuchin; but I found on him no tincture of the religion of a prince." [107] When one has read a few thousand letters written by a man on all occasions and to all manner of persons, one can say a few things confidently. James was not superstitious, unless his Catholic faith is considered so. When he refers to religion, it is to holy life as well as to correct faith, to God, not to relics or images, as his own Anglican chaplains bear witness. His life has been, so far as even the watchful English government could tell, virtuous in the extreme — whatever the gossips of Bar may have told Mr. H. W. Wolff in the 1890's.[108] The English minister at Venice confessed, in commenting on the scandalous behavior of some Jacobites at Pesaro in 1717, "The Pretender's sanctity of life, and his attending punctually the functions, give great joy to his Holiness." [109] Since the minister would have heard any breath of scandal, his negative is of great value; and British envoys were not appointed to give the Pretender character references. No, indeed. It may be assumed that the statement was as true two years earlier, when Bolingbroke hinted at sensuality in the Bois de Boulogne; but this is not superstition or bigotry, let us hope.

The Pope thought enough of the quality of the Pretender's religion to invite him to stay at Avignon, a Papal territory, or in any other part of the States of the Church. It was to Avignon — at first it was imagined for a short time — that James resolved to go.[110]

[107] Bolingbroke, 269.
[108] There was a tradition at Bar that he kept a mistress there. Wolff, "The Pretender at Bar-le-duc," *Blackwood's Magazine*, CLVI. This is the probable origin of Mr. Andrew Lang's acceptance of such a liaison as "undeniably" genuine.
[109] Quoted in Graham, II, 3.
[110] James to the Duke of Lorraine, near Châlons, March 21, 1716, H.M.C. *Stuart Papers*, II, 35.

5

PLOTTING

(1 7 1 7 – 1 7 2 7)

1. THE STATE OF EUROPE; THE SWEDISH PLOT

Had there been any reasonable alternative, refuge in the Papal States would not have attracted James III. His father had avoided withdrawing into Italy at the Peace of Ryswick; and after the conclusion of that of Utrecht the Duke of Lorraine had withstood pressure from England for his guest's expulsion, which would have meant, since the Empire was bound not to receive him and France had already requested his departure from St.-Germain, that he would have to go southward, into either Spain or Italy. Possibly the Chevalier judged rightly in setting aside Bolingbroke's advice, that Lorraine had formerly sheltered him with French approval, and could not persist when the Regent, after Louis XIV's death, took the side of England and observed the clauses of the treaty with England relating to the Pretender more rigorously than his uncle had done. That Orléans was now set upon the conciliation of George I is obvious from the compulsory retirement of Jacobite officers and subsequent events. This determination was founded on excellent reasons.

The King of Spain, grandson of Louis XIV and uncle of the young Louis XV, had become, in the course of an epidemic, next heir to the French crown. In quick succession Philip V's father, the Dauphin, his brothers, the duc de Berry and the duc de Bourgogne, and his nephew, the duc de Bretagne, had died. Philip's claim was barred by the terms of the treaties of Utrecht; nevertheless, the opinion of French legists was that the next heir could not renounce his right. But granted that the renunciation

would hold, the heir was the nephew of Louis XIV, the duc
d'Orléans, Regent of France. The dispute would have had little
significance if Louis XV had begun his life in good health, but he
was ill much of his first ten years, and might have succumbed at
any time to one of the diseases which combed through royal
families as well as others in the eighteenth century, leaving the
French monarchy as a prize in a contest of strength or agility
between his uncle and cousin. The hatred between Philip V and
the Regent engendered by a quarrel, when the latter commanded
an army in the Peninsula and had laid himself open to a charge
of treachery, added a further complication — that the Regent
could expect disgrace even if he acknowledged Philip's claim and
stood aside to allow Spain and France to be ruled by one king.
This last, of course, would have caused war with England, the
Netherlands, and the Empire. Since it was cheaper for England
to support the Regent than to fight another war on the scale of
that of the Spanish Succession, George I and the duc d'Orléans
were bound together. Only one obstacle stood in the way, the
presence of the Pretender in France, or in its satellite, Lorraine.
James must go.

Spain was also anxious to conciliate England, as a part of the
early policy of Cardinal Alberoni, the chief minister of Philip V
at this time, for the revival of Spanish trade, as well as to gain
support for the king of Spain as a candidate for the French throne
if Louis XV should die. Philip was even willing, if absolutely
necessary, to give up Spain for France. Therefore James could not
enter Spain. Portugal was a close ally of England. The Empire
and the United Provinces were closed to him by the system of
alliances resumed and strengthened after the death of Queen
Anne. Switzerland's Catholic cantons would have offered asylum,
had it not been that the smallness of these states made safeguards
against assassination impossible, except in their most remote
districts, such as Bellinzona or Sion,[1] which were as inaccessible
from England before the introduction of improved transportation as Italy itself.

James chose Avignon as the nearest place to England open to

---

[1] John Carnegy to Mar, Lucerne, Dec. 18, 1716, H.M.C. *Stuart Papers*, III,
325–26. See also Carte MSS. 257, foll. 6–10.

him, and the only real alternative to Italy. By way of Commercy, Châlons, and Lyon, he travelled slowly to that place, arriving on April 2, 1716.[2] Mar accompanied him, and several others came immediately after, making a court,[3] not only of Catholics, but of Protestants as well. Ormonde, the Earl of Panmure, the Marquess of Tullibardine and the escaped Earl of Nithsdale were all there. Charles Leslie read prayers at the Pretender's house, as he had done at Bar, "but in this country we must not make a noise about it," [4] services having been prohibited by orders from Rome.[5] There was, of course, an informer, who wrote to Cardinal Gualterio, "They live there with the freedom of their religion to the scandal of good Catholics, and among themselves in so barbaric a manner that they fight each other very often about the smallest things." [6] There were many duels, from boredom, drink, and ancient bitternesses, and the Chevalier was hard put to it to keep the peace, as his father had been before him.[7] Most of the Jacobites abroad were poor, now as before, and suffered, if not hunger, certainly shabbiness and discomfort. Those who were wise followed the old path and sought military employment in one of the continental armies.[8] Catholics found a good number of opportunities, in Lorraine, Tuscany, and to some extent the Empire, but especially in Spain.

Avignon could not be a final haven, for the Regent wished to conclude a treaty of alliance with England, and it was understood that he must force James into Italy. He desired the Pope to ask the Pretender to leave; a refusal would have endangered the enclave of Papal territory in France. "On prend Avignon quand on veut," Cardinal Bernis was to write in 1773,[9] a saying

---

[2] H.M.C. *Stuart Papers*, II, 7, 34, 45; H. Tayler, ed. "Jacobite Papers at Avignon," *Miscellany of the Scottish Hist. Soc.*, V (Edinburgh, 1933), 300–301.

[3] Tayler, "Jacobite Papers," 305–07.

[4] H.M.C. *Stuart Papers*, II, 216. In a list of the suite, Leslie, Barclay, Hamilton, Patterson, and "Woord" are classed as "docteurs," separate from physicians and priests. Tayler, "Jacobite Papers," 306.

[5] Tayler, "Jacobite Papers," 301.

[6] Add. MSS. 20,311, foll. 369–70.

[7] E.g. in the ugly affair between two sons of Lord Salisbury at St.-Germain, Dangeau, III, 292.

[8] As Lord Andrew Drummond did. H.M.C. *Stuart Papers*, II, 193.

[9] Quoted by A. Sorel, *L'Europe et la révolution francaise* (Paris, new printing, 1946–49), I, 54.

already true in 1716. James replied to Clement XI's invitation to come to Italy that residence in Rome would ruin his credit in England [10] by identifying him with Ultramontanism, but in the autumn representatives of France and England signed preliminaries of a treaty at Hanover, with clauses that provided that James be made to reside beyond the Alps,[11] probably for just that reason. His illness of a fistula, which prostrated him so that for two months he could not even write with his own hand,[12] made an operation necessary, and postponed the movement into Italy. The Regent was obliging about the delay.[13] At the commencement of 1717 he promised a pension of 750,000 livres a year as a consolation for retirement.[14]

Before the signature of the preliminaries there had been grandiose plans, involving King Charles XII of Sweden. Certainly some kind of intrigue with Sweden through Count Belke, a Swedish major-general in the French service, extended as far back as 1705.[15] Twelve battalions had been spoken of in 1715 as Charles XII's contribution to the Scots; [16] but vainly, because the "great Swede" was fighting for his own life and possessions at Stralsund.[17] Sir John Erskine of Alva was sent to the continent on a mission to Sweden, but failed to arrive there before the collapse of the Jacobite army. James's interview with Sparre, the Swedish envoy at Paris, has been mentioned; Sparre was reprimanded by Charles for consenting to it. While Denmark, Russia, and Prussia made war on Charles, he wanted no enemies; what he wanted was money.

To find it he chose a minister of Franconian birth, George Henry Goertz von Schitz, who was to go to Holland, borrow money on Sweden's credit, and invest it in ships, which were badly needed at that time. The Dutch were not eager to part with money on such slender security as Sweden could give. The Regent

[10] Add. MSS. 20,292, fol. 96.
[11] Maria Beatrice to Mar, Oct. 14, 1716, H.M.C. *Stuart Papers,* III, 77–78.
[12] *Ibid.,* III, v.
[13] *Ibid.,* III, 159.
[14] Note on engagements between Louis XV and James III, written 1764. Affaires étrangères, Mémoires et documents, Angleterre 75, fol. 175.
[15] H.M.C. *Report* XV, app. IV, 259, 307.
[16] H.M.C. *Stuart Papers,* I, 413–14.
[17] *Ibid.,* II, 128.

of France, who was next approached with a request for 100,000 crowns, pointed to his own difficulties, which were probably real enough.

Independently for the moment of Goertz's notions, the Swedish ambassadors at Paris and London, Sparre and Gyllenborg, agreed in September 1716 that the actions of George I were so friendly toward Sweden's enemies that his destruction would be of use to her.[18] Gyllenborg reported that Englishmen hostile to Hanover had approached him, but had insisted that he show express authority to work with them in arranging for the loan of 10,000 men from the Swedish army.[19] Later he was offered £60,000 for the purpose if he could obtain Charles's personal promise to fulfil his part of the bargain. Father Thomas Southcoat would once more collect the money.[20] Now this happened to be more than three times Goertz's desired 100,000 crowns,[21] as they must have known. Ormonde, as spokesman for the English Jacobites, was drawn into the question and wrote to Goertz to make a formal agreement, which the latter regretted to be impossible without danger of betrayal.[22] The decision was not in the Pretender's hands, because the money was not his; Goertz's effort was made among his English followers.[23]

Goertz hoped that direct authorization by Charles would not be necessary, saying that if the troops could not be sent the money would be repaid by the following May, but even the most optimistic Jacobite ought to have known that Charles could not repay influential creditors, let alone impotent ones. Goertz was bold, and wrote Gyllenborg on November 23 to obtain the Jacobites' plan for raising money and send it to him.[24] He did have authority

[18] Sparre to Gyllenborg, Sept. 25, 1716, C. S. Terry, *The Chevalier de St.-George.* (London, etc., 1901), 314.

[19] *Ibid.*, 314–15.

[20] *Ibid.*, 317–18; H.M.C. *Stuart Papers*, II, 360; III, 182.

[21] For the conversion rate, see Dicconson's "Account . . . ," Carte MSS. 211, foll. 323–24. The French crown (écu) was worth 5 livres. French coinage depreciated in value until 1724. A. Blanchet and A. Dieudonné, *Manuel de numismatique française* (Paris, 1912–36), II.

[22] Letter of Nov. 12, 1716, cited in J. F. Chance, "The 'Swedish Plot' of 1716–17," *E.H.R.*, XVIII (January 1903), 93. This article is drawn upon for much of this account of the plot.

[23] H.M.C. *Stuart Papers*, II, 477.

[24] Chance, *E.H.R.*, XVIII, 94.

to raise money for his king, and saw no reason to reject English gold for some tiny scruple. At about this time, also, Sparre and Gyllenborg found themselves cut off from Sweden, and decided to write home no more until interception seemed less probable,[25] so that it is to be doubted that the king ever knew to what extent his agents had committed him. Goertz assured the Jacobites that an invasion was certain, since Charles's interest would hold him to the plan better than an agreement in writing, but the English, he said, must reduce the appropriation for armaments by Parliamentary action, leaving the country bare, and keeping the English fleet out of the Baltic during the next year. It is obvious that both of these objects were important to the Swedes, whether or not the ten to twelve thousand troops promised [26] could ever be found for the invasion.

Count Gyllenborg then sent word that 20,000 "pièces," probably pounds sterling, were collected, and that 8000 more had been paid to Sparre. Goertz was now in Paris, and replied in January 1717 that his plans for getting 100,000 crowns from other sources had disappeared; he sent a set of full powers to Gyllenborg and authorized receipt of the English money, but warned him not to write home what he was doing.[27] Goertz was then able to borrow 100,000 francs (livres) on the strength of these promises, and was allowed credit in Holland up to the value of 1,000,000 florins (probably also livres). Gyllenborg did not receive the money himself, but told Goertz to expect it from Queen Maria at St.-Germain.[28] It had been collected partly by Southcoat and partly by Atterbury.[29]

The final agreement between Goertz and General Dillon at Paris was that "Robertson," i.e. James, was "to give Saxby [Charles XII] or Longford [Goertz] *a milion French* and Saxby is to *transport into England by the twentieth of Aprill or sooner eight thousand foot, five hundred horse mounted,* and *three thousand five hundred horsemen,* with their *accuterments* . . . . *therty*

[25] *Ibid.*
[26] *Ibid.*, 96–97.
[27] *Ibid.*, 97–98.
[28] Chance, *E.H.R.*, XVIII, 98.
[29] H.M.C. *Stuart Papers*, III, 307, 338, 401, 436–37.

thousand armes," and so on.[30] Finding these things was simply impossible; the whole project shows how little was clearly known in France and England about the state of Charles' fortunes, or, perhaps, anything else east of the Elbe. The Swedes tried to hurry payment of the money,[31] but it came slowly, and on January 29, Old Style, Gyllenborg was arrested in his house, his papers seized, and his quarters searched, in frank violation of the law respecting ambassadors. His correspondence had been opened and his cipher known for a long time, and when matters reached this stage, and other reasons made it desirable, George I and his cabinet intervened. Goertz was arrested in Holland after a short period in hiding, on February 19/March 2.

The plot, such as it was, had exploded. Charles Caesar, Sir Jacob Banks, a Major Smith, and Henry Jerningham, a goldsmith of Covent Garden, were arrested with Gyllenborg.[32] All were later released,[33] as were the ambassadors.

There are several things to be observed in all this. The king of Sweden was never committed to assisting James III. It is possible that he knew nothing of Goertz's schemes; certainly that is what he said later. Goertz's character was doubtful, and his errand was a search for money from almost any source on almost any terms. The eagerness of some of the English Jacobites gave him an excellent opportunity for a swindle, and he took it. Fortunately for them their promises were slow of fulfilment, but as it was, 175,000 livres — about £12,000 — had been given to the Swedes,[34] and James was to dun the government of Sweden for repayment for twenty years or more. Had the full payment been made, the total would have been nearly £80,000. Why did the English government interrupt Goertz when he was conveniently bleeding the Jacobites white?

Mr. J. F. Chance [35] suggests that the new Stanhope-Sunderland government, recently formed in the room of Townshend and his

---

[30] Mar to George Jerningham, Jan. 27, 1717, *ibid.,* III, 481. Italics indicate decipherment.

[31] H.M.C. *Stuart Papers,* III, 511.

[32] *Ibid.,* III, 530.

[33] J. Menzies to L. Inese, Feb. 11/22, 1717, *ibid.,* III, 538.

[34] *Ibid.,* IV, 97.

[35] *E.H.R.,* XVIII, 105.

friends, was afraid that the circumstances of its rise might bring on a parliamentary crisis. The disclosure of the plot to Parliament, on February 20/March 3, 1717, concealed its harmlessness and rallied the English to patriotism and support of the new ministers. Even so, the supply for measures against Sweden, which George I would have wanted taken, plot or no plot, was only passed by a majority of four, when it was voted, on April 9/20. The plot was also a useful excuse for English participation in the hostilities in the Baltic, in which George I's German dominions were already involved by his purchase of Bremen and Verden, part of Denmark's spoils in the Northern War. This conjecture is a very plausible one.

2. THE PRETENDER IN ITALY

In the midst of the excitement of the plot, when its outcome was still doubtful, James was forced to leave Avignon and cross the Alps. Departing on February 6, he passed over on the 21st into the territory of the King of Sicily (later of Sardinia), who refused any sort of assistance.[36] Mar went from Avignon to Paris after accompanying the Pretender for a short way on his journey, to confer with Sparre and Queen Maria.[37] Bologna was supposed at first to be the place of residence of the court,[38] but James evidently had changed his mind *en route,* or on seeing Bologna, for he continued as far as Pesaro, where he arrived on March 20. There it was that he learned, on March 26, of Goertz's arrest.[39] The full fraudulence of the transaction was not known until the following summer, so that it must have cost him a great deal of anxiety for his own interest as well as for his friends.

Already he had drawn up a declaration, which was later printed, dated "Pezzaro," March 21, 1717.[40] It is remarkable for two things only. Anticipating a restoration of James by Charles XII, it con-

---

[36] H.M.C. *Stuart Papers,* III, 535–36.
[37] Mar to James, March 4, 1717, *ibid.,* IV, 91.
[38] Add. MSS. 20,292, fol. 111.
[39] H.M.C. *Stuart Papers,* IV, 138. Pesaro was "well-walled and therefore easy to take care of." Carte MSS. 257, foll. 6–10.
[40] H.M.C. *Stuart Papers,* IV, 128–31.

firms the Declarations of July 20 and October 25, 1715, but with this addition:

> We do likewise renew and confirm all the promises made by Us in Our aforesaid Declarations to protect, support and maintain Our subjects of the Church of England and Ireland in the full and free exercise of their religion, and to secure the said Church as by law established, and all the members thereof in as full enjoyment of all their legal rights, privileges and immunities, and in as full and peaceable possession of all their Churches, Universities, Colleges and Schools as ever they enjoyed them, under any of Our Royal Predecessors of the Protestant Communion.

This is an "entire knot." There were *no* promises to the Church of Ireland in either of those declarations; indeed, an extension of those to the Church of England to her sister church was crossed out of the October one, as we have seen. To confirm the promises before made where none had been made is nonsense, but even nonsense is intended to mean something. It is possible that the Pretender wished to convey a meaning which he was not at liberty to set down. In the case of the phrase "subjects of the Church of England," this is so, on his own word. "The difference of protecting the Church of England or the members of it has been an old dispute, but coming from me certainly means the same thing," he wrote in 1728.[41] Similarly it is possible, and from James III's character not improbable, that he was not simply seeking to delude his Protestant friends by pretending to have made promises which he had not made, but took this occasion and this means of granting to the Church of Ireland what had already been given to the Church of England without provoking remonstrances from the priests of whom he was shortly to assert his independence. This is only a conjecture, possibly an over-ingenious one, but based on the sound fact that the Pretender is always found wishing to do more than his spiritual advisers felt safe. In due course he was relieved of much of his difficulty by the highest Catholic spiritual authority, but that was not yet.

The other cause for comment was the reference to Parliament of the public debt and public engagements contracted since the

---

[41] James to Daniel O'Brien, Aug. 2, 1728, Windsor Stuart Papers (henceforth cited as W.S.P.) 118, no. 142.

Revolution. In the October 25 Declaration, only those made since Anne's death were liable to repudiation: "Let all publick ingagements be looked upon as sacred, and be preserevd [sic] inviolate which have been enterd into until the death of Our Dear sister; for We cannot suppose it is expected We should have any regard to the Acts of this riotous assembly, which under the authority of the Usurper [George I] stiles itself a Parliament." [42] Now, to the first restoration Parliament the duty is given of finding means "to ease the nation of the intolerable burdens under which it now groans." This is not the first instance of a tendency to shift the responsibility to the shoulders of Parliament.

The stay at Pesaro passed very quietly, for the journey from Avignon had reduced James to sitting "by the chimney side," [43] until May. At the end of that month he was at Rome on a ceremonial visit, receiving all possible courtesies: audiences with the Pope, calls from cardinals, even a delay of one hour in the procession of the Holy Sacrament so that he could see it. It was his first visit to Rome, and Rome's first glimpse of him. The monarch and the city regarded each other with curiosity until July,[44] when he departed to Urbino, where a new residence had been arranged for him.

His main immediate concern was marriage. Various princesses were single, and it might seem that it would not be troublesome to choose a suitable queen from among them, but if James were to have children he intended to educate them in his own religion, so that a Protestant marriage was almost out of the question; his bride must also be of princely rank, and of a family friendly to the Pretender's hopes. Thus, although marriage with an archduchess, of the Hapsburg family, had been seriously considered after the conclusion of the Peace of Utrecht,[45] the Imperial House was now considered to be opposed to the Pretender on all points except religion. Rank excluded the very wealthy Lady Petre, otherwise acceptable.[46] A Princess Palatine had been excused from

[42] Carte MSS. 180, fol. 341.
[43] H.M.C. *Stuart Papers,* IV, 140.
[44] "Journal du sejour," Carte MSS. 208, foll. 338–59v.
[45] Wolfgang Michael, *England under George I,* trans. A. and G. E. MacGregor (London, 1936–39), II, 171.
[46] H.M.C. *Stuart Papers,* IV, 149.

the inconvenient honor by her father, who was afraid that George I might give him trouble from Hanover if he followed his natural desires for her promotion.[47] Oxford, through Mar, begged the Pretender to choose a Protestant Princess of Hesse,[48] but this scheme collapsed also. Passing through Modena in the spring, James had been much struck with a young cousin of his; [49] in the summer, taking a dispensation for marriage within the forbidden degrees for granted, he asked the Duke of Modena for her hand.[50] The Emperor's hostility was too strong for the Duke, however, and he sent his nephew a "reponse courte, signifiante, et positive" [51] in September 1717. And many letters came every month from England and Scotland begging James to find a suitable queen and beget heirs for the perpetuation of the house of which he was the sole survivor.

Ormonde, doubtless because of his Protestantism, left James when he went to Rome, and joined Mar at Paris. The Czar of Russia, Peter I, was then in western Europe, accompanied, among others, by Dr. Erskine, a loyal Jacobite. Peter, it would appear, was ready to make peace overtures to Charles XII, perhaps through an emissary of James, who might, Mar hoped, be able to obtain a price for his mediation.[52] Since Ormonde had been named by the English government as an important rebel, the Regent would in any case soon request that he withdraw from France; Mar suggested that he should go to the Baltic as Peter's agent.[53] "A good round sum of money," Erskine was assured, could be found for any ruler willing to support the Pretender with arms. Ormonde went off to Danzig, by way of Prague, preceded by George Jerningham, who was to ask Charles XII for permission for Ormonde to advance further.[54] Permission was refused. Eventually the duke turned off to Mitau, where he was to talk to Peter about a Russo-Swedish peace, an alliance of those countries for James's benefit

---

[47] The Elector Palatine to Owen O'Rourke, Sept. 8, 1716, *ibid.*, IV, 68.

[48] *Ibid.*, IV, 389.

[49] *Ibid.*, IV, 162, 516.

[50] *Ibid.*, IV, 284.

[51] *Ibid.*, IV, 547.

[52] Mar to James, May 14, 1717, *ibid.*, IV, 241.

[53] *Ibid.*, IV, 260-61.

[54] Jerningham's instructions, June 5, 1717, *ibid.*, V, 546-48.

(and the ruin of George I), and the possibility of a marriage between the Chevalier and Peter's daughter,[55] raised first by the Czar himself.[56]

Some were sanguine now, but not those to whom secrets were entrusted. It was only George Flint, a journalist and the author of *Robin's Last Shift*,[57] who wrote

> Our cause is sacred; the great Swede appears
> And in that cause demands our hearts and spears,
> Sure he and such a cause dispel our fears.
> Let us but arm, the business is done,
> For I am sure that we are six to one. . .[58]

Others were not sure; and the advantages of peace, and, of course, the love of money were the motives of Charles and Peter. Only under very improbable circumstances would they have invaded England, or found it possible, without a great fleet which neither had, to do so. The Scottish Jacobites had not yet raised their heads,[59] and the English were cowed. The hundred thousand pounds thought necessary for influencing crowned heads was also out of reach.[60] Ormonde remained in the Baltic region until late in 1718, then returned to Paris with nothing to show for his tedious and expensive journey.

Not that this deceptive prospect did not have its effect on policy: the recent controversy about Bishop Hoadly's doctrines, followed by the dissolution of the Convocation of the Church of England to avoid proceedings against him, provided an excellent opportunity for tickling the vanity and smoothing the ruffled pride of some of Hoadly's antagonists. James wrote to Charles

[55] *Ibid.*, V, 4, 36, 43, 95–96, 176, 222, 312.
[56] *Ibid.*, V, 154.
[57] Reprinted in bound form, London, 1717. For Flint and his publications, see Mr. Laurence Hanson's *Government and the Press, 1695–1763* (London, 1936), 59, 64.
[58] H.M.C. *Stuart Papers*, IV, 304.
[59] Lockhart, II, 6.
[60] Cardinal Aquaviva hoped to obtain it from Philip V in January 1718. H.M.C. *Stuart Papers*, V, 616–20. About 300,000 Roman crowns (scudi) were hoped for from the Pope in February. This would be a little less than £100,000. James to Cardinal Imperiali, Feb. 6, 1718, Add. MSS. 20,292, fol. 191. See also M. W. Bruce, "Jacobite Relations with Peter the Great," *Slavonic Review*, XIV (January 1936), 343–62, for the whole Russian complication.

Leslie,[61] who had gone back to France from Pesaro in June 1717,[62] "by the best information I can have the intrinsic spiritual power of the Church, or power of the Keys as exercised by the Apostles and most pure and primitive Church in the first three centuries has ever been thought an essential right of the Church of England, so that it may inquire into the doctrines of its own members and inflict ecclesiastical censures, not extending to any civil punishment." This right he promised, if restored, to maintain. The letter was copied and circulated,[63] and may have given some comfort to Anglican orthodoxy.

Notwithstanding its reasonable and moderate character — the Pretender does not say what he thinks of the Church of England, only what he has been told, and denies it the right to civil punishments — it provoked uncharitable comment from certain Catholics, and resulted in the dismissal of Father Lewis Inese, a servant of James and his father for many years, from political business, as the Pretender explained to Père Honoré Gaillard at the end of February 1718: [64]

> Alas! all Catholics are not saints, and there are only too many among them who have still more ambition than true zeal. With such people the solid foundation of religion is little regarded; and when they think of the situation in which it has pleased Providence to put me, of the necessity under which I lie of living among Protestants, of the necessity under which I shall lie of giving them preference in posts, honors, &c., and of the little part they themselves will have in [public] business, this great resemblance to the primitive church is unbearable to those who lack its true spirit. . .[65] Who does not know the prudence and even charity with which the Protestants here behave toward the Catholics? Who does not know that there is no longer any question of my personal religion. . . ? I am a Catholic, but I am a king, and subjects of whatever religion should be equally protected. I am a king, but as the Pope himself has said to me I am not an apostle, I am not obliged to convert my subjects except by my example, nor to show an obvious partiality for the Catholics which would only injure them effectually in the long run.

[61] Letter dated Urbino, Nov. 29, 1717, H.M.C. *Stuart Papers*, V, 244.

[62] *Ibid.*, IV, 346.

[63] Mar to James Murray and Atterbury, Dec. 24, 1717, *ibid.*, V, 320, 322. See also V, 252.

[64] Letter dated Fano, Feb. 28, *ibid.*, V, 513–17.

[65] This passage is cited by Michael, II, 141, as a complaint about having to live among Protestants. My quotation, I hope, remedies this error. Gaillard's career is described by the editor of Torcy's *Journal inédit*, 305n.

This letter, not designed for publication (there is no other copy to my knowledge), speaks for itself. Another defense of the letter to Leslie was made to Cardinal Gualterio, the Protector of the English nation, when he took his royal charge to task, repeating the complaints of previous objections to the Pretender's policy.[66] The defense [67] left no doubt that from that time James would say, and mean, what he pleased, with no references to confessors.

This did not scandalize as many Catholics as one might think. Father Archangel Graeme had written to Mar in October 1717 that he would "make it my business to convince the world by my actions and words that a true Roman Catholic King of England is obliged in conscience to observe his coronation oath and maintain the Protestant Religion as it's established by law in the three kingdoms . . . not out of any liking for the Protestant Religion . . . but merely out of a principle of honour and honesty, which obliges every man to stand to his legal oath, or at least not to take it with a design to break it." [68] Hereafter it grows still harder to prove the Pretender priest-ridden, for priests are almost never employed in political affairs again.[69]

3. MARRIAGE; THE SPANISH WAR

The marriage question naturally had not ceased to be considered during 1717, but had become more urgent. The Pretender was nearly thirty, and had had no younger brother or sister since the death of Louisa Maria in 1712. Any accident might bring his line to an end, and failure to have male children would make "accidents" more possible. Besides, he had only a pension of 10,000 Roman crowns from the Pope,[70] a residence at Urbino, and some other resources less regular in payment — pensions from France and *rentes* on the Hôtel de Ville, the latter a mere 3281 livres

[66] Add. MSS. 20,295, foll. 234–36.
[67] James to Gualterio, March 11, 1718, H.M.C. *Stuart Papers*, VI, 133–35.
[68] *Ibid.*, V, 105.
[69] An exception is Bishop James Gordon in the 1740's. W.S.P. 226, no. 63.
[70] Paulucci to Gualterio, Rome, April 14, 1716, Add. MSS. 20,311, foll. 356–57.

annually.[71] A wealthy marriage would increase his meager revenues, and the Pope would probably increase his Roman pension to provide for his family.

Prince James Sobieski's daughters were first mentioned as suitable in a postscript to Mar's instructions to Charles Wogan, who was sent out to Baden and Saxony to view young princesses of the German states in late November 1717.[72] By the end of the year, other prospects had been eliminated, and Wogan was directed to hasten his steps to see them at Prince James's estate of Ohlau in Silesia.[73] Prince James was the son of the famous King John of Poland, and heir to his estates, but not to his crown, which was elective; he resided at Ohlau by choice.[74] Wogan found the youngest, Princess Maria Clementina, to be fifteen years old, generally attractive, though short, "devout," and with "a good mixture of haughtiness, . . . but cunning enough to disguise it." [75] Her dowry was satisfactory; for a royal match Prince James was willing to make it twice that of her sister, who had 400,000 crowns to marry the Duke of Modena.[76] She was a Catholic, and her rank, if not equal to that of an hereditary ruling house, was higher than that of some other princesses considered. James gave orders to propose marriage to her in late June, 1718.[77] The marriage contract was drawn up by the direction of Prince James and the Pretender's accredited representative, James Murray of Stormont.[78] The dowry was finally set at 600,000 livres in French *rentes,* 800,000 livres in Polish estates, and 250,000 livres owed by the Elector of Saxony to Prince James. Besides this, there were jewels not counted. Had all this money been realizable, it would have been an immense sum; but as it was, at least 900,000 French livres changed hands, and probably a good deal more. Moreover, the Pretender's children were to be heirs to a large part of the

[71] For the pension see Dangeau, XVII, 304; for the *rentes* Dicconson's declaration, Carte MSS. 208, foll. 316–17.

[72] H.M.C. *Stuart Papers,* V, 235.

[73] *Ibid.,* V, 243.

[74] *Ibid.,* V, 503.

[75] *Ibid.,* VI, 95–96.

[76] *Ibid.,* VI, 96, 390–91, 558.

[77] *Ibid.,* VI, 573–76.

[78] Abridged, *ibid.,* VII, 77–78.

entire Sobieski inheritance on Prince James's death, as he had no sons. The marriage was expected to take place within three months, but the intervention of the Emperor and a Spanish offer of assistance retarded it for over a year.

Alberoni, chief minister of the King of Spain from the fall of the princesse des Ursins until 1719, desired to be a cardinal, and Queen Elisabeth of Spain, whose marriage with Philip V he had arranged, pushed his pretensions. Clement XI had no desire to promote him. Although the ambitious priest had tied Spain to England with a commercial treaty, designed to revive Spanish commerce and industry, while allowing England lucrative privileges, the Protestant line could not help him at Rome, and he turned to obtain the favor of James, which was known to be considerable. The only cardinal made on his nomination before this time was Melchior, Cardinal de Polignac, whom he had proposed as a gesture of friendship to France in 1713. He was able to urge Alberoni on Clement XI with success. Quite justly he made a great show of his power on this occasion, since Clement XI had flatly declared that Alberoni would have no red hat in his lifetime,[79] and Gualterio wrote to Nairne after the ceremony of voting on the promotion:

I have never seen a promotion succeed amidst greater embarrassment than this one. The Pope, who either was very displeased at making it, or wanted to seem so, gave all the signs of disgust and affliction. The votes of the cardinals were for the most part favorable, but given with such circumspection that it was easily seen that they condescended rather from interest than from good will. It was the least important ones who said something in praise [of it].[80]

James also took Alberoni's side from interest, desiring at least a good sum of money, and possibly a Spanish fleet and army. No power ever goes to war but for what it supposes to be its own good; circumstances were needed to presuade Spain to such a drastic step. The Austrian governor of Milan happened to seize the person of the Spanish Inquisitor-General, Molinez, passing through that state on an overland journey to Spain, at about the time of Alberoni's promotion. The violation of a safe-conduct granted to Molinez, and his death in the hands of the Austrians,

[79] *Ibid.*, IV, 448.
[80] Letter of July 14, 1717, Carte MSS. 257, foll. 95–97.

of old age as much as anything else, was the formal cause of war between Spain and the Emperor, which proved remarkably successful for Spain, causing some surprise, in view of Alberoni's unpreparedness. In July a Spanish army, conveyed from Barcelona to Sardinia, commenced an occupation completed within three months. This action upset the balance established at Utrecht, and disturbed several powers, especially England, who wished the Mediterranean to remain as it had been arranged. The Pretender naturally hurried to propose, through Cardinal Aquaviva d'Aragon, the Spanish representative at Rome, diplomatic action which would eventually lead to a triple alliance of Sweden, Russia, and Spain against Spain's enemies, from which James was to profit, as well as a direct grant of £100,000 to the Jacobites.[81] Alberoni's reply was to beg James to be patient.

He had a great deal on his hands. At the beginning of 1717 a Triple Alliance of France, England, and the United Provinces had been formed, which now opposed the Spanish annexation of Sardinia. France was willing to go to war, despite the relationship of the kings of France and Spain, if Spain would not renounce unilateral action. Torcy and others were not eager for this, but the Regent, asserting himself, got what he wanted. England took the diplomatic lead: Cadogan, Marlborough's lieutenant in the recent war in Flanders, was sent to Spain to offer the right of succession in Parma and Tuscany to the first son of Philip V's second marriage, the Infant Don Carlos, if Sardinia were surrendered by Spain to Savoy, as compensation for its cession of Sicily to the Emperor. Alberoni may have been tempted, but was not convinced. A Spanish army landed in Sicily on July 1, 1718, and met with success similar to that of the Sardinian expedition.

Already a British fleet had sailed under Byng in June, to act as a counterpoise to the Spanish fleet in Italian waters. On arrival of news of the Sicilian invasion, Lord Stanhope, a Secretary of State, was dispatched from England to reach an agreement, if he could. He was hardly out of Spain, after refusal of his demands, when word came to Spain of the destruction of the Spanish fleet by Byng at Cape Passaro. England and Spain were thus at war.

[81] A copy is Add. MSS. 20,292, foll. 189–190; another is printed in H.M.C. *Stuart Papers*, V, 616–20.

Alberoni had not awaited this aggressive action to encourage the Jacobites, and the English knew it.[82] Whatever his intentions in doing so had been, he had now good reason to satisfy these beggarly exiles, and perhaps a safe way. In October, Ormonde returned from the Baltic, where Russia and Sweden had been wrangling about peace terms, and the duke had sought unsuccessfully to thrust himself and James's claim into the picture; Alberoni sent for him to come to Spain and act as the Chevalier's general. He accepted and called the Keiths to follow him; they assembled in Spain [83] and were given plans for two simultaneous descents, in England and Scotland, the forces to be commanded by Ormonde and the Earl Marischal. Alberoni had already sent Sir Patrick Lawless,[84] an Irishman in the Spanish service, to Sweden to lead Charles XII to coöperate. Ormonde wanted 8,000 men, but was allowed only 4,000 foot and 1,000 horse, with 300 mounts, 10 field pieces, and arms for 15,000 foot. The Scottish command was to have at least 300 men, and 2,000 fusils.[85] The Pretender was to follow Ormonde to England, after a safe landing.[86] James Keith went quickly back into France in early 1719, to gather the Scottish exiles there — Tullibardine, Seaforth, Campbell of Glendarule and Brigadier Campbell were among them — so that they might join Marischal in Scotland, and embarked at the mouth of the Seine for the Hebrides.

James was delighted to hear of Alberoni's preparations, because his marriage had been indefinitely postponed. Clementina Sobieska, on her way to Italy through the Tyrol, had been arrested on the Emperor's orders,[87] and her father had been warned by an Imperial emissary, Count Praschma, that he would lose favor at

[82] Colonel Stanhope to Earl Stanhope, Madrid, April 27, 1718, Graham, II, 353–54.

[83] W. K. Dickson, *The Jacobite Attempt of 1719* (Edinburgh, 1895), 2–33; Keith, 36–39.

[84] Known in Spain as Don Patricio Laules, he rose to be a lieutenant-general in the Spanish army, was accredited to the court of France from 1720 to 1725, and died as governor of Majorca. Morel-Fatio, ed. *Recueil des instructions données aux ambassadeurs . . . Espagne* (Paris, 1894–99), III, 423.

[85] Dickson, 60; Keith, 41.

[86] Dickson, 63.

[87] Jean du Hamel de Breuil, "Le mariage du Prétendant," *Revue d'histoire diplomatique*, IX (1895), 58–60.

Vienna (he resided in the hereditary dominions of the house of Austria), if he persisted with the marriage plans. Prince James replied that the marriage had been concluded by proxy, and wrote a private letter to the Emperor reminding him that the extermination of the Stuart race would make Hanover more independent of the Empire, and leave England at liberty to disregard Imperial interests in Italy. News of the arrest set him "hors de lui," said Praschma, and gave fears that he would be carried off by a stroke.[88]

James had gone as far as Bologna to meet his bride, to whom he was not yet united, as Sobieski said, and he received the news of the arrest with indignation. "Plunged in gloom . . . overwhelmed . . . astounded," he did not demand, he said, the protection of the Pope for the institution of marriage, "for one must have renounced religion and honor not to take my cause in hand." [89] He returned to Rome on November 9.[90] It was given out that he would remain there during the winter, at the Muti Palace, which the Pope gave him for a town house.[91] When it was clear that Alberoni was committed, he gave authority to James Murray of Stormont for a marriage by proxy to Clementina, if she should reach the Papal States in his absence, and left Italy.[92] He set out on February 8 for the coast, and sailed that evening.[93]

Mar, who had joined him in Italy after the obvious failure of the Swedish plot, went overland as far as Voghera, near Milan, where he and the second "Duke" of Perth were arrested, a companion having been mistaken for the Pretender by the Imperial authorities. They were held from February 7 to March 5, but did not go on after their release because Davenant, George I's resident at Genoa, was waiting for them. Instead, they returned to Rome.[94]

---

[88] *Ibid.*, 67–70.
[89] James to Don Carlo Albani, Oct. 18, 1718, H.M.C. *Stuart Papers*, VII, 401.
[90] *Ibid.*, VII, 508. Clement XI acted according to his bond. Letters to Prince James, the Emperor, and the Pretender, Clement XI, *Opera Omnia*, "Epistolae et Brevia Selectiora," cols. 2311–14, 2315–20.
[91] H.M.C. *Stuart Papers*, VII, 646; Carte MSS. 258, foll. 290–93.
[92] Carte MSS. 208, fol. 321r and v.
[93] Dickson, 207.
[94] *Ibid.*, 207–15; Carte MSS. 244, fol. 97; Tindal, IV, 583.

James, protected to some extent by this mistake, reached Rosas, after an unpleasant sea voyage, on March 9, 1719.[95]

The English government had not been kept ignorant of the Spanish designs, nor could they be. The excellent intelligence of Cardinal Dubois, the French foreign minister, notified him, and he notified Craggs, the English Secretary of State, in a letter of January 16, 1719, of James's expected meeting with Ormonde, of the place of embarkation, and the planned strength of the expeditions.[96] A more detailed report he forwarded on March 8,[97] prophesying a landing at Bristol. Four battalions of foot and eighteen squadrons of cavalry were consequently sent into the West Country to keep the peace and defend it against an invasion.[98] Two naval squadrons were designated to cruise off Land's End, and four battalions of Dutch foot were requested to meet the emergency.

The troops which Ormonde was to command had already sailed from Cadiz on March 7, and Marischal had left Los Pasajes on the eighth. The larger squadron took a circuitous route, to avoid the English fleet, only arriving off Finisterre on March 28, when a violent storm of three days' duration dispersed the fleet, and wrought havoc among the men and animals aboard before the ships straggled back to Vigo and Corunna in the middle of April. All of the troops had to be disembarked; many horses had been jettisoned during the storm; and several of the ships were very much the worse for wear.[99] Alberoni did not immediately lose heart, but the reports of damage finally forced him to postpone any other expedition until August.[100]

The Scottish expedition had already reached Scotland, meeting Keith's contingent of exiles at Stornoway in late March, Old Style. The Earl Marischal's Spanish troops disembarked on the mainland, but the unexpected "delay" in Ormonde's landing cost

---

[95] Giulio, Cardinal Alberoni, *Letters intimes au comte I. Rocca*, ed. Émile Bourgeois (Lyon, 1892), 627.
[96] Dickson, 223–24.
[97] *Ibid.*, 225.
[98] Craggs to Stair, Whitehall, 9/20 March, 1718/19, *ibid.*, 234.
[99] Reports from Vigo and Corunna, April 9–13, 1719, *ibid.*, 243–46.
[100] *Ibid.*, 247, 250.

him the support of all but about one thousand men.[101] Tullibardine assumed command, after a dispute with Marischal, and
led the tiny force at Glenshiel on June 10, where the Hanoverian
side triumphed, the Highlanders fled to the hills, and the Spaniards surrendered. There were few prominent men made prisoners, most of them hiding for a few weeks until they could be
got off on ships.[102]

The war went very badly for Spain. Lawless had got to Russia,
and had obtained a conditional promise of alliance from Peter I,
but the provisos — a Spanish subsidy for Russia and a Prussian
alliance — could not be met in Spain's exhausted state, and Prussia was to bind itself to Hanover and England by the Treaty of
Berlin, signed on August 5, 1719.[103] Spain was left alone before
her enemies.

The French invaded the Pyrenean region and captured Los
Pasajes without effective opposition, under the command of Berwick, who was almost alone, among French marshals, in his will-
ingness to fight Spain. From the Pretender's point of view, he did
his duty damnably well. The best of the Spanish troops were
bottled up in Sicily by the English fleet. Peace was imperative, and
James must therefore leave Spain. The rescue of Princess Clementina from Innsbruck by Charles Wogan on April 27, and her
successful escape to Venetian,[104] and thence to Papal territory,
gave him an excuse to withdraw as if voluntarily, to consummate
the marriage which James Murray had hastened to perform. The
news arrived in Spain in June; [105] when the Pretender had given
up hope for the time being, he embarked at Vinaroz on August
14.[106] Landing at Livorno, he celebrated a personal marriage
ceremony at Viterbo on September 1,[107] wrote to Ormonde of

[101] Keith, pp. 45–51; Lockhart, II, 19.

[102] Besides Dickson and Keith, see C. S. Terry's *Chevalier de St.-George*,
457–96. Lord George Murray, the chiefs of Lochiel, Clanranald, Mackintosh,
and Sir John Mackenzie were present at Glenshiel, with those previously
mentioned.

[103] Louis Wiesener, *Le Régent, l'abbé Dubois, et les anglais* (Paris, 1891–99),
III, 132–35.

[104] Du Hamel de Breuil, *Revue d'histoire diplomatique*, IX, 85–93.

[105] Dickson, 253–54.

[106] *Ibid.*, 165, 258.

[107] Wiesener, III, 82. Wiesener places his landing on August 19, fine sailing
indeed, but cites no source.

his happiness on the 5th,[108] and asked Alberoni for money on the 14th; [109] but it was not long before Alberoni was overthrown to make room for peace with England and France.

There was another lasting effect of the Spanish attempt. Mar, trying to join James in Spain by the overland route, was arrested at Geneva in May, by request of the British government.[110] He had already, when in Paris in 1717, visited Lord Stair, who said that he "flung out several things as I thought with a design to try whether there was any hope of treating," but got no response.[111] He had offered James his resignation, conditional on the re- covery of England,[112] but was pressed to hold on. Since he had reserved to himself a place in the cabinet where he might be, he hints, a secret adviser on all subjects, it would probably be more decent, constitutionally, to give him an open appointment. Now he made an unwarranted merit of this offer (remember the con- dition) when asking Stair to procure his enlargement to enter France.[113] Stair recommended this step to Craggs, and suggested a pardon or pension if Mar should make his submission.[114] This was eventually granted, in spite of George I's very reasonable prejudice against Mar. As Stair argued, "It is not a shilling matter to us whether he leaves the Pretender's cause, because he thinks it a bad one, or whether he leaves it because he thinks it cannot any longer be supported. . . It is very plain, in three or four months time, it will come to be all the same thing. All the Jaco- bite mouths are open against him already . . . if he should not behave himself as he ought, what do you venture? You are masters of stopping the pension." [115] Mar, being released in June 1720,[116] went to Paris, where he consulted General Dillon on the propriety

[108] Dickson, 260.

[109] Ibid., 261–62.

[110] H. Tayler, ed., The Jacobite Court at Rome in 1719 (Edinburgh, 1938), 53; Dangeau, XVIII, 55.

[111] Hardwicke, II, 561.

[112] Stuart Erskine, ed. Mar's "Legacies" (Edinburgh, 1896), 146–49. This is a more accurate text than that of A. and H. Tayler, The Stuart Papers at Windsor, 46–47, where it appears as previously unpublished, and remarkably mangled at that. I have compared it with the original at Windsor.

[113] Mar to Stair, Geneva, May 22, 1719, Hardwicke, II, 567–69.

[114] Ibid., 572–73.

[115] Ibid., II, 588.

[116] Dangeau, XVIII, 309.

of accepting a pension. Dillon evaded the question, but privately thought it strange Mar should need to ask.[117] James III was asked for permission to accept, and was led by reflection both to grant it and to suspect Mar.[118] Colonel John Hay, son of the Earl of Kinnoull, and James Murray, son of Lord Stormont,[119] assumed his functions at the court, to the discomfort of some, who thought them both too young, and Murray officious.[120]

4. CONCESSIONS, A PENSION, AND A RED HAT

Mar was not immediately dropped. An arrangement possible only under those conditions was adopted. At Paris lay the natural center for information and control of the English Jacobites, very important at that time because of the rapid progress and dissolution of the South Sea bubble. A group of three leading Jacobites, Mar, General Dillon, and Lord Lansdowne, were all there after July 1720, when Lansdowne, who had emptied his pockets by extravagant spending and speculation, withdrew from England to live more cheaply in France.[121] Queen Maria being lately dead, this group took over a great deal of business, to the exclusion of Hay and Murray, who were in charge, except nominally, at Rome. It had been hoped that one or other might be made Secretary, but Mar's friends and others made this impossible; Murray was sent away to France in 1721.

The South Sea Company had for long provoked comment among the Jacobites as elsewhere: some speculated, but, on the whole, cautiously, as befitted men who felt that stability of any kind depended on return to political order — that is, the hereditary succession in the Stuart dynasty. Many certainly heard rumblings long before the collapse, especially rumors of stocks puffed by means of political corruption. "Our Ministers of State," Montagu Wood wrote to Samuel Carte in early 1719, "have laid aside all Honour, & Honesty, & Publick spirit, & are become

---

[117] Carte MSS. 231, fol. 51. Mar said later that Dillon advised him to accept, but I incline to believe Dillon. Lockhart, II, 179.

[118] John Hay to Lockhart, Sept. 8, 1725, Lockhart, II, 202.

[119] James to Tullibardine, April 29, 1720, H.M.C. *Report* X, app. I, 92.

[120] Pitsligo's narrative, Tayler, *The Jacobite Court at Rome*, 55f.

[121] Handasyde, 169–70.

perfect Stock-Jobbers." [122] Wood, however, bought in again, after selling his shares, and advised Carte to do so. When the fall of stock prices came, Jacobites in Parliament made political capital of it, with James's full approval.[123] Lansdowne sent him from Paris a draft of a declaration which he hoped would serve on this occasion, beginning, "The cry of our people having reached our ears";[124] James signed it on October 10, 1720, and returned it for distribution. Atterbury, who had now completely superseded Oxford in London affairs, seems to have managed this. Dillon reported (from hearsay) that it met with an enthusiastic reception among the friends of the Pretender in England as being "reputed his own work." [125] That it was not his own work ought to have been guessed from the absence of the assurances to the Church of England or anything like them, mention of public engagements, or of a toleration. Perhaps Dillon meant that the author was evidently not a priest, and that is true enough.

The last previous declarations of the traditional sort were dated Madrid, March 31, 1719,[126] were printed in Spain, and had little more to say than that of Pesaro in 1717. The one for Scotland is the more interesting: it takes full advantage of the "strange laws," the "multiplicity of new taxes," and the rebels of the '15 having been "carry'd in procession into another kingdom, there to receive their doom," and so on. There is no significant addition of any other sort. The 1719 and 1720 declarations do not clash: the assurances of 1719, taken bodily from that of 1717, complete with the promises supposed to have been made in 1715, but which had not been so made, are perfectly consistent with the more general and sounding exhortation penned by Lansdowne.[127]

The Jacobites among the opposition in Parliament responded to the invitation to do their duty by placing whatever obstacles

[122] Letter of March 19, 1718/19, Carte MSS. 244, fol. 97.

[123] "D. Macarty" [Oliver Plunket?] to John Hungerford, M.P., Paris, Sept. 22, 1720, Carte MSS. 230, fol. 209.

[124] W.S.P. 49, no. 45; printed from a copy among the Fintry MSS. in H.M.C. *Var. Coll.*, V, 242–43. I follow the latter's spelling. For authorship, see Handasyde, 176.

[125] Dillon to James, Nov. 25, 1720, W.S.P. 50, no. 48.

[126] W.S.P. 43, nos. 16 and 18.

[127] Lansdowne refers to "that ancient Constitution We wish to see restored," which is curious, but not even he can have favored a return to the past.

they could in the way of ministerial legislation, under the leadership of the Earl of Orrery (the Boyle of the Battle of the Books) in the Lords, and William Shippen in the Commons,[128] counting on the assistance of agitated public feeling, and hoping that the Chevalier could find foreign troops to assist a rebellion, if one should break out as a result of the South Sea excitement. To gain a domestic ally, the Jacobites, with the remarkable exception of Shippen ("an Enthusiastick & a Phanatick in his own honest way, and one dare never trust him with a reason if there were ne'er so good a one," Menzies said),[129] joined the friends of the second Earl of Sunderland to save him from impeachment for his shady connection with the South Sea Company before the passage of the South Sea Act.[130] The Scots, at a distance from this center, had been organized under a council of responsible "Cavaliers" by Lockhart in early 1720;[131] its members included Lockhart, the Earls of Eglinton and Wigton, Lord Balmerino, the former Bishop of Edinburgh, Captain Harry Straiton, MacDonald of Glengarry and Harry Maule, later titular Lord Panmure.

Mar's prolonged absence made the appointment of a new Secretary of State urgent; the work of his office had devolved entirely upon the Pretender and a few clerks who wrote nothing except by his dictation. Mar was consulted for a proper successor, but gave only vague replies.[132] That an Englishman was desired accounts for the final decision to appoint Lord Lansdowne, who was to receive Mar's seals at Paris, and use them for James if there were an invasion.[133] Commissions were issued to the Earl of Strafford, Lord North and Grey, Sir Harry Goring, and Mar.[134] Lansdowne declined to go to Rome to act publicly,[135] but was granted the titles of Earl of Bath and Duke of Albemarle in the autumn of 1721.[136] Goring was expected to form and execute a conspiracy

[128] Orrery to James, Jan. 16, 1721, W.S.P. 51, no. 53.
[129] J. Menzies to James, Paris, April 7, 1721, W.S.P. 53, no. 13.
[130] Ibid.
[131] James to Lockhart, Feb. 15, 1720, Lockhart, II, 29–31.
[132] James to Mar, April 28, 1721 and Mar to John Hay, May 19, W.S.P. 53, nos. 63 and 111.
[133] James to Mar, Albano, Aug. 11, 1721, W.S.P. 54, no. 98.
[134] Warrant Book M 20, W.S.P., entries 96, 98, 106, and 89, respectively.
[135] Handasyde, 183.
[136] W.S.P. warrant book M 20, entries 92 and 93; Handasyde, 183, 187.

for the seizure of Bristol; whether or not this was ever made definite cannot be known, but it was never exposed.[137]

Mar's brain had not ceased to function, however his sentiments may have been inclined. He took up the question of Scotland in November 1721. With the purpose of securing autonomy, he advanced the suggestion, *inter alia,* that prerogative be diminished in that country, to make its authorities independent of the influence which the English ministers must always have on the mind of the sovereign of two such unequal countries.[138] James had limited his confidence in Mar, but considered his proposals seriously, and granted a good number. In a letter of January 1, 1722,[139] he conceded septennial Scottish Parliaments, abolition of the Lords of the Articles, assent to a new Act anent Peace and War, which would require parliamentary consent before making either, parliamentary nomination of officers of state, judges, bishops, and Privy Councillors, mutual exclusion between the English and Scottish Parliaments, improvement of Scottish royal justice, and independent Scottish representatives at certain royal courts, those of France, Spain, Vienna, and "Holland." Besides this, the Scottish Parliament was to regulate expenditures, both civil and military, and ministerial salaries. This would have seemed revolutionary before the Union, which James wished to abolish, and was to serve as a measure of compensation for the loss of the less autocratic English government, but it was not all.

Another letter, of January 20 and 29,[140] promised the conversion of all land holdings under the crown to "ffew" or "blench," eradicating the oppressive "ward" or military tenure, with the incident of wardship, among others. "Few" holdings were those in consideration of payments in kind, money, or service; "blench" holdings were those which required nominal payments of some sort.[141] Those who held land of subjects were to be allowed to purchase their holdings at a price to be set, and become tenants

---

[137] Handasyde, 188.
[138] Mar to Hay, Paris, Nov. 17, W.S.P. 55, no. 115.
[139] W.S.P. 56, nos. 141–141B.
[140] W.S.P. 57, no. 77.
[141] After 1747, ward holdings held of the Crown were converted to blench holdings; at the same time ward holdings held of others became few holdings. My distinction is a rough one.

of the Crown, also by "ffew" or "blench"; as holdings were pur-
chased of superiors possessing jurisdictions of "justiciary" or
"regality," these superiors were to be forced to sell such jurisdictions to the Crown, which would be obliged to buy. An addition to this letter allowed Scotland a separate army of 2,000
regulars and 15,000 or 16,000 Highland militia, and a small naval
squadron for the protection of Scottish trade. The last, and most
unwilling, concession was made in a letter of February 5 [142] — a
promise to arrange for the King of France to take into his service
"a certain number" of Scottish troops. Mar's intention here is
obscure, but in the other requests granted by the Chevalier de
St.-Georges, it was clearly to make Scotland autonomous, and more
able to defend her autonomy than she had been since the Bishops'
Wars.

Mar's reply was fulsome. "Never was a finer nor more valuable
New-years gift made by *a Prince to his people* than what you
was pleased to send me by last post," he wrote on March 30.[143]
It was his last successful effort to influence policy. His request
made earlier in that month for similar grants to Ireland [144] was
quietly dropped, and his titular promotion to an Irish dukedom
later in the year would seem to show that Irish independence was
not much on James's mind, nor on his.

The Pretender was occupied with projects of invasion and ways
to obtain troops and ships for it, which he had never ceased to
ponder since the return from Spain.

The foreign minister of the Regent, the abbé Dubois, offered
the first opportunity, at least to get money, in November 1719,
when the abbé's unreasoning and ceaseless efforts to obtain the
red hat of a cardinal led Cardinal Gualterio to propose to Lafi-
teau, the abbé's agent at Rome, that James nominate Dubois.
In return James would receive the payment of the French pension promised in 1717 to get the Pretender to leave Avignon.[145]

---

[142] W.S.P. 57, no. 137.

[143] W.S.P. 58, no. 113. For a slightly different version of Mar's proposals,
and also James's three letters, see Mar's "Legacies," 194–205, 206–212.

[144] Mar's "Legacies," 213–14.

[145] Boutry (*Intrigues*, 41) asserts that James had nothing else to live on,
which, if true (it is not, as we have seen) would have left him on the point
of starvation, because it had never been regularly paid.

Dubois hesitated, but replied that he would accept if the name of the Chevalier were not mentioned during the process, and arranged to pay 300,000 livres instead of the pension.[146] James treated this as a small sum, and made the nomination free of charge, leaving to the abbé's sense of justice, as he put it, the choice of a gift appropriate to such an occasion.[147] The gift proved to be 50,000 Roman crowns,[148] about two years of the proposed pension in a lump, or 600,000 French livres at the current rate of exchange,[149] then very unfavorable to France. In return, James promised unremitting solicitation of Pope Clement XI,[150] acting so sincerely as to draw on his head the humiliating scene in May 1720, when the Pope complained to Gualterio of the "King of England," "qui lui devait tant d'obligations et qui au lieu de reconnoissance, ne lui apportait que des ennuis." [151] In the promotion of September 1720, Dubois was passed over, as might have been expected.

In January the Pope gave way to James, provided that France would pledge herself to protect Papal interests in Italy then in dispute, "provided that Your Majesty continues in your present favorable disposition, . . . and not otherwise." [152] Dubois naturally balked at terms the exact magnitude of which could not then be known.[153] On March 19, Clement died. The conclave which assembled on April 1 to choose his successor was adroitly managed by the French interest, so that the new Pope Innocent XIII, formerly Michelangelo, Cardinal Conti, had made one of those engagements, "by nature abominable, most expressly forbidden . . . and little distinguished from all the other kinds of simony," to make no one a cardinal before Dubois.[154] The struggle was not over: the promise was broken by the promotion of the Pope's nephew; but on July 25, after pleas, menaces, and bribes had done

---

[146] Wiesener, III, 369; Émile Bourgeois, *La diplomatie secrète au 18e siècle, ses débuts* (Paris, 1909), III, 310–11.
[147] Wiesener, III, 371.
[148] *Ibid.*, III, 372.
[149] Bourgeois, III, 312.
[150] Wiesener, III, 376.
[151] *Ibid.*, III, 380–81.
[152] Clement XI to James, Jan. 14, 1721, *ibid.*, III, 393–94.
[153] *Ibid.*, III, 395.
[154] Polignac's relation, 1724, quoted by Boutry, 34n.

their work at the Curia, Dubois heard that the hat was his.[155] The resumption of payment of the pension, at 24,000 Roman crowns a year, was promised to James on June 12 by the maréchal de Villeroy in impersonal terms.[156] Dubois wrote a very respectful letter to his sponsor early in that month, and then broke off direct relations with him.[157]

5. THE ATTERBURY PLOT AND THE DISGRACE OF MAR

By that time another opportunity to work on Peter I was furnished by the Treaty of Nystad, signed August 30, 1721, which brought the Northern War to a close, and left the Czar free to participate in general European affairs. Only when the new Pope was approached for money to assist the English Jacobites was it taken seriously, for Innocent XIII found it, Hay wrote to Gualterio, "une chose impracticable que les amis du Roy peuvent reussir dans aucune entreprise . . . quant la france et l'Espagne sont actuellement en negociations pour faire des ligues avec l'Electeur d'Hannover a son exclusion." [158]

The unwillingness of these two powers might be offset by the benevolence or assistance of the Czar. For this reason the Chevalier wrote on November 21 to Admiral Thomas Gordon, formerly a naval officer under Queen Anne, now a favorite officer of Peter,[159] asking him to request the use of some of his "many idle workmen" (soldiers) and "materials of all kinds." [160] General Dillon, a general of repute at Paris, closer to the English Jacobites, then took up the correspondence. Both Gordon and Sir Harry Stirling, another Scot then in Russia (the Scottish influence at the court of Peter was truly remarkable), attempted to turn the Czar's mind into Jacobite channels,[161] but without success during

---

[155] Ibid., 59n.

[156] Ibid., 42. It had earlier been promised by the abbé de Tencin to commence in April 1721. Affaires étrangères, Memoires et documents, Angleterre 75, fol. 175. This came, in French money, now somewhat stronger, to 150,000 livres. Bourgeois, III, 327.

[157] Wiesener, III, 409–10.

[158] Letter of Aug. 22, 1721, Add. MSS. 20,303, fol. 29.

[159] See H.M.C. Report X, app. I, 185–87.

[160] Ibid., 159.

[161] Dillon to [Gordon], Paris, Dec. 26, 1721, ibid., 171; M. W. Bruce, Slavonic Review, XIV, 346.

the first half of 1722. Thus there were no foreign troops to be had before the Jacobite agitation was detected and frustrated.

One need not marvel at the detection itself, when informants reported such indiscretions as public discussion, as John Mellor of Erthig did to Solicitor-General Yorke from North Wales: "The Jacobites in our parts are strangely animated of late & they endeavour to carry their Points by Heat & Fury and they are so bare faced, as to drink the Pretender's health in public Companys." [162]

The breaking of the conspiracy, or conspiracies, began with the arrest of George Kelly, a Jacobite with a long record, on May 10/21, 1722.[163] Nothing followed until August, when a number of minor plotters, of whom the most important was John Sample or Sempill, were detained.[164] Thomas Carte fled on August 13, and Atterbury was arrested on the twenty-fourth. Shortly after came the apprehension and confinement in the Tower of the Duke of Norfolk, Lord North, and the Earl of Orrery.[165] Shippen's house was searched, but nothing was found. Parliament was called upon to suspend *Habeas Corpus* for a year, and the Duke of Wharton, a "brilliant but erratic" nobleman and dilettante, sometimes a Jacobite, voted for the suspension. Christopher Layer, a lawyer, who had made his own plot, almost entirely apart from the others, and without authority, was brought to trial for enlisting men in Essex for the Pretender, was condemned by the court of King's Bench, and suffered death in May 1723.[166] Philip Neynoe, a clergyman and a client of Orrery, chief witness for the government against his patron and his friends, drowned himself in the Thames, either in remorse or, as is more credible, in attempting to escape,[167] so that Orrery escaped punishment for lack of evidence.

[162] Letter of Feb. 27, 1722, printed by Philip Yorke, *Life and Correspondence of Philip Yorke, Earl of Hardwicke* (Cambridge, 1913), I, 76.

[163] H.M.C. *Report* XV, app. VI, 39.

[164] Tindal, IV, 660.

[165] Warrants for their reception, H.M.C. *Report* XV, app. VI, 43.

[166] *The Whole Proceeding upon the Arraignment . . . of Christopher Layer, Esq.* (London, 1722) and an anonymous *Life of Christopher Layer* (Norwich, 1723) with the *Report from the Committee appointed by the House of Commons* [to examine Layer] (London, 1722). Some notes in the *Whole Proceeding* attributed to James III are probably forged.

[167] Henry Pelham to Francis Hare, Sept. 22, 1722, H.M.C. *Report XIV*, app. IX, 234. For Neynoe's history, see W.S.P. 100, no. 45.

According to Tindal,[168] the evidence revealed that it was hoped to smuggle groups of officers into the country, corrupt the troops, begin election riots by careful agitation of the South Sea affair, and seize important places such as the Bank of England and the Tower. The plot was said to have failed for lack of money, lack of skill in the conspirators, the suspected faith of the regent, within whose jurisdiction most of the Jacobites must move, and the Chevalier's cowardice, which was said to have led to the proposed employment of his son, a child of two, in his stead.[169] The whole truth is not accessible, but the Windsor Stuart Papers speak of no such use of the future Young Pretender. The phases outlined are plausible, because such plans had certainly been used before, and the reasons given for failure, being those which so often frustrated Jacobite efforts, are also credible, except that the Pretender was no coward. That accusation stems from the report of a spy, and of an anonymous spy at that, and thus requires little consideration. Thanks to the Stanhope system of alliances, there was not one country in Europe — Spain, Portugal, France, Holland, the Empire, or Denmark — from which James could have embarked for England, or into which he would have been admitted, known or in disguise. He could not stir out of Italy, or go south into Naples, or north into Lombardy; without spies reporting it he could not even leave Rome, for he was closely watched there and at Albano, where he spent his *villeggiatura* every year.

James was, moreover, ignorant of most of what was done in his name. He had to leave details of plans to Jacobites at London or Paris, and was in great confusion when he heard of the detection of his friends, because he was not quite sure where they had got to; Hay wrote to Mar on June 30, 1722 that he was "mightily impatient till the post comes in to know whether this plot be a sham or not." [170] Also, if Norfolk had been involved the Pretender did not know, for he wrote in December to Dillon "I never had in my life a Cypher with the D. of Norfolk." [171] Later it could be

[168] IV, 666–67.
[169] *Report from the Committee* . . . , appendix B, 11.
[170] W.S.P. 60, no. 98. See also no. 29 of that volume.
[171] W.S.P. 63, no. 177.

proved that Sir William Ellis, the Pretender's financial officer, was involved in Layer's plot, but without the knowledge of James or his chief assistant, Hay.[172] Layer's actions were almost entirely unknown, although he had visited Rome in 1721 and met the Pretender. Hundreds of young men had done the same.

The question of the evidence against Bishop Atterbury has become a matter of controversy once more. The dog Harlequin, sent to Atterbury as a gift from Jacobites abroad, was mentioned in intercepted letters written by Mar to one "Illington," which identified "Illington" as the possessor of the dog, and therefore with Atterbury. The Honorable Stuart Erskine, editor of Mar's "Legacies," defends him,[173] as the victim of prejudice — that is, the "Harlequin affair" gave Atterbury "a fixed notion" of Mar's guilt, as well it might — but does not explain how he came to write such careless letters, and continued in carelessness so far as to send them by post, which almost guaranteed their interception. Mr. Maurice Bruce in a recent article [174] explains that Mar *need* not have betrayed the conspiracy, because the Regent had already warned the English government in April,[175] and that he *could* not have betrayed it because Sir Luke Schaub spent £500 on obtaining information in Paris, which he says would not have been necessary if Mar had been a traitor, so that Mar was guilty of no more than folly.

In answer, we can say that the Regent, to whom the Jacobites had applied for help, knew a great deal, but could not be produced in court against Atterbury, and that no secret service in good working order depends on one informant for its intelligence. We are not sure that Schaub's money did not go to Mar but, if not, Lady Lansdowne, whose extravagance had eaten up her husband's fortune, was suspected by James Murray of espionage for the government. She was certainly too friendly with Colonel Churchill when he was in Paris for intelligence in May 1722.[176] Five

---

[172] Hay to Mar, Jan. 5, 1723, W.S.P. 64, no. 134.
[173] *Publications of the Scottish History Society*, XXVI, 150.
[174] "The Duke of Mar in Exile," *Transactions of the Royal Historical Society*, 20:61–82 (1937).
[175] *Ibid.*, 66–67.
[176] Handasyde, 195. For Mar's account of Churchill's visit, see Lockhart, II, 180–81.

hundred pounds would have seemed little to her. Hay visited Paris later, and heard that she had been offered a pension of £2000 for her knowledge.[177] Nor was she the only possible spy about. Yet, Mar did write the letter, and Atterbury was condemned to exile on the strength of it. Mr. Bruce calls for "Historical Revision," but without more convincing evidence than that he has advanced we must abide by the convictions of Mar's contemporaries — Lockhart, Hay, Lord Falkland, and James himself — who thought him guilty.[178]

The plot had an immediate effect in the cutting off of Mar from knowledge of new ciphers and correspondence, which he felt and complained of in October 1722,[179] but did not yet cause his public disgrace. That he brought upon himself by a further act of folly or malice. Excluded from confidence though he was, he presented to the Regent of France in September 1723 a Memorial urging Orléans to restore the Stuarts on the condition of a grant of complete autonomy to Ireland and Scotland. The Regent's diplomatic alignment being known, he must have understood that he was putting a weapon into the hands of George I's ministers, Townshend and Walpole. Orléans certainly received it without anger. Hay, visiting Paris, saw a copy of it, or of parts of it,[180] met Atterbury at Brussels later, and put together the whole story of Mar's guilt. It had long seemed strange that Atterbury's name should have come out: James had ordered a search of the papers of Hay and of David Kennedy, one of the Chevalier's secretaries, for evidence of treachery,[181] but had found none. The pension, Atterbury's betrayal, trial, and exile, and this attempt to damage James's reputation by offending English prejudices — all pointed to a guilty connection with the English government. James received a copy of the Memorial without reply, but wrote to his friends to suspend all communication on confidential affairs, first with Mar, then with Dillon [182] and Lans-

[177] W.S.P. 79, no. 91.
[178] Lockhart, II, 186; Falkland to James, Aug. 29, 1722, W.S.P. 61, no. 151; James to Atterbury, Dec. 19, 1724, W.S.P. 78, no. 128. Mr. Bruce uses Lockhart to attack Hay, but not to attack Mar, of whom Lockhart thought as little.
[179] W.S.P. 62, no. 75.
[180] Hay to Lockhart, Sept. 8, 1725, Lockhart, II, 206.
[181] W.S.P. 62, no. 99.
[182] James to Atterbury, Dec. 19, 1724, W.S.P. 78, no. 128.

downe,[183] as they seemed to be susceptible to his influence. These later decisions may seem harsh; but Mar had shown on two occasions that he could not be allowed to know what was going on, and Lansdowne later made his peace in England and received a pension from George II.

So it was that Hay replaced Mar as intermediary in correspondence with Great Britain. Dillon lost his functions as agent at the French court to Atterbury and Colonel Daniel O'Brien.[184] Mar's official papers were handed over to Atterbury, and Dillon's also, but after a long delay.[185]

Two results followed the fall of Mar. The first, a very temporary one, was a flutter of interest at the French court, in the foreign affairs of which André-Hercule Fleury, Bishop of Fréjus, had assumed an important role. On January 8, 1725, Fleury wrote a formal note to James, with compliments and inexpensive good wishes, which survives in its answer, equally formal, dated January 30.[186] Hay judged this ready entrance into correspondence to be a direct result of Mar's dismissal, which left Fleury without eyes to see into Jacobite affairs. A meeting took place between Atterbury and Torcy,[187] now out of all important office, and genteel letters were exchanged with the duchesse de Bourbon, wife of the Regent's successor, but the futility of it all was shown when the French ceased to take interest in them, having presumably learned enough of Jacobite designs from other sources.

The other consequence was the rupture between James and Maria Clementina, which took time to appear, and will be discussed elsewhere.

On the surface, England was left, after the subsidence of the excitement of the plot, much as it had been. Under it, the condemnation of Atterbury to exile for life, and the weakness and dilatoriness of the leaders — Lords Arran, Gower, North, and Orrery — in the face of the emergency, dealt the party a sharp blow. Jacobites in Parliament were politically isolated and dared

[183] Hay to Atterbury, Jan. 2, 1725, W.S.P. 79, no. 9; Hay to Orrery, Rome, Jan. 24, 1725, *ibid.*, no. 91.
[184] Hay to Atterbury, Nov. 7, 1724; W.S.P. 77, no. 154.
[185] James to Dillon, Feb. 3, 1725, W.S.P. 79, no. 136.
[186] *Ibid.*, no. 114.
[187] Hay to Atterbury, Jan. 30, 1725, *ibid.*, no. 116.

not vote according to their convictions; the lower orders were not tempted to meddle in politics if they remembered that George Kelly remained in the Tower without trial, as he did until 1736, when he escaped. Again there had been appeal to parliamentary justice, or trial by majority vote, in Atterbury's case.

> To make Legall Proof t'was needful of yore
> One witness with two legs and one with two more
> This dog is worth both. Proof runs on all four
>   Which nobody can deny.

> But the Case is the same to the Comons they Said
> Whether Speaking or Dumb or forthcoming or fled
> Whether two leg'd or four leg'd or living or dead
>   Which nobody can deny.

> Whether Guiltless or Guilty it signifyes not
> Tho' they canot Convict they can punish by vote
> And who e're disbeleives is one of the Plot
>   Which Nobody can deny.[188]

To some, although to how many is a problem beyond solution, the *True Briton's* clumsy ode, published in October, 1723, had a clear application, and Atterbury seemed a "Bulwarke of the Roman [read British] State, In Acts in thought a God"; but most men without a stake on one side or the other would not have cared much. Jacobitism was dangerous to its followers, and represented no vital interest of the people as a whole; it was easier to be neutral at heart and take what came from the ruling party. Parliamentary determination of causes was certainly not customary, but there were precedents, and no one who minded his own affairs would bring the Commons down on his head. So the thoughts of many Englishmen may have run, in the time of prosperity which followed and ended the South Sea crisis.

That the period had been dangerous to the ruling dynasty is not to be denied. "As England had never yet undergone such great disappointment and confusion, so it never had so loudly called for confiscation and blood," Mahon writes; [189] and he might have granted that enemies of Walpole's settlement or of the directors of the company could easily become enemies of George I and his

---

[188] "Mr. Pope's ballad on the Plot of 1722," Carte MSS. 230, foll. 24v, 25.
[189] *History of England from the Peace of Utrecht. . . ,* II, 20.

family, whose hands were not clean. The Jacobites were not deluding themselves; they knew that these classes of malcontents were not coextensive. They fished in these waters with full knowledge that foreign assistance was necessary.[190] Carte records a conversation with Sir John Hind Cotton in 1737, in which Cotton said that when Peter the Great died in February 1725, once more disappointing Jacobite agents in Russia,[191] "Jack Chetwynd came to Sr. Robt. [Walpole] & told him, he was just come from the Secretary's office, where an Express was just arrived with an account of the Czar's death. Upon wch Sr. Rob. said, Then by God K[ing] G[eorge] is the luckiest man alive. To wch Sr John answered, of a King, Sr Robert, for of a Subject, you know one as lucky." [192] Perhaps the opportunity had already gone by at that time; it grows harder to find the pulse of the movement in England from the time of the exile of Atterbury, and one must look henceforth to Scotland for vigor and decision.

6. DIPLOMATIC OPPORTUNITY

Colonel John Hay had been admitted to the Pretender's confidence years before, and had been recommended to Lockhart in a letter of August 31, 1724,[193] but he was not declared Secretary of State in Mar's place until March 5, 1725, in a letter from James to Atterbury.[194] He then assumed the title of Earl of Inverness, granted to him in 1718.[195]

As Secretary of State he had greater difficulties than ordinary: several leaders in England, such as Lord North, Lord Orrery, and the Duke of Wharton, had cut off their communication with Rome in a fit of prudence, and in Scotland Lord "Dun," probably Dundonald, Sir John Erskine of Alva, and Colin Campbell of Glendarule had followed their example.[196] Lansdowne was out of

[190] Cf. Mahon, II, 46.
[191] Bruce, *Slavonic Review*, XIV, 361.
[192] Carte MSS. 266, fol. 32.
[193] Lockhart, II, 130–31.
[194] W.S.P. 80, no. 117. See also Hay to Lockhart, March 10, Lockhart, II, 149.
[195] W.S.P. warrant book M20, entry no. 80.
[196] Lockhart, II, 133, 222.

favor, and turned his friends against Hay and the new system; in conjunction with Dillon and Mar, he formed a group of malcontents at Paris, known as the "triumvirate." [197] Mar left nothing undone to destroy party unity: he published a defense of his Memorial to the Regent before it was attacked, sent Glendarule to Scotland to win friends for himself and make enemies for James, and was probably directly responsible for the disagreement between James and his wife.

The issue was a bedchamber controversy. Mrs. Sheldon, Dillon's sister-in-law, had the care of Prince Charles, born in 1720, during the first five years of his life, originally by Mar's suggestion. She was a particular friend of Maria Clementina. In accordance with custom, and also to replace Mar's friend, the Prince was to be given, about that time, male attendants — governor, under-governor, preceptor, and grooms. James himself had been given a governor when he was eight. The Queen, having become attached to Mrs. Sheldon, did not wish to let her go; the "spirit" she had displayed in youth became now a kind of stubbornness. Mrs. Sheldon built up a dislike of the Hays and the new governor, James Murray, as evil advisers, who had caused James to put away his best friends — Mar and Dillon. Moreover, she played upon Clementina's devotion to her Church by pointing out that Murray was a Protestant, and would be a danger to the faith of her child, in spite of the choice of a Catholic under-governor, Thomas Sheridan,[198] who would be the principal direct participant in Charles' education.

Her jealousy was probably owing to the intrigues of the malcontents,[199] inspired by Mar's pension dangling before him. The motive of the English government in seeking to bring about a breach is not far to seek. Every division on any level was a blow

[197] Atterbury to James, Jan. 29, 1725, W.S.P. 79, no. 111. Mahon, II, 134, construes this term as meaning Inverness, James Murray, and Lady Inverness, but cites no source. Perhaps he was influenced by Lockhart, who uses the word so.

[198] Son of the Sheridan who wrote the *Historical Account* and died in 1712. The senior Sheridan, originally a Protestant, was a Catholic before 1709, and probably before the christening of his children in 1692 and 1694 according to the Catholic rite. Thomas the younger was educated at the Collège Louis-le-Grand. See Lart, I, 124; H.M.C. *Stuart Papers*, I, 148.

[199] Lockhart, II, 221.

at the Jacobite cause but this on the highest level must naturally
set the queen's adherents against those of the king. Perhaps at
first no more was intended than to suspend the payment of the
papal pension by means of a domestic dispute. When, however,
in November 1725, Clementina left her husband and retired to a
convent, his enemies gained far more than that. At this point the
deserted husband, according to Mr. T. F. Henderson, of the
Dictionary of National Biography,[200] lapsed into "mingled melancholy and dissipation." Mr. Henderson, however, produces no
evidence; I do not believe that there is any. Lockhart testifies, "I
have been often assured by persons on whom I may depend, that
whilst they lived with the King they coud observe nothing in him
tending that way." [201] To tell the truth, less exciting than old
rumors, the Chevalier de St.-Georges spent the years 1725, 1726,
and 1727 in that feverish, not melancholy, letter-writing which
filled hours of every day of his life. His object was to heal
the breach and repair the harm Clementina had done. Had he
been successful, he might have drawn advantage from the diplomatic crisis in which Europe wallowed at that time, as a result of
the duc de Bourbon's cancellation of Louis XV's engagement to
the Infanta of Spain. So infuriated was Elisabeth Farnese, mother
of that princess, that she darted and plunged from one alliance
to another for several years through the mazes of European
politics until she was satisfied with compensatory principalities
for her children; in the meantime James III might find a way to
England through some chink opened in the system of Stanhope.

Hay was able to pick up the threads again with the Englishmen and Scotsmen who had been frightened by the Atterbury
trial. James Hamilton, "a litle pert insignificant fellow," [202] and
certainly a man of no education, seems to have assembled Orrery,
Charles Caesar, formerly treasurer of the navy under Anne, and
Colonel William Cecil, a younger son of the family of the Earl
of Salisbury, at a London meeting, and led them to act through
him, by offering to do all the work.[203] It was a very unsatisfactory

[200] X, 639.
[201] II, 340.
[202] Lockhart, II, 348.
[203] J. Hamilton to James, March 19/30, 1725, W.S.P. 81, no. 7.

arrangement,[204] but nothing better could be done at the time. The Duke of Wharton, who had played at Jacobitism since a visit to Avignon in 1716,[205] was in league with James once more in April 1725.[206] A new Scottish correspondent, John Corsar, replaced Captain Straiton, who died in May,[207] and Orrery overcame his shyness at about the same time.[208] Reorganized in this way, the Jacobites were soon bombarding every power in Europe with memorials, except the Dutch, whom they left alone, presuming a fixed alliance with the house of Hanover.

The duc de Bourbon had set Europe in an uproar when he sent the little Infanta, incapable of marriage for years yet, back to Spain, so that he might protect his own position from the possibility of the succession of his cousin, the son of the Regent Orléans, by marrying Louis XV to a nubile princess immediately. It is true that the court of Spain was already chafing at the slowness of the Congress of Cambrai in reaching a settlement of the claims and counter-claims of the Emperor and Philip V; but this stinging blow threw the Queen of Spain, who governed her husband absolutely, into the arms of his former rival, the Emperor Charles, and brought peace and an alliance between them in a few weeks. The new alignment forced Bourbon to tighten his alliance with England, and opposed the greedy Queen Elisabeth once more to George I, so that she had a mind to use the man whose birth had placed him in a position to reduce the King of England to his native electorate — if so supported as to tip the scales of public opinion and private interest toward the Stuart house.

So it came about that with Madrid, and with the court of Vienna allied with Madrid, correspondence was particularly frequent and long in the middle of 1725, and hopes drawn from it correspondingly high.[209] "It is hard to imagine that from the present Confusion of Affairs, some event should not happen which

---

[204] W.S.P. 94, no. 61.
[205] H.M.C. Stuart Papers, III, 37.
[206] Lockhart, II, 149.
[207] Ibid., II, 155.
[208] Orrery to James, May 7, W.S.P. 82, nos. 18–18B.
[209] E.g. Atterbury to James, March 16, W.S.P. 81, no. 28; Ormonde's instructions, April 21, ibid., no. 126.

may determine some fforeign power to embrace my intrest,"
James wrote to Orrery, but "How desireable therefor would it be
that my own subjects might be able to profit of the present con-
juncture, in acting by themselves for their own delivery." [210] He
knew the need to convince foreign rulers of England's desire for
"delivery," you see. Once more a great crusading alliance for the
vindication of the rights of sovereigns was imagined, including
Austria, Spain, and perhaps Russia.

At this time Bolingbroke, who wished those who came after to
believe that he vowed in 1716 nevermore to wield his sword or
pen in the Pretender's service, offered to enter into friendship
with his former master if he could deal with anybody but Atterbury; at least Murray wrote to James to that effect from Paris,[211]
and Murray had known Bolingbroke from his service in Parliament under Anne, and had been given the Secretaryship for
Scotland by him ten years before.

Murray offered James's mediation of the dispute with Spain to
France,[212] and James tried to obtain the privilege, perhaps to sell
to a friend, of sending one ship a year to the Spanish colonies.[213]
Wild projects of one kind or another flew across Europe as fast as
horse or ship could carry them. James had nothing to do with
much of this hurly-burly. Atterbury heard a rumor that James
might marry his young son to the rejected Infanta,[214] as he would,
if it could have been arranged,[215] but it had never even been
considered by the Spanish court. The first definite plans were
made in June for an expedition to Scotland. Atterbury would
handle any details about it at Paris.[216]

The reason for the selection of Scotland for such an undertaking
was simply that the collection of the Malt Tax and the compulsory disarming of the Highlanders [217] had aroused a feeling of
resentment there that promised support, if the Highlanders could

[210] *Ibid.*, no. 95.
[211] *Ibid.*, no. 104.
[212] Murray to Hay, Paris, April 23, 1725, *ibid.*, no. 131.
[213] *Ibid.*, no. 114.
[214] W.S.P. 82, no. 26.
[215] Ormonde's instructions, W.S.P. 81, no. 126.
[216] James to Atterbury, June 15, 1725, W.S.P. 83, no. 3.
[217] Lockhart, II, 159–64.

be joined by foreigners or Englishmen, for they were too weak to stand alone.[218] When the Scots were called upon to do their duty, it was with a promise of foreign assistance,[219] and an order to retain their arms. That summer having brought no success in Jacobite diplomacy, the Mackenzies, on the instructions of their chief, Seaforth, surrendered many of their arms and broke the front of loyal clans.[220] These, at least, reserved their newer and more valuable arms from the surrender, giving up only worthless ones, as far as possible.

The English sent over the Duke of Wharton, whose debts had made his residence in England uncomfortable in any case, to treat for them as well as for the Pretender at the court of Vienna in July. Wharton was present at meetings of Spanish representatives and Imperial ministers, and hoped to lead them to conclude an alliance against George I (and therefore for James III);[221] he pretended to be a tourist, but did not deceive anyone. The Nuncio at Vienna, Grimaldi,[222] who was expected to work with him, found it sad that his zeal was not matched by his maturity.[223] It had been intended that the duke should return to England with information,[224] but his indiscretion abroad and his extravagance at home had ruined his position.[225]

Hopes based on France fell to the ground when Atterbury wrote that Bourbon had tied France fast to England [226] from fright (which, incidentally, destroyed much work formerly done by Dubois to retrieve French prestige after the death of Louis XIV), but that had been expected. Wharton, on the other hand, encouraged the Pretender to believe the assurances of Ripperda and Sinzendorff, the ministers of Spain and Austria who dealt with him,[227] and it would have been hard for more experienced men

[218] *Ibid.*, II, 187.
[219] W.S.P. 83, nos. 5–12, 25; Lockhart, II, 187.
[220] Lockhart, II, 218; Gen. Guest to the Duke of Gordon, "Innerness," Sept. 30 O.S., 1725, *Publications of the Spalding Club*, XVI (Edinburgh, 1846), 279.
[221] Wharton's representations, W.S.P. 83, nos. 87–88.
[222] Girolamo Grimaldi (1674–1733), Nuncio 1721–1730, and a cardinal in the latter year.
[223] Grimaldi to the Papal Secretariat, Aug. 4, 1725, W.S.P. 85, no. 6.
[224] James to Ormonde, Aug. 4, *ibid.*, no. 10.
[225] The Duchess of Wharton to the duke [Nov. 1725], W.S.P. 87, no. 95.
[226] W.S.P. 83, no. 67.
[227] W.S.P. 85, no. 149; vol. 86, nos. 52 and 79.

to see their way through the plausible utterances of those wily and inconsistent politicians. Charles VI and Philip V were on the verge of the conclusion of an alliance; if this bargain were reached, it would be to the interest of those two rulers to break up the Anglo-French coalition. The Emperor could thus humble Hanover, and Spain could chastise France; both would be free to apportion Italy — this to be an Imperial province, that to be the appanage of a son of Philip V and Elisabeth Farnese. But if the Austro-Spanish alliance were not exactly what the two powers desired (and no one could depend on Elisabeth's temper or capacity for satiation) neither of them would be willing to take irreversible steps to change the balance of power. Nevertheless, Spain might well have grasped at the proffered reward for her assistance, possession of Port Mahon and Gibraltar, and Charles VI might have thought the recognition of the Ostend Company and a guarantee of the Pragmatic Sanction [228] worth the effort and expense necessary to restore James III. Were these promises, as Mr. Basil Williams says, a betrayal of English interests, "the most fatal blow conceivable to the commercial power of England"? [229] Perhaps, but can anyone honestly say that he knows what might have been?

7. CLEMENTINA'S RETIREMENT

Into this beehive fell the stone of the retirement. At first Clementina's complaints had only been of the dismissal of Mrs. Sheldon; later they included certain slights, never specified in writing, suffered at the hands of the Earl and Countess of Inverness. These charges were quickly construed by some ill-wishers to mean that the earl was a complaisant husband, and his wife the Pretender's mistress. Clementina never said so. Finally, to involve Benedict XIII, she objected to the Protestant governor, Murray, created Earl of Dunbar. Already in August Cardinal Imperiali, Protector of Ireland at Rome, had protested against Dunbar's employment,[230] but had been reminded that the Catho-

---

[228] Wharton's representations, W.S.P. 83, nos. 87–88.

[229] "The Foreign Policy of England under Walpole; 1721–27," *E.H.R.*, XV (April 1900), 268.

[230] W.S.P. 85, no. 109. Giuseppe Imperiali (1651–1737), a cardinal since 1690, was said in 1730 to have missed elevation to the papacy by one vote.

lic under-governor would have the greatest share in the education of the "Prince of Wales," and the only authority in his religious instruction.[231] James, however, attributed the retirement to the workings of a sinister influence upon her mind. Let us examine these possible reasons separately.

As to Inverness, his lady, and slights put upon the queen by them, we have both direct and indirect evidence that these could not have been serious, nor of long standing; probably until after the decision had been taken to break with James. Gualterio, who knew the household well, wrote in January 1726, "La longue habitude que j'ay dans la maison Royale, quoique j'aye toujours evité de me meler dans le domestique, ne m'a pas fait voir rien qui pût offenser la Reine du côte de ce Milord." [232] His wife, while still Mrs. Hay, had been the occasion of a nasty letter from Mar of December 7, 1722, to the effect that the Queen was jealous of her.[233] He had responded by offering to Clementina in a hastily-written letter, not mentioning Mar's name, to send his wife away from Rome "if [it] should be only insinuated by yr. Majtie to be agreeable to you." [234] Mrs. Hay did indeed visit her family in England later, but probably not because of jealousy on Clementina's part, for when the lady was stopped in England to prevent her planned return to Rome, the Pretender's wife wrote in her own hand to the duchesse de Bourbon to obtain French intervention for her release, because "the cares and services of Mrs. Hay will be of great comfort to me during my confinement," [235] Clementina then being pregnant of her second son, Prince Henry. This was only a year before the withdrawal, but two years after the question had first arisen. Clementina, then, was a fool, a pander to her husband's pleasures, or convinced that nothing was really the matter.

As to the Protestant governor, what raised that question, since

---

[231] Letter of Aug. 29, 1725, W.S.P. 85, no. 113. Dureng (357–58) has adopted the baseless notion that Atterbury had persuaded James to rear his son in the Anglican religion.

[232] Letter to Fleury, Jan. 16, 1726, Add. MSS. 20,322, foll. 130–31.

[233] W.S.P. 63, no. 132.

[234] W.S.P. 64, no. 93, faultily printed by Miss H. Tayler in *The Jacobite Court at Rome in 1719*, 217–18; and in her *Stuart Papers at Windsor*, 66–68.

[235] Letter dated Albano, Nov. 7, 1724, W.S.P. 77, no. 152.

Dunbar's position was to be honorary, is beyond mortal man to say. But raising it at the Papal court was the easiest way to hurt the Pretender and bring him to terms, for Pope Benedict could not well keep his hands off if he thought that the education of his pensioner's children was to be of a Protestant sort. His position demanded it, and Clementina's friends would not let the matter alone. She retired to a convent in November 1725, and there cardinals and Roman ladies visited her, heard her story, or rather stories, and spread them about. In December the Pope yielded to pressure and sent to ask James to dismiss Dunbar and re-employ Mrs. Sheldon. Had James given in, he would have been faced with desertion by his Protestant friends, but the Pope controlled his purse, and had the power of the keys. He lost his temper and "replyed that I had no occasion for The Popes consent or advice in an affair which concerned my privat family." [236] Please notice that the Hays are not mentioned. When the rumor of this reached a spy of the English government, he represented the Pope's messenger as having accused James of adultery with Mrs. Hay, and James as having threatened to kick the bearer of the message, a bishop, out of a window.[237] The Ormonde-Atterbury-Marischal Protestant group was pleased with the report they received, probably less highly colored, and the Catholic Daniel O'Brien wrote to Hay on December 24, "Le pape se conduit fort singulieremt dans cette ocation sa derniere demarche me paroit . . . tres avantageuse au roy en ce qu'il fait voir . . . que la reyne na plus eu de meilleure raisons pour autoriser sa retraitte que celle du gouverneur protestant . . . la fermeté de S[a] M[ajesté] dans cette conjoncture lui fera suremt beaucoup d'honneur." [238]

But it brought little comfort. The Pope suspended the payment of the Chevalier's pension, and the King of Spain, moved by his wife, did the same [239] with a pension James had had from the

---

[236] James to Atterbury, Rome, Dec. 5, 1725, W.S.P. 87, no. 154.

[237] A. C. Ewald, *The Life and Times of Prince Charles Stuart, Count of Albany* (London, 1875), I, 25. Here, as elsewhere in Ewald, I find a regularity of spelling and grammar unusual in 18th century sources.

[238] W.S.P. 88, no. 113.

[239] Gualterio to Fleury, Rome, Jan. 9, 1726, Add. MSS. 20,322, fol. 123. The Spanish pension was still not restored in 1734. H.M.C. *Report* XIV, app. II, 238.

time of Alberoni. It was a good public ground on which to fight,[240] but the necessity of the fight in itself did no end of harm.

But the Protestant governor was not the cause of the withdrawal. The English government was the party most interested in it. Mar, it was early suspected, had struck at James through his wife, and the Pretender was the first to know it: "The Queen neither hath nor indeed can bring any reason for leaving of me, and her pretended motives all center in matters quite out of a wife's sphere, & entirely subservient to D[uke] of Mar's projects."[241] To Ormonde he wrote in December: "It would seem that project has been long layd and by letters of D. of Mar's I can see That his view has been for several years to remove Lord Inverness by the Queen's means."[242] Gualterio was the earliest to mention Cardinal Alberoni, who now lived at Rome, in this connection, with Mar.[243]

The Pretender could not pick his ground, it became apparent, because of the interest of some persons, particularly English spies in Italy, in muddying the waters. "Walton," whose real name was Stosch, sent reports to England which were very handy in attacks on the Pretender's morals: Clementina had been slighted, scorned, betrayed, confronted with her husband's mistress, and otherwise mentally tortured. These are now preserved among the State Papers, Foreign, Italian States, for the use of persons who can evaluate them.[244] Let no one be misled: such treatment of wives was not unknown in the eighteenth century, but on no grounds except these spy's reports and loose rumor can it be attributed to the Pretender, and only Mar mentioned suspicion of a connection between him and Mrs. Hay before this time. Hay's letter in 1722, Clementina's anxiety to have Mrs. Hay back in 1724, and the Protestant governor's wrangle all suggest that infidelity was not the grievance, but that it was made to appear so. Clementina nursed all her injuries in ostentatious self-pity, but did not pub-

[240] Hay to Archbishop Tencin, Jan. 30, W.S.P. 90, no. 47.
[241] Letter to Atterbury, Rome, Nov. 19, W.S.P. 87, no. 97.
[242] *Ibid.*, no. 138.
[243] Add. MSS. 20,322, foll. 130–31.
[244] Mr. A. C. Ewald drew upon these for material on Prince Charles' childhood, but did not attack the Stuart Papers, the extent of which he seems to have ignored.

lish an accusation. What was not published was improvised. The
scandal of separation was greater than it would be now, and two
of James's most loyal friends, Lockhart and Atterbury, took his
wife's side.[245] Walpole must have been delighted.

The breach also destroyed any hope of Spanish assistance. Sir
Charles Wogan, who had been promised a promotion in the
Spanish army, told James years later that after the arrival of the
news of the breach he was received "like a Dog in a nine-pin-
Alley," and told to "think himself happy in keeping what he had
got." [246] When such a tirade was vented on dependents, the im-
placability of the Spanish court toward James III can be con-
ceived.

In late February 1726, the harassed Pretender offered to replace
Dunbar with Ormonde, and Ormonde (as agent in Spain) with
Marischal, and to send Lady Inverness away indefinitely, while
retaining her husband as a political necessity.[247] The Princess of
Piombino carried these terms to the immured queen, and carried
back their rejection. Clementina's desires extended further than a
reshuffling of Protestants about the court, and her main object
was evidently not the removal of the Countess. She may have been
insane, although it would be rash to suppose it, in spite of her
peculiar behavior in later life. There is an alternative possibility
— that Clementina, excitable as she was, and disappointed in her
husband's failure to make her queen in more than name, was
being played upon by Alberoni.

That cardinal had taken his place at Rome after the death of
Clement XI, and had risen to high positions under Innocent XIII
until 1724, when the election of Pope Benedict XIII had reduced
him to a less favorable position. Alberoni found time to visit
Clementina for hours on end,[248] pretending to urge reconciliation.
It was suspected at that time that his real desire was to postpone
it — did he hold up for her emulation a picture of the conduct of
the dauntless Queen of Spain? — and this was confirmed on her

[245] W.S.P. 89, no. 18; vol. 91, no. 121; Lockhart, II, *passim*. Lockhart's disapproval was based on the supposed officiousness of Hay and Murray.
[246] Wogan to James, Ba[rcelona], June 22, 1741, W.S.P. 233, no. 170.
[247] Undated W.S.P., box 1, no. 60.
[248] Mahon, II, 135; William Coxe, *Memoirs of . . . Sir Robert Walpole*
(London, 1798), II, 573.

death by papers which James burned without showing to any-one.[249] So he says, and I believe him.

Cessation of the Pope's payments forced economy on the Chevalier, which meant withdrawal to a cheaper place of residence. At Bologna he would be nearer the Emperor and have fewer expenses, and if some chance opened his way to England he would have a shorter distance to travel. The Pope attempted to avoid the removal by offering, in September 1726, to mediate a reconciliation, if James would send away his Protestant "predicanti," the successors of old Charles Leslie. James accepted, and offered to send them to Florence, but the Pope seized the occasion to demand the dismissal of Dunbar as well.[250] James refused, for where, then, would demands end? *Predicanti* and all, the court was installed at Bologna in early October,[251] on an allowance of three-fifths of the old pension, the rest going to Clementina for her separate maintenance.[252] Retaliation was taken in the form of denial of the Pretender's right of nomination of Catholic bishops for his dominions, unchallenged in recent years.[253]

8. THE DEATH OF GEORGE I; RECONCILIATION

Good news came that winter to the effect that the Emperor would, if war with England should begin for other reasons, restore James,[254] and that the whole "triumvirate" was at work, or so Lansdowne said, to mend the breach in the royal family,[255] but the stay at Bologna must have been very unpleasant. Hay became suspicious and irritable; being well informed by spies, he heard every word circulated about him and multiplied it in his belief that he knew only a portion of the whole machine which moved against him. The spleen engendered in him by the persecution of Spain and the Pope he vented on Atterbury, the incompetent

---

[249] W.S.P. 177, nos. 23 and 49.

[250] Inverness to Graeme, Sept. 21, 1726, W.S.P. 97, no. 74.

[251] W.S.P. 97, no. 156.

[252] Add. MSS. 20,313, fol. 261.

[253] H.M.C. *Stuart Papers*, I, *passim*; W.S.P. warrant book M17. According to the latter, in 1722–25, James nominated eight bishops and archbishops.

[254] John Graeme to Inverness, Dec. 28, 1726, W.S.P. 101, no. 8.

[255] *Ibid.*, no. 70.

James Hamilton, and Barclay, one of the *predicanti,* indiscriminately.[256] Wharton had failed in Spain, but "Sir John" Graeme, at Vienna, was put into direct relations with the English Jacobites;[257] agents were instructed;[258] and Jacobites in Parliament or otherwise influential were once more marshalled to trouble the ministry of George I. The last effort was disappointing.[259] More reliance was placed on the Emperor if war should come; the court could then move to the Austrian Netherlands and the Chevalier could embark at Ostend.

The Emperor could not fight England without Spain, however; and Spain would not agree to help James while the separation continued, although Father William Clarke, the Catholic King's confessor, used his influence, such as it was, to bring him around.[260] Hay had done all he could. In March 1727, James accepted his resignation,[261] and called John Graeme to Bologna from Vienna to replace him as Secretary of State.[262] Hay was sent to meet the Duke of Liria, formerly Lord Tynemouth, Berwick's eldest son and a grandee of Spain, who was then passing through Italy on his way to serve as Spanish ambassador to the court of Russia, and to give the duke letters[263] and verbal messages for his use as a Jacobite agent there. Then the discarded secretary was to retire with his wife to the neighborhood of Pisa.[264]

His withdrawal was followed by Mar's submission,[265] but not yet by reconciliation with the cloistered Clementina, which, James wrote to Gualterio on May 7, might not occur while Benedict XIII lived.[266] Graeme was installed before the end of that month, disappointing Lord North and Grey, who was supported for the post by Lockhart. He was the son of James Graeme or Graham,

[256] W.S.P. 94, no. 61; vol. 103, nos. 129, 159.
[257] Hay to James Hamilton, Nov. 6, 1726, W.S.P. 98, no. 156.
[258] Hay to Peter Redmond, Nov. 26, W.S.P. 99, no. 94.
[259] Orrery to James, Jan. 28 O.S. and J. Hamilton to James, Jan. 29 O.S., W.S.P. 102, nos. 68, 71.
[260] W.S.P. 103, no. 37; the comte de Rottembourg's secret instructions, Morel-Fatio, III, 137.
[261] W.S.P. 105, nos. 51, 52.
[262] James to Graeme, Bologna, March 28, 1727, *ibid.,* no. 61.
[263] E.g. Admiral Gordon's credential letter, H.M.C. *Report* X, app. I, 162.
[264] W.S.P. 105, no. 105.
[265] Mar to James, May 5, W.S.P. 106, no. 88.
[266] *Ibid.,* no. 90.

solicitor for James II in Scotland, who was an important Jacobite in Hooke's day; and was himself esteemed to be "a young gentleman of good parts" at the time of his elevation.[267] North and Grey went to Spain as a major-general instead, probably because he had taken Clementina's side in the separation.[268] Graeme proved to be weak and rather incapable, in the long run, and was generally regarded as a creature of Hay.

The conclusion of peace preliminaries at Paris at the end of May crushed Graeme's expectation that Spain would readily combine with the Emperor and the Jacobites when Hay was sent away, and the advantage of George I's death in June[269] was lost before it was known. While uncertain of the state of affairs, the Pretender had left Bologna on July 4,[270] at the first word of his rival's demise, and travelled as fast as he could to Lorraine, where he stopped to catch his breath on the 18th. There he wrote to Atterbury at Paris to know in what state his English affairs lay, and whether he could expect encouragement from France.[271] He was not allowed to enter France, nor could Atterbury and Daniel O'Brien even obtain French neutrality,[272] because of the dependence upon England, in which Cardinal Fleury, chief minister after the dismissal of the duc de Bourbon, found the foreign policy of Louis XV. As part of his plan for re-establishment of French freedom of action, the cardinal did order resumption of the French payments, suspended probably since the end of 1724.[273] One does not starve people one may some day be able to use. The Duke of Lorraine was forced to send James away, just the same,[274] for the day of use was not yet come.

The English Jacobites wrote desperately, and somewhat comically, that he should attempt nothing that summer, although England was as dissatisfied with George II as with his father "but as yet dissatisfaction has not had that [time?] to spread itself

[267] Lockhart, II, 337–38, 343.
[268] Wharton to North, Feb. 2, 1726, W.S.P. 90, no. 59; Lockhart, II, 344.
[269] Strafford to James, London, June 21 O.S., 1727, W.S.P. 107, no. 97.
[270] W.S.P. 108, no. 10.
[271] W.S.P. 109, no. 18.
[272] W.S.P. 108, no. 98.
[273] *Ibid.*
[274] The Duke to James, Lunéville, Aug. 8, W.S.P. 109, no. 46.

amongst the common people, wch it certainly will very soon. . ." [275] Avignon was the best place open to him to await events at the coming peace congress, and if Philip V could be persuaded to use his influence with France to let James stay there,[276] permanent residence north of the Alps might follow. The royal party arrived at Avignon on August 20.

Clementina had before this "returned to her duty," to the relief of everyone, even Alberoni. The cardinal, whose hopes were then for pensions and benefices in the gift of the King of Spain, had been detected in his intrigue, which he continued to represent as benevolence. He wrote to his Parmesan friend and go-between with Elisabeth Farnese, "What has come of it, count? that malevolent persons have made the Queen of Spain believe that my counsels were those which impeded such a reunion." [277] It had taken long enough to convince her, and her conviction was immediately followed by the reconciliation. Had it come earlier, the same result probably would have been reached in a much shorter time. He had admonished Clementina that the Protestant governor was the Pope's affair, although she was still uneasy about him in 1727. Why had he not so admonished her earlier? Nor did she return to her husband in the best mood for friendship. "What a misfortune, count," said Alberoni, "that a soul full of God, because truly of angelic behavior, who has served as a model to all Rome and to this convent where she has lived with so much piety and in such an exemplary fashion, should not be allowed to live quietly and at peace." [278] That peace for her lay in the convent, not in wedlock, is probable, but she had undertaken marriage, and now peace for everyone else lay in her return to it.

She went to her husband's empty house at Bologna in the middle of July, with the ill-concealed wishes of her adviser that she would leave it again if she did not get all she wanted: "If the king knows how to manage this princess, he will get from her what he wishes, because she is an angel incarnate: but if he thinks to treat her as on other occasions, she goes resolved to repeat her

[275] Strafford to James, Aug 1 [O.S.], *ibid.*, no. 2. See also vol. 109, nos. 6, 19, and 22.
[276] James to Ormonde and Philip V, Aug. 22, *ibid.*, nos. 101, 102.
[277] Alberoni, *Lettres intimes,* 662.
[278] *Ibid.*

step [*fare la seconda di cambio*] without further hope of remedy.
I hope, however, that, the wicked instruments being removed,
there will be born between the royal consorts that love, peace,
and union which can render them happy. . ." [279] It was as "wicked
instruments" that Alberoni viewed the Hays, and his assurances
that his visits were intended to bring about that "love, peace, and
union" were pretty obviously false, at least as long as the Hays
were about the court; but he did not deceive the Pretender or the
Queen of Spain, as has been shown. His motives are doubtful.
If he was the distinguished person at Rome who informed the
English government of plots in 1722 and was mentioned in a
document published by the Committee of the Commons which
examined Layer,[280] the pieces of the puzzle which survive would
all fit: he would have been in the pay of the English ministry for
several years when his opportunity came to do it invaluable
service. He may, equally well, not have been the "distinguished
person." Even if not, he had conferred benefits only upon George I
by his actions, not upon Spain or the Emperor, and least of all
upon the Pope, who was made to appear a persecutor in the eyes
of the world. James had been his friend since 1718, and had recently helped him to recover some of his Spanish revenues,[281] but
the man who had contrived the fall of his benefactress, the princesse des Ursins, did not let that stand in his way.

While the Pretender remained at Avignon, he proposed that
his wife should come there, but she refused,[282] showing her attitude toward the reconciliation. Graeme and Hay had joined him,
but Hay had returned to Pisa. Graeme's presence proved a
trouble, because of recent miscarriages of communications,
through which letters of George Lockhart of Carnwath, the most
important Scottish Jacobite, had been betrayed by a messenger
named Strahan. Corsar, the chief correspondent, was captured,
but Lockhart got away to Holland. He wrote demanding

---

[279] *Ibid.*, 658.

[280] *A Report from the Committee* (London, 1722), App. A, 4, and App. B,
11. The contemporary reports of the spy "Walton" (Baron Philip de Stosch)
recount private meetings with Alberoni; one of these may have been doctored
as to wording and date for publication.

[281] W.S.P. 85, no. 136.

[282] Atterbury to Keith, Nov. 17, 1727, H.M.C. *Report*, IX, app. II, 219.

Graeme's removal as a possible traitor.[283] Bowing to necessity, James sent "Sir John" to Spain in October, at first for a few months,[284] but when he found that he could do as well by himself, he extended the time, and finally settled Graeme at Avignon, when James himself had returned to Italy. Lockhart was later informed of Strahan's treachery by Lord Islay and Duncan Forbes of Culloden, and acknowledged his error, if not to James himself, at least to posterity.[285]

Graeme was never recalled, but retained the title of Secretary for many years. James knew him to have been wronged, but did not want a Secretary, for any appointment would irritate some faction; from this time he carried the burden of correspondence alone. Murray (or "Dunbar"), who had kept his position as governor, and was at that time at Bologna occupied with pacifying his hysterical queen, is sometimes said to have been a minister without a title, in complete charge; but there is no reason to believe this common talk, since in the voluminous correspondence now surviving there is no evidence to support it. Dunbar did not correspond with agents of the Pretender whom he did not otherwise know; to those he knew he wrote only personal letters, never directives. His position was probably that of a major-domo, regulating servants, inspecting accounts, and in general supplying the wants of James III and Maria Clementina.

The Prince was left to Sheridan's tutelage, which was pretty bad, but it was not Dunbar's fault, since he dared not intervene for fear of his mistress's temper. While she was at Bologna she seems to have attempted to drive him to resign by treating him scornfully.[286] She did not succeed, for James had a servant more loyal than his wife.

[283] Lockhart, II, 331–32; W.S.P. 111, nos. 32, 47.
[284] James to Hay, Avignon, Oct. 20, 1727, *ibid.*, no. 95.
[285] Lockhart, II, 398.
[286] Dunbar to O'Brien, Oct. 28, W.S.P. 111, no. 147.

6

DIPLOMACY AND OPPOSITION POLITICS

(1 7 2 7 – 1 7 3 6)

1. PARLIAMENTARY JACOBITES

The threats of France [1] and Clementina's instability [2] cut short the second stay at Avignon. The Pope made a decent resistance to French pressure,[3] but the outcome was never in doubt. James left quietly late in December 1727, was at Milan on January 3, and at Bologna on the 7th.[4]

Mrs. Sheldon retired into a convent before his arrival, and other adjustments were made.[5] The conditions for domestic peace, though not friendship, seem to have been fulfilled on both sides, but Clementina showed from this time to her death signs of a religious fervor which approached mania,[6] and which prevented the birth of more children, although she more than once fancied herself pregnant.[7] "She leads a most singular life," her husband wrote, "she takes no manner of amusement, not even taking the air, and when she is not at Church or at Table, is locked up in her room, & sees no mortal but her maids or so; she eats meat this lent, but fasts to that degree that I believe no married woman that pretends to have children ever did; I am very little with her, I let her do what she will. . . She has quite left off dressing &

---

[1] Gualterio to James, Corgnolo, Sept. 20, W.S.P. 110, no. 82.
[2] Liria to Admiral Gordon, Petersburg, Jan. 13 [O.S.], 1728, H.M.C. *Report* X, app. I, 166.
[3] W.S.P. 111, no. 26.
[4] W.S.P. 113, no. 62.
[5] *Ibid.*, no. 55; H.M.C. *Report* X, app. I, 166.
[6] Dunbar to O'Brien, Feb. 17, W.S.P. 114, no. 44.
[7] H.M.C. *Report* X, app. I, 162; W.S.P. 131, no. 7.

parure. . ." [8] This regimen brought on scurvy, from which she suffered for years,[9] and which ended her miserable life with an early death.

She had returned too late to aid James's relations with Spain. Ormonde had secured a token payment from Philip V, through the efforts of Father Clarke,[10] but not the pension granted before. A protest was circulated against the deliberations of the Congress of Soissons, and expostulating "Memorials" were presented to the principal European courts at the same time.[11] Ormonde remained at Madrid for the time being; Owen O'Rourke, an Irish officer formerly in the Duke of Lorraine's service, had replaced Graeme at Vienna.[12] Atterbury and O'Brien quarreled over trifles until the bishop gave up the struggle and retired to the country.[13] James and Prince Charles took advantage of the lull to tour Northern Italy, meeting Hay at Parma. Reinstatement as secretary was suggested, but he refused and returned to Pisa.[14]

In February 1728 it was found necessary to replace Lockhart with Lord Dundonald,[15] neither so regular nor so useful as his predecessor, who made his peace with the government of George I and returned to England in May, but abstained from political activity thereafter.[16] Dr. Blaikie is wrong in assuming that he had no successor.[17] James Hamilton continued his epistolary work in England, but lacked the skill of Atterbury and others who had once done it — no wonder, for as he confessed, "My own misfortune . . . [was] not being at a Schoole since I was Ten Years of age." [18] James would have preferred a better agent, but there was no suitable material. Orrery was loyal, and had gone as far as Christ Church, Oxford, but he was timid and ineffectual. Sir

[8] James to Hay, March 1, W.S.P. 114, no. 116.
[9] James to O'Brien, Dec. 20, 1734, W.S.P. 176, no. 21.
[10] Ormonde to James, March 6, 1728, W.S.P. 114, no. 130.
[11] W.S.P. 116, nos. 142, 164; vol. 117, nos. 11, 12, and 14.
[12] W.S.P. 105, no. 61.
[13] Atterbury to James, March 30, W.S.P. 115, no. 56.
[14] James to Ormonde, June 20, W.S.P. 117, no. 88.
[15] James to Dundonald, Feb. 18, W.S.P. 114, no. 47.
[16] Lockhart, II, 397, 403.
[17] Origins of the 'Forty-Five, and other papers. . . (Edinburgh, 1916), p. xxiii.
[18] W.S.P. 130, no. 115.

Henry Goring had the not entirely original idea of commencing a series of Jacobite sheets and pamphlets,[19] but he saw it rejected, and was quiet. James's conscience was, here again, the objection: "The truth is," he wrote to O'Brien, "that in relation to *pamphlets* & such sort of *papers*, It is I think in general neither decent nor proper that they should *come out* in any way by *my* authority, neither can Christopher [James] approve of any thing where *truth* is not *observed*." [20] Some publications appeared independently, and we shall see that James actually did approve of one publication, in which he presumably hoped that the truth would be observed, but he did not openly endorse any papers until 1743. He was probably right about declarations, which could do little good and a great deal of harm, until his insight into European politics was much improved. One which was in the press in the summer of 1728 was suppressed, and its plate destroyed, by his orders.[21]

As to parliamentary action, the Jacobites were divided "whither the *discarding of Mr. Walpole* would be for the advantage of their *cause* or not, some think if *he* was out of employment, he would be a powerful Mall-content, against his Successors and that *he* then would push heartily *for the Kings Restoration*. others say he is now so beated [baited] by the *Whigs* that *he* can *have no safety* but in *bringing home the King*. . . The generality of the *Jacobits* are warm for having Sir Robert out of power, because they dispair of any good service from him to the King or Country." [22] Of course, the Jacobites could not alone bring about Walpole's overthrow, but close watch was kept by Hamilton, who reported parliamentary affairs regularly.[23]

Rome would be as convenient for this kind of correspondence as Bologna, now that a settlement had been reached. James paid a visit in February 1729 to pave the way for the return of the court; having been received favorably by the Pope, he wrote

---

[19] W.S.P. 118, nos. 85, 119.

[20] Letter of Jan. 18, 1729, W.S.P. 124, no. 46. Italics are deciphered by the code clerk.

[21] O'Brien to James, Aug. 23, 1728, W.S.P. 119, no. 89.

[22] Hamilton to J. Edgar, London, Dec. 18 [O.S.], 1728, W.S.P. 122, no. 109. Italics are deciphered by the recipient.

[23] E. g., in early 1729, W.S.P. 125, nos. 34, 115; vol. 126, nos. 18, 163.

orders, in March, for the household to prepare to move in May.[24] Inverness was again invited to resume his place,[25] but evidently feared to test Clementina's forbearance.

Fleury, being still diplomatically dependent on England, and having no belief that the Jacobites could succeed, had not given any sign of abandoning Hanover for Stuart: "ce seroit se flatter mal apropos dimaginer que pendant le ministere de Mr. le cardinal de fleury, v[otre] m[ajesté] puisse esperer que lon se determine jamais icy, afaire rien de bon en sa faveur, amoins que par quelque coup imprevu le sistheme entieremt ne change." [26] That much was known, but Spain's policy was unfathomable. The desires of the queen were for Port Mahon and Gibraltar, and the establishment of her sons, who seemed unlikely to rule in Spain, in independent principalities in Italy. If she were thwarted, there might be war, provided she found allies, but with and against whom no man could say.

To stir her up, the English Jacobites in Parliament attempted to obstruct a pacification which would give her what she wanted. Hamilton wrote to Edgar, "*The Kings friends* have done all that is possible *here* to prevent the *Usurper* giving *up Gibraltar &* *Port Mahon*, and if *Spain* will *comply without these* it must be oweing to the *ffrench* influence." [27] Even Scotland had given up thoughts of action independent of foreign assistance, so that "*everybody that wishes the King's cause are gaping to know the event of ſſoreign affairs*," as Dundonald wrote in May. It was his view that the Pretender would have an opportunity if the ministry gave up Gibraltar and brought on its own fall, but that the Jacobites must not enter into any sort of coalition, which would take from them some of their strength.

The parliamentary Jacobites were not, however, opposed to the return of the Mediterranean strongholds on principle, for they authorized James to promise that, if he were restored, they would help to arrange the surrender of the places, and do anything else which James might have promised to Spain or the Emperor.[28]

---

[24] W.S.P. 124, no. 172; vol. 125, no 16; vol. 126, no. 1.
[25] James to Hay, March 12, W.S.P. 125, no. 158.
[26] O'Brien to James, May 1, 1729, W.S.P. 127, no. 78.
[27] Letter of April 30, 1729, *ibid.*, no. 63.
[28] James to O'Rourke, May 14, W.S.P. 128, no. 5.

Moreover, the Pretender gave Ormonde a free hand in the middle of May to promise the furtherance of the claims of Don Carlos in Italy, if Spain would put him in a position to do so.[29]

Spain preferred more certain support, and within the year the spirits of the Chevalier were down again. Father Clarke's influence had been overestimated, he found: "As for ffather Clerk I look upon him to be a Cypher & that he was promoted & is kept in to be one."[30] Clementina was disappointed of her imagined pregnancy in the autumn.[31] Then, at the end of the year, came the word of the conclusion of the Treaty of Seville by England, France, and Spain, bringing to an end the diplomatic turbulence which had been inaugurated in 1725.

At the beginning of 1730 Ormonde's work at the court of Spain and O'Rourke's at Vienna were allowed to lapse pending appearance of more favorable circumstances,[32] while orders were sent to the parliamentary Jacobites through Hamilton to use the terms of the treaty to embarrass the government.[33] It was hoped that this action, vigorously carried out, and rightly represented by an English representative more skilful than Wharton, would impress the court of Vienna and encourage it to oppose the settlement made by the treaty. Another instrument for stirring up trouble was the Jacobite group in the governing bodies of the City of London, led by Alderman Barber,[34] which used the irritation caused by modification of the city's charter a few years back to bring over converts to Jacobitism. Wharton had been the first to play upon the City's feelings in this way. Now the Pretender's aldermanic friends set to work to unite their Tory colleagues in opposing the government. This policy had its effect on the Excise Bill crisis, of which it is one of the less well-known causes.

The Jacobites acted in Parliament according to their instructions. In February, "we had a debate upon the seventeen thousand odd hundred of our own troops. Mr. Shippen, in his speech . . . said he hoped he should never see these kingdoms so Germanised

[29] *Ibid.*, no. 9.
[30] James to Ormonde, Aug. 6, W.S.P. 130, no. 20.
[31] W.S.P. 132, no. 11.
[32] Letters dated Rome, Jan. 7, 1730, W.S.P. 133, nos. 58, 60.
[33] J. Edgar to Hamilton, Jan. 10, *ibid.*, no. 71.
[34] W.S.P. 134, no. 145.

as to become military; he went on with giving reasons that such
a number of troops were inconsistent with our constitution; then,
says he, force and violence are the resort of usurpers and tyrants,
whose only security is in a standing army." [35] Shippen knew exactly how far he could go, and was not punished. The Jacobites
also joined Wyndham and other Hanover Tories influenced by
Bolingbroke to disrupt English relations with France.[36]

Walpole could not be ignorant of these plans for an "ostensible"
opposition for the encouragement of foreign powers; he strove to
divide the Jacobites from the opposition Whigs by assuring them
of his good will toward the Pretender, so that James found it necessary to issue a special warning: " 'tis fit my friends should know
that I have not the least reason to think That Walpole or any
other of the present Ministers are anyways favorably disposed
towards me." [37] Colonel Cecil, according to Dr. William King of
St. Mary's Hall, Oxford, did not take this caution as seriously as
he should, but was "cajoled and duped by Sir *Robert Walpole* to
such a degree as to be fully persuaded that Sir *Robert* had formed
a design to restore the House of *Stuart*. For this reason he communicated to Sir *Robert* all his dispatches." [38]

Of course there were many knaves, as well as dupes. There had
always been spies at St.-Germain, Bar, Bologna, and Rome. Mrs.
Strickland, who was said to have betrayed Maria Beatrice's confidences to William's ministers; [39] John Ogilvie, a spy in the pay
of Harley before 1710; "Walton," who superintended the work
of several spies in Italy in the 1720's and 1730's; and Sir William
Ellis, who was once rejected as an agent in 1700 because his price
was too high,[40] but later seems to have served for an unknown
consideration [41] — always there were scoundrels and starvelings.
Walpole may have known Cecil's orders through other means,
since there were plenty who were willing to sell anything they

[35] Col. Charles Howard [to Lord Carlisle], Feb. 3, [1730], H.M.C. *Report*
XV, app. VI, 66–67.
[36] *Ibid.*, 68–69. This is my own interpretation of a confused text.
[37] James to W. Cecil, Dec. 13, 1730, W.S.P. 140, no. 195.
[38] King's *Anecdotes of his Own Times* (London, 1818), 37. Italics are King's.
[39] Madame de Caylus, *Souvenirs* (Paris, 1881), 167.
[40] Cole, 112, 117, 126.
[41] H.M.C. *Report* XV, app. IV, 314.

knew or would make up, as did "La Roche," who told the English government in 1727 that the Pretender had been in Cologne and Liége,[42] which was absurd. Still, King was right insofar as Cecil's gullibility was concerned, and James knew that he could not be told much or relied upon for advice.

2. THE DUCHESS OF BUCKINGHAM

Pope Benedict, who had supported Clementina, died in 1730, and was replaced by the more friendly Cardinal Corsini, who took the name of Clement XII, and began his rule with several kind gestures, particularly a gift of 10,000 Roman crowns and promotion of several of the Pretender's priests.[43] The new Pope advised Clementina to permit Hay's return, but she resisted, and fear of upsetting her delicate mental balance forced James to leave her alone during the autumn of that year.[44] On the day after Christmas he let it be known that "Inverness" was to be recalled to court, but not to his former post.[45] He returned, and was received kindly by Clementina and the Pope, but a few days later took a "new Resolution to go away again, In which the Queen has no share." [46] It may have been prearranged, although Hay had written to Atterbury for his opinion of the new retirement,[47] because he did not await the bishop's answer. Mrs. Hay remained at Pisa throughout her husband's short stay at Rome.[48] The object of this play-acting, if such it were, must have been the final reunion of factions. At any rate, Atterbury, after nearly three years of inactivity, was brought back into the fold, and returned to Paris.[49]

A less healthy sign was the introduction into Jacobite schemes of the "half-mad" Duchess of Buckingham,[50] Berwick's sister, in

[42] H.M.C. *Report* XI, app. IV, 199–200.
[43] W.S.P. 138, nos. 47, 126.
[44] James to Hay, Sept. 16, 1730, W.S.P. 139, no. 63; James to Hay, Oct. 20, vol. 140, no. 23.
[45] W.S.P. 141, no. 54.
[46] *Ibid.*, no. 148; vol. 142, no. 55.
[47] H.M.C. *Report* X, app. I, 179.
[48] W.S.P. 141, no. 164.
[49] *Ibid.*, no. 22; vol. 142, no. 86.
[50] The description is Dr. King's, 38–39.

the company of Viscount Cornbury, eldest son of the Earl of Clarendon and M.P. for Oxford University. After the death of James Hamilton in August 1730, this pair proposed that James come to terms with the Whig and Tory opposition by promises of posts in his household, orders, pensions, offices, and titles to the leaders. These things were the easiest in the world to give when out of power; James made no objection to compiling a list of persons to be bought and the prices thought likely to fetch them.[51] William Pulteney was to have the Garter, an earldom, and possibly the revived office of Lord Treasurer; the Duke of Argyll was to retain his Hanoverian employments and have a further pension of £2000; Bathurst was to be a marquess and Secretary of State; Bolingbroke was also to be a marquess, but to be sent away as ambassador to France; Lord Gower was to be a Lord of the Bedchamber and an earl. Shippen, Wyndham, Lord Wilmington, the Dukes of Dorset and Somerset, the Earl of Berkeley, Daniel Pulteney, and Sir John "Rushwout" [52] were also on the list with others.

At once this seems ridiculous. Surely these men would not even consider such offers; but Pulteney obtained that earldom after Walpole's fall, and little else, because his heart was set on it, and Gower was accused by Dr. King of having sold himself to the Whigs for his own promotion.[53] Possibly these could be worked upon, although there were no doubt limits to their desires for titles; but some of the men on the list, like Argyll and Wilmington, could never have been brought over by this or any other device; and reliance on Bolingbroke, whose bitterness at his own past folly had turned to hatred of the Chevalier, would have been lunacy. James never took the project seriously; he was only to admit Ormonde and Atterbury to the secret of it,[54] and probably never found it worth while to tell anyone else. The Marquess of Blandford, who had been brought into the plan on the English side, was urged to get money from his grandmother, the old,

---

[51] James to the duchess and others, Jan. 31, 1731, W.S.P. 142, no. 99.
[52] Sir John Rushout, 4th Bart., of Northwick Park, Worcs., M.P. for Evesham, and an opponent of Walpole.
[53] King., 47–48.
[54] "L[ord] C[ornbury]'s paper," Jan. 1731, W.S.P. 142, no. 112.

wealthy, indestructible Duchess of Marlborough,[55] for the expenses of this or of some other plot.

Some of the persons to be benefitted were told of the rewards promised them (that could not hurt them, and might even cheer some of them up): Cornbury learned that he was to be a Lord of the Bedchamber, Ormonde that he was expected to be Governor to the princes, and Atterbury that he would be Archbishop of Canterbury, and receive "some other mark of my favor." [56] All of this suggests that there was a definite plan, which seems not to have survived anywhere, for a *coup d'état,* of which the first and "principal point as for England, is to gain as many persons considerable by their ranks and employments as is possible." [57] Officers in the army and fleet were to be promised their current ranks and commands if they behaved well and joined James. Posts in the government and household, however, were to be promised but sparingly. James II had tried to conquer England when he had the power, and to trick it when he imagined that he had the wit; James III had tried to woo her with promises made conscientiously in his early years, and to carry her off her feet in a popular rising in 1715, but had since been forced to base all his hopes on a foreign invasion to encourage the loyal party to take arms. Now, once only, he appears to attempt to buy the leaders of the country, bidding against George II.

He did not promise to change his own or his family's religion. "In two words, I and my children are catholics, and it is in vain to expect a change. . . What have my Protestant Subjects to fear after all the assurances I have, and shall be willing to give for the security of the Church of England; Or would they have the Royal ffamily to be the only persons in England constrained in points of Religion [?]" [58]

If the *coup d'état* should need a foreign regular force, Fleury was to be asked for it; Atterbury was approached by the French ministry in May 1731, for information of Jacobite plans,[59] which

[55] James to R. Arbuthnot, Feb. 3, *ibid.*, no. 122.
[56] W.S.P. 145, no. 35; vol. 144, no. 49; vol. 145, nos. 35, 36.
[57] James to the Duchess, Rome, May 13, 1731, W.S.P. 145, no. 58.
[58] W.S.P. 145, no. 58.
[59] Atterbury to James, Paris, May 28, *ibid.*, no. 145. See also Paul Vaucher, *Robert Walpole et la politique de Fleury* (Paris, 1924), 39–55.

furnished an opportunity to see him, with Dillon and Colonel Arthur Brett, an adherent of the Duchess of Buckingham. Orrery had chosen these as agents for the English Jacobites, who wished to govern the "treaty," if there were to be one.[60]

James decided against Dillon,[61] and secured his replacement by Daniel O'Brien, in conferences with Fleury and the *garde des sceaux*, Chauvelin.[62] The Duke of Berwick, however, in his last effort for his half-brother, gave him the good advice to abandon hope for foreign forces, regardless of promises, but to win the trust of the English Protestants.[63] Perhaps he knew already something of Fleury's plans for any future hostilities — he was destined to command a French army on the Rhine and be killed at Phillipsburg in 1734 — and how little attention was given in them to the aspirations of the Chevalier de St. Georges. Whatever his source, he was right: the French ministers had practically terminated their meetings with O'Brien and Brett in October 1731, and no more had been done than at the beginning of the year for foreign troops. Neither did the alternative, a rebellion, seem probable, when Lord Dundonald wrote querulously to tell his master that the reason why he had not written to Rome in the last nine months of 1731 was that there was nothing to write of in Scotland.[64]

The duchess's plan had proved a mare's nest. Fleury sent a Captain Hardy, deputed by the English to present plans, about his business, because he had brought insufficient detail.[65] The French regarded the matter as closed, whatever the party may have thought of it. In the summer of 1732 it was quiet and watched for opportunity. The Earl Marischal had come to Rome, but now left Italy; [66] and Ormonde gave up his dull post at Madrid to join Inverness and John Graeme at Avignon.[67] Inverness accepted Catholicism in late 1731, to Atterbury's disgust.[68] Ormonde being

[60] W.S.P. 146, no. 22; vol. 147, nos. 12, 48.
[61] W.S.P. 146, no. 95.
[62] James to O'Brien, Aug. 8, W.S.P. 147, no. 148.
[63] *Ibid.*, no. 155.
[64] Letter of Jan. 9, 1732, W.S.P. 151, no. 5.
[65] W.S.P. 154, no. 106.
[66] W.S.P. 155, no. 152; H.M.C. *Report* IX, app. II, 222.
[67] W.S.P. 156, no. 40.
[68] W.S.P. 151, no. 10; H.M.C. *Report* X, app. I, 178–81.

an old man, and Inverness useless, the English government did nothing to have them expelled.

At this time Atterbury and Orrery both died. It was natural that they should both have spent their lives in a cause with more sentimental appeal than hope of success. What is strange is that men of such "parts" could have judged badly so often, or that men thought shallow could feel so deeply. The Pretender sensed the loss keenly, for it left as chiefs in England only Cecil, the duchess, and Cornbury. It was not time for weakness or stupidity.

3. THE EXCISE BILL CRISIS

The approaching crisis of the Excise Bill was discerned in February 1733 by Captain Hardy. He suggested that if the French could be brought to see the popular irritation, occasioned by a drastic reform of the English government's haphazard but customary financial structure, as a sign of discontent with the Hanoverian dynasty — which to some extent it no doubt was — they might be persuaded to risk a few men and a little money.[69] The opposition to the Bill was consequently well reported [70] and encouraged. Not only were the Jacobites active, but Bolingbroke and his friends, linked almost openly with the French ambassador, Chavigny,[71] and a number of opposition Whigs. This being the case, the division on bringing in the bill on March 14, 1733 showed a trend against Walpole which surprised only a few of his friends. As the bill passed through subsequent stages the public became so aroused as to be hardly amenable to reason by the middle of April. The City of London gave instructions to its members against the bill; its Jacobite Lord Mayor, John Barber, used the moment for a "loyal" gathering in his house.[72] Lord Scarborough told Walpole that he could not vouch for his regiment. When the Common Council of London agreed to petition against the bill, the minister decided to drop it, and communicated his decision to the Commons on April 22, O.S.[73]

[69] W.S.P. 159, no. 132.

[70] *Ibid*, no. 145; vol. 160, nos. 21, 25, 41, 69.

[71] Anne-Théodore Chevignard de Chavigny (1687–1771), envoy of France at London since 1731. See Vaucher, *Robert Walpole*, 61n.

[72] W.S.P. 160, no. 21.

[73] Vaucher, *La Crise du ministère Walpole en 1733–34* (Paris, 1924), 19.

The posts across Europe were very slow, the ways unsure, and waiting tantalizing. Prince James Sobieski offered his family's influence to his son-in-law in the coming election of a King of Poland; James declined, suggesting Prince Henry, a boy of eight, as a possible candidate: "Je vous avoue que mon coeur et mon inclination me portent tout entier pour ma propre patrie; dont les loix et les interests ont toujours fait mon etude principale." [74] Whether the preoccupation with events in England or recognition of a fool's errand was responsible for this decision, it was wise.

Chavigny saw Bolingbroke and Jacobites on many occasions in the following months. Chavigny was convinced that Walpole was not alone in his peril, that George II's crown was also at stake, but felt that the Jacobites were out of the picture because of the personality of the Chevalier. Montijo, the Spanish ambassador, thought as he did, and believed that France and Spain together could do the work of a restoration, for which Chavigny believed that a son of the Pretender would be a better choice, if he could be removed from his father's tutelage. [75]

To that the main body of real Jacobites was opposed, but their hopes soared, all the same. A set of declarations was prepared, as always in emergencies, which were never distributed. [76] The Scottish Declaration, with pledges "to advance Trade, Relieve the Poor, and . . . be particularly sollicitous to Settle, encourage & maintain the Fishry of the Nation," and its offer of freedom from feudal obligations to vassals of "such as . . . obstinately persist in their Rebellion," is first. One to the City of London promises return to the older Charter, and, inexplicably, "to employ the properest & most Secure methods . . . that Trade & Commerce may once more flourish again [sic], and Our Native City be Restored to its ancient wealth & Splendor." Evidently merchants of the City had, as Sir Lewis Namier says, been making their flesh creep with tales of the decay of trade.

[74] Letter dated Rome, March 28, H.M.C. *Report* X, app. I, 164.
[75] Chavigny to Chauvelin, London, April 23, Affaires étrangères, Correspondance Politique, Angleterre (henceforth cited as Corr. Pol. Ang.) 380, foll. 89–95.
[76] Declarations to Scotland and England, April 23, 1733, W.S.P. 161, nos. 3, 6; to the City of London, *ibid.*, no. 4; to the army and fleet, *ibid.*, nos. 8, 10; Letter to the Universities, *ibid.*, no. 13. All are MS.

The declaration designed for England begins with a list of grievances which comes close to a compilation of complaints made in such publications of the constitutional opposition as the *Craftsman*.

We have seen the Treasures of the Nation applyed to satiate private avarice, and lavished for the support of German Dominions, or for the carrying on ambicious views, always forreign, & often contrary, to the true intrest of the Nation. We have beheld with astonishment an universal corruption & dissolution of manners [77] . . . And a tacite connivance given to all Irreligion & Immorality by the Convocations not being allowed to sit. . . The Manufactures of England are visibly going to decay. Trade has been neglected, & even discouraged.

As an answer to this list of real and imaginary problems, James promised, at last "to Protect Support and Maintain the Church of England as by Law established, in all her Rights, privileges and immunities whatsoever; We shall constantly allow the Convocation to sit and act according to Law during each Session of Parliament." Besides, Parliament was to be kept free and uncorrupted, and to settle with James "all that may relate to the wellfare of the Kingdom, both in civil & Ecclesiastical matters." A toleration would be granted; and it was hoped that "Party-division and distinction" would be abolished by a policy of promotion and reward of "men of merit & probity, who are true Lovers of their Countrey, & of the Church of England as by Law Established," suggesting the later doctrine of Bolingbroke. The princes, Charles and Henry, would be brought to England for their education, it was stated, "in those principles of love for their Countrey, & esteem for the people, Laws & Government of it." A bloodless revolution would please the Pretender better than civil war, he concludes.

The other declarations consist of recognition of the vested interests of the army, navy, and universities, if they behave so as to merit it.

When the bill was withdrawn, the news was received jubilantly. At Oxford an indignant Reverend Mr. Meadowcourt wrote from

[77] This is a frequent Jacobite complaint. See J. Maxwell of Kirkconnell's *Narrative of Charles Prince of Wales' Expedition to Scotland. . .* (Edinburgh, 1841), 5–7.

Merton College: "The night that the news came here that the excise bill was dropp'd, bonfires were made, moppets with stars and blue garters were burnt. . . The next night the mob was entertained again with bonfires and moppets. Great number of gowns-men appear'd openly in the streets, throwing money amongst the rabble, and reviving the old cries of Ormond, Bolingbroke, king James for ever, &c." [78] The use of Bolingbroke's name suggests that the mob was either not so much Jacobite as opposition, or was ignorant of the events of the preceding seventeen years.

The labor of Walpole's enemies was now to keep up the heat they had made. Their ability to get the people on their side was demonstrated, but they needed both measures to combat and counter-measures to propose; on these they were divided, and on nothing so much as the Pretender. "Ils avouent bien qu'ils ne peuvent avoir pis que ce qu'ils ont," Chavigny wrote to Chauvelin on May 22, "mais ce n'est pas la peine de changer Si ce n'est en mieux. Ils se replient Sur les enfans, et voudroient etablir Sur eux leurs esperances. . ." Lord Mayor Barber displayed portraits of the young princes in his rooms.[79] Chavigny inclined more and more to that plan. Loyalty to James had been dissipated by forty-five years of exile, during which public affairs had come into the hands of men who "ne Sont attachés a la famille de Stuart ny par des obligations personnelles, ny par des engagemens d'honneur, ny par des sermens." The public debt of nearly fifty millions had created a gigantic interest in its security. The best the Jacobites could do was to hide in the crowd of the opposition for the time.[80]

The principal Jacobites now — Ormonde, O'Brien, and Cornbury — had not let the French interest pass. Cornbury went over to France in June and persuaded Chauvelin to promise an expedition to England within the year.[81] The dropping of the bill had not, it appeared, closed the opening for a well-supported

[78] Coxe, *Walpole*, III, 137.
[79] Corr. Pol. Ang. 380, foll. 201–03.
[80] Letter to Chauvelin, June 30, 1733 (misdated July 1), Corr. Pol. Ang. 380, foll. 328–329.
[81] W.S.P. 162, no. 124; vol. 163, no. 8.

invasion.[82] War between England and France seemed certain, and not only to James: later in the year, Keene, the English ambassador at Madrid, obtained a copy of a secret treaty signed on November 7 by France and Spain, the terms of which called for a joint war with England, among other things, for the restitution of Gibraltar.[83] Walpole did not want war. The opposition, under Chavigny's spell, wished to enter the Polish Succession war then commencing between Austria and France, on the French side, while George II wanted to fight in alliance with Austria, and chafed at Walpole's caution when the two continental powers resorted to arms in October, and England remained neutral.

There was no certainty, of course, that Walpole could always control the situation: Chavigny continued to play with the notion of restoring Prince Charles or Prince Henry, and Bolingbroke was in the thick of his deliberations.[84] Lord Gower feared, the ambassador wrote to Chauvelin, that France might either precipitate a civil war in England, or attempt to conquer her; "Rassurés sur ces craintes, edifié de nos principes d'equité et de moderation, Il delibere serieusement sur les moyens de menager une revolution." Among all those who had reason to fear a change or to hope for it, there was no one who did not foresee it sooner or later.[85] These were not Jacobite desires, however. If he had had any, Cecil wrote later, Chavigny discarded them when Bolingbroke persuaded him that most Tories did not look over the water for leadership.[86] Cecil must have known, if he had taken time to think, that the French knew that the strength of the Pretender's real friends had declined, and that the opposition was a new and independent faction. That Chavigny's opinions were largely based on suggestions of Bolingbroke, however, is probable. It was upon the advice of the ambassador that Fleury bestowed a subsidy on that noble lord.[87]

Chavigny did not determine French policy: the French govern-

[82] Hardy to O'Brien, April 17 O.S., W.S.P. 161, no. 37.
[83] Vaucher, *Robert Walpole*, 75.
[84] Corr. Pol. Ang. 381, foll. 8–31v; fol. 84.
[85] *Ibid.*, foll. 113–116v.
[86] Letter to James, Dec. 30, 1733, W.S.P. 167, no. 32.
[87] Bolingbroke to the marquis de Matignon, June 30, cited by Vaucher, *La Crise*, 37; Chauvelin to Bolingbroke, July 20, *ibid.*, 38n.

ment had for some time been informed of the Jacobite weakness and lack of leaders, and knew itself unable to provide the fourteen thousand men necessary; [88] thus it was delighted by George II's decision, made in November,[89] to remain neutral. Fleury and Chauvelin awaited it, in spite of the tempting report of David Avery (later proved to be unauthorized) that six of the principal aldermen and twelve Common Councilmen of the City were anxious for the Pretender's return,[90] until enthusiasm, Cecil wrote in December, had melted away.[91] As always, the Jacobites were left alone when they were weak.

4. THE PRETENDER AS MEDIATOR

Early in the next year O'Brien returned to the attack upon the French, no doubt to their dismay. Chauvelin bluntly told him on March 29 that France could not attack England without the advantage of surprise before a declaration of war. The election struggle provided material for endless discussions at London, Rome, and Paris as to how Walpole's possible defeat should be exploited. A man named "Cockburn," who may or may not have been one of several Jacobites of that name, turned out reams of reports on the political state of England,[92] but did not encourage his master, who began to perceive the hopelessness of trying to bring over the opposition Whigs: "It would seem a Paradox, but it is but too true That I have less reason to hope well now in my great affairs than I have had this great while." [93] Walpole, pressed hard by his enemies in the developing struggle, asserted that the Jacobites were the major force in the opposition, and that he feared the Pretender would be the only gainer by his fall.[94] A Latin prophecy was circulated which pointed to a restoration in 1734:

[88] O'Brien to James, Oct. 9, 1733, W.S.P. 165, no. 111.
[89] Vaucher, Robert Walpole, 85.
[90] W.S.P. 165, no. 233; vol. 166, nos. 2-2A, 82.
[91] W.S.P. 167, no. 32.
[92] E.g. W.S.P. 168, no. 122, on the tea, coffee, and chocolate excise, and W.S.P. 169, no. 119, on withdrawals from the sinking fund.
[93] Letter to Inese, Rome, April 28, 1734, W.S.P. 170, no. 17.
[94] Coxe, I, 425; Vaucher, Robert Walpole, 65.

Cum Marcus cantabit Hallelujah,
Et Antonius Veni Creator,
Et Joannes Baptista Coenabit,
Tum regnabit et triumphabit rex in Anglia Jacobus III.[95]

Regardless of the coincidence of fixed and movable feasts, and the credulity of those who would accept a prophecy made up, it is probable, by some scribbling cleric for party use, the year passed without either the eclipse of Walpole or the emergence of any good reasons for the Pretender's friends to expect any profit if it should ever come. The election, it is true, reduced the numbers of Walpole's Whig majority, and the Jacobites united with the rest of the opposition, Whig and Tory, to harass the government. Their assistance was very welcome to some quite sincere supporters of the Protestant succession, especially those from Scotland. Robert Dundas, for instance, complained, "Such a set of Peers [as those chosen in 1734 to represent Scotland] I think we never had set up and forced through. . . . As to the elections of our commoners . . . such liberties were taken by the sheriffs and returning officers, and such barefaced things done, as power and a majority can alone screen and justify." Again, "there are a far greater number of opposers in the House of Commons . . . and, to be sure, the generality of the whole nation [is] quite dissatisfied both with our M - - - - r and his measures, but, as they have a majority in the house, corruption and oppression in elections will probably increase it." [96]

Not only did the Scots resent the rapid annexation of the Scottish representation to the government for right or wrong, but Walpole's corrupt practices and quasi-illegal actions provoked the aged Duchess of Marlborough: "It amazes me, that the people should so soon forget that King James lost his crown, who was a good manager for the public, without breaking any law, but what proceeded from his weakness of having a mind that everybody should attend him in heaven by establishing popery here." [97] The duchess seems to have come full circle since 1688.

<hr>

[95] Mahon, app. to II, lxix.
[96] G.W.T. Omond, ed., *The Arniston Memoirs* (Edinburgh, 1887), 81.
[97] Sir George Henry Rose, ed., *Selections from the Papers of the Earls of Marchmont* (London, 1831), II, 31.

The Jacobites, dissident Whigs, and Hanover Tories, then, drew together more closely in early 1735 than before. Jacobite peers, including Lords Dundonald, Gower, and others, met with Dundas, Lords Stair, Carteret, and Bathurst, and the Dukes of Montrose, Queensberry, and Bolton.[98] Stair wrote at the end of the following year to Lord Marchmont, "It is very true, that in the opposition we have made to the ministers' measures, we have had the assistance of many persons, who have been called by name of Tories; but I am very far from being ashamed to take the assistance of Tories to preserve our constitution." [99] He knew very well that some of his "Tories" — for example Sir John Hynde Cotton [100] — were notorious supporters of James III.

Nor was this coalition unimportant, for there is reason to believe that Walpole would have done much to prevent it. Avery, whose mission to France in 1733 may have been made at Walpole's desire, suggested to O'Brien in the summer of 1734 that Thomas Winnington, then a junior lord of the Admiralty, might be a proper channel of communication with his chief. O'Brien did write to Walpole, and told James what he had done. The Pretender, at any rate, was not deceived; his reply was that "wherever Walpole is concerned, one cannot bee too cautious and circumspect; his character and his circumstances make it impossible to depend on him, though it would be still good to gain him, if one runs no risque by it." [101]

Thomas Carte, an accomplice of Avery in whatever he was doing, although perhaps without knowledge of its full implications, encouraged the Jacobite agent at Paris to believe that "particular affronts" had estranged Walpole from George II.[102] It was vainly hoped that Winnington would arrange an interview with O'Brien at some neutral place; and, although Avery claimed to have seen Walpole at his London house, and to have been told by the minister himself that the object of all his thoughts was an agreement with the Pretender,[103] James refused to write directly

[98] *Ibid.*, II, 57–67; Omond, 83–84.
[99] Rose, II, 81.
[100] Graham, II, 275.
[101] Letter of Sept. 1, 1734, H.M.C. *Report* XV, app. II, 235.
[102] W.S.P. 174, no. 68.
[103] O'Brien to James, Paris, Nov. 7, *ibid.*, nos. 186–186B.

to Walpole, because he did not believe that Avery was the bearer of a sincere proposal. Walpole either had some "ill design," or else Avery was lying.[104] When he was sent back to England with a warning from O'Brien that it was useless to return without some proofs of the sincerity of the minister,[105] he disappeared for years from Jacobite correspondence.

James had judged rightly, and acted on his judgment by sending a letter to his friends in England urging those in Parliament to join the opposition.[106] It was the best he could do.

Shortly after, in January 1735, Clementina died, leaving two sons, Prince Charles and Henry, Duke of York, and a claim to the Sobieski estates and other possessions. Her marriage had been acclaimed in 1719 by supporters of the Stuarts as a stroke of policy, and by the world in general as a feat of daring. Her life had been short, disturbed, and, in its own way, devout; but she had been a curse to her husband for the last ten years of her life, and her death was a relief to all who knew her.

Spain and France had had a certain amount of success in their war with the Emperor: Spain had done very well, having employed an army under Liria (who now succeeded his father as Duke of Berwick) to occupy the kingdom of Naples for Don Carlos; France had done less well, and had given up the cause of Stanislas Leczynski in Poland for the more important purpose of securing something for herself. To this end she was disposed to act independently of her ally.

The Jacobites at Paris and Rome learned of this disposition soon enough. Already Horatio Walpole and Lord Waldegrave, English ambassador at Paris, were concerned in the mediation of peace between Louis XV and Charles VI. Fleury stated his terms, very high ones, in December 1734. There seemed to be every expectation that the Emperor would refuse them, but Fleury set them even higher in February 1735. The English made counter-suggestions for a pacification at the end of that month, finally rejected in early April by the French *conseil royal*.[107] Fleury, then,

[104] James to O'Brien, Dec. 1, W.S.P. 175, no. 108; James to O'Brien, Dec. 6, *ibid.*, no. 138.
[105] O'Brien to James, Dec. 27, 1734, W.S.P. 176, no. 52.
[106] *Ibid.*, no. 90.
[107] Vaucher, *Robert Walpole*, 111–35.

decided against mediation by England, and cast about for more convenient means. These lay ready to hand in the Jacobites. They had not been ignorant of Walpole's attempt in the winter, but had been resigned to the conclusion of the war through the English and Dutch as instruments. In February Chauvelin had refused any comfort to O'Brien.[108] Before the end of April, however, he told him that France was willing to treat with the Emperor through new channels, and desired that the Imperial ministers should be so informed.[109] This was accordingly done by O'Rourke, the Pretender's agent in Vienna, in the middle of May; but already that court had asked the Pretender to discover French views on preliminary conferences. James's letters to this effect reached Chauvelin at the end of the month.[110] This suggests collusion, perhaps the result of a hint in the customary annual complimentary letter of Fleury, as a cardinal, to the Emperor.

James naturally threw his resources in to the gap with enthusiasm, with dreams of a mediator's reward ranging from the secure possession of the Ohlau estate when Prince James Sobieski should die to the satisfaction of his need for foreign troops. An archduchess might even be obtained for marriage to Prince Charles, who was now fifteen.[111] In June he offered the services of Daniel O'Brien and Owen O'Rourke to the French for more definite advances to the Emperor.[112] On the other hand he almost simultaneously encouraged the Imperial court to offer to send an emissary to a meeting with one from France.[113] The Emperor, he knew, would like to bring the Maritime Powers into the discussions, but it was thought that if he did not succeed he would ask for the dispatch of an envoy to Vienna. O'Brien offered himself in that capacity, but was not accepted.[114] Fleury was willing to send an instructed agent to Italy or elsewhere, but not to Vienna.[115]

[108] O'Brien to James, Paris, Feb. 14, W.S.P. 177, no. 142.
[109] James to O'Rourke, Rome, May 14, W.S.P. 179, no. 83. This letter dates the commencement of the approaches to Vienna several weeks earlier than May 30, when Professor Vaucher believed it to have begun.
[110] Vaucher, Robert Walpole, 147.
[111] O'Rourke to James, Vienna, July 2, 1735, W.S.P. 180, no. 144.
[112] Ibid., no. 65.
[113] Ibid., no. 92.
[114] Vaucher, Robert Walpole, 147.
[115] O'Brien to James, Paris, July 11, W.S.P. 181, no. 8.

Bologna was mentioned, but rejected by Chauvelin, who suggested instead Lorraine or Basle. O'Brien was asked to find a trustworthy messenger to carry letters to the ministers at Vienna — something of a tribute to his discretion,[116] and perhaps a contradiction of Professor Vaucher's belief that Fleury did not want to use Jacobites in his enterprise.[117] It may be that he was willing to use less well-known agents than the man who had been James's *chargé d'affaires* at Paris for more than a decade.

This plan was dropped, but a letter dictated by Chauvelin to O'Brien on July 23 was sent to Rome and forwarded, proposing a meeting of emissaries "en lieu tiers." [118] This letter was the end of negotiation by way of Rome. A parallel work had been done by the Count of Wied as French agent at Vienna since May 18, when he first presented a message from Fleury to the Imperial Chancellor, Sinzendorff.[119] The Pretender first learned of the Emperor's preference for other means of discussion in September,[120] and preliminary articles were signed on October 3. Fleury did not announce this conclusion until the beginning of November, but O'Rourke, at Vienna, had obtained information about it two weeks before.[121]

The eminent Professor Vaucher is of the opinion that the whole correspondence "n'a jamais été prise au sérieux" at Vienna or at Paris, but was to be dust in the eyes of the Jacobites, whose activity might otherwise be indiscreet and troublesome. He may be right, but the "concealment" was rather elaborate for such a result, and discovery by Spain that France was disregarding her obligations as an ally by attempting to make a separate peace, either through the Jacobites or otherwise, would have endangered their relations, perhaps before France had obtained the advantages for which she strove. A completely irresponsible set of intriguers would not, in all probability, be trusted with such a thing. It is similarly improbable that the Imperial ministers would have wished a failure to make peace. One would be safe in be-

---

[116] O'Brien to James, Paris, July 15, *ibid.*, nos. 33–33A.
[117] *Robert Walpole*, 147.
[118] A copy taken at Rome is W.S.P. 181, no. 67.
[119] Vaucher, *Robert Walpole*, 148–49.
[120] *Ibid.*, 147; James to O'Brien, Sept. 21, 1735, W.S.P. 182, no. 162.
[121] Letter to James, Oct. 22, W.S.P. 183, no. 106.

lieving that Fleury and Sinzendorff were not sure that the Wied channel would be satisfactory, and wished to keep at least one other open until they were. Even after the signature of the preliminaries O'Rourke did not despair, as he would have done if he had thought himself a dupe, but predicted the very alliance of France and the Empire that James so much desired.[122] It was as certain as death that he could do nothing without it, for as he wrote to Ormonde at the end of November, his friends were too disunited to restore him alone.[123] He might have added that they were too few.

Fleury had, it appears, more important aims; and General George Hamilton, now in favor at Vienna, had no more influence there with Count von Starhemberg in this matter than O'Brien had had at Paris.[124] So 1735 was brought to an end and 1736 began.

And so that year continued. France and Spain did not agree on the peace: O'Brien first received this information from the secretary of the Spanish ambassador at Paris,[125] and then from the ambassador himself, with a hint that James ought to promise the restitution of Port Mahon and Gibraltar. James made no difficulty about those terms in September, when the ambassador conveyed his opinion that an invasion should be made that year or never, public opinion being ripe, the Dutch lethargic, and Spain properly equipped for such an undertaking.[126] He did not insist that Jamaica should be promised to Spain, although she wanted it, because of the certain unpopularity of such a bargain. Nevertheless, in October the project was postponed until spring.[127] There was a similar, but less long-drawn-out failure at Vienna,[128] and the Pretender conceded that further work was futile until the expected conclusion of the final peace terms.

[122] *Ibid.*
[123] W.S.P. 184, no. 92.
[124] *Ibid.*, no. 104A; vol. 185, no. 106.
[125] O'Brien to James, April 2, 1736, W.S.P. 186, no. 116. (Another letter written by him earlier that day is in no. *115*.)
[126] O'Brien to James, Paris, Sept. 2, W.S.P. 189, no. 95.
[127] O'Brien to James, Oct. 22, W.S.P. 190, no. 145.
[128] James to O'Brien, Oct. 17, *ibid.*, no. 109; Vaucher, *Robert Walpole*, 178.

7

RUIN

(1 7 3 7 – 1 7 4 6)

It would seem that James III's pretensions had reached the condition of a suit in Chancery, with its monstrous expense, great numbers of barristers and solicitors, and innumerable pleadings and proceedings — with no end, the papers being always referred back "for the present." The man had grown old in a cause which had commenced when he was scarcely born, and had never considered that it would be wise to withdraw. Any man now (historians have only to look back, not to prophesy) can see that he was in its clutches, wasting his energies in claims when his only profit must have lain in renunciation. James had to foresee, not to recall; his temperament and training were absolutely averse to compromise with the forces of absolute evil, as he saw it, which upheld the Revolution Settlement.

Let us consider. James had been reared by an absolutist father, and in a particularly Puritan way. To him there was no question that a king's prerogative was to command, as the subject's duty was to obey. The king might, as James often did, yield portions of that prerogative to the representatives of the people, or to ministers responsible to those representatives, but the prerogative was his until he gave it up freely; it could not be wrenched from him by force. Such an usurpation was the sin of taking from a man that which belonged to him, and by the constitutional theory taught to James, everything belonging to the royal power was, and must be, the property of the right heir by the customary

English rules of succession. How much more than encroachment was dethronement a sin — a sin spread to all ranks in England, with its guilt tainting the common life to bring upon all Englishmen destruction, temporal or eternal, or perhaps both. Renunciation carried in itself here, a guilt, that of the great refusal to strive to put things right, and to relieve the nation of a burden under which, unwittingly, it labored.

Besides, there were now the young princes to consider. Prince Charles had rights which James could not surrender for him. Every year that passed brought him closer and closer to the world stage, upon which, as yet, his father had only allowed him to appear once, on an excursion in 1734 to the siege of Gaeta, in the company of his cousin, the Duke of Liria and Berwick. This kind of action was intended to show signs of spirit in the boy, and a letter purporting to be the work of Liria was printed and distributed in England. It was now proposed by O'Brien that he should make a tour of Europe, with a stay in Flanders, where Englishmen might meet him as they passed on their way to Spa or Aix-la-chapelle.[1] The journey was not even pondered: there was still no country bold enough to receive any member of that family.

Thus the strength of the party in England was James III's main concern. He had come to believe that a paper not directly authorized to speak for him might be a great convenience, in August 1736,[2] if the right man could be found to be its editor, and worthy contributors could be brought to lend their pens. In October Charles Molloy, "a man of good character, & who has been already used to such sort of matters," offered his services as editor if James would help defray his expenses. Colonel Cecil was therefore asked to speak to some friends on that head.[3] Molloy had formerly contributed to *Fog's Journal*; he proposed to begin a new paper early in 1737. Whether he only intended from the first to get money from the Jacobites, or found that with the collaboration of Chesterfield and others, even perhaps Pope,[4] he

[1] Letter to James, Jan. 28, 1737, W.S.P. 193, no. 133A.
[2] James to O'Brien, Rome, Aug. 29, 1736, W.S.P. 189, no. 80.
[3] W.S.P. 190, no. 12. For a further elaboration of this matter, see my note in *The Review of English Studies*, vol. IV, no. 14 (April 1953), 144.
[4] O'Brien to James, Paris, Feb. 4, 1737, W.S.P. 194, no. 10B.

could afford independence of his backers, is not certain. *Common Sense, or the Englishman's Journal,* as it was called, showed, regardless of intentions, more of the marks of the opposition Whig than of the Tory. Of the known contributors only Dr. William King was a Jacobite. *Common Sense* was not one of the Jacobite successes: England went on her way unmoved.

The Scots had been only in irregular correspondence since the appointment of Dundonald as chief manager. On May 29, 1737, he died; Colonel James Urquhart communicated the news to James Edgar,[5] the Pretender's chief secretary, and was himself appointed to succeed Dundonald in August.[6] The Porteous riots showed Scotland to have at least some rebellious elements, and might, James thought, be used[7] to persuade Spain or some other nation (Spain was most interested in contriving George II's ruin) to intervene, but his followers in England were timid, insisting on having 12,000 regular troops,[8] and Spain was paralyzed: as Liria-Berwick said, "The Ministry in Spain is taken up just now with nothing else but with seeking meanes to find mony to pay the debts and carry on the current expences for Patigno has left the finances in such desorder that it is a down wright labyrinthe." [9]

John Gordon of Glenbucket, a laird, but no chieftain, well-known and respected in the Highlands, was commissioned by Macdonald of Glengarry and General Alexander Gordon of Auchintoul[10] to go to Rome at the end of 1737 to get authority for a rebellion with or without foreign assistance, which the Pretender would join.[11] Glenbucket brought his information to O'Brien in Paris in late November, causing fears in the agent's

---

[5] Letter of June 6, W.S.P. 197, no. 108.
[6] Edgar to Urquhart, Aug. 8, W.S.P. 199, no. 184. Urquhart (1691–1741) was the son of Jonathan Urquhart of Cromartie. Blaikie, *Origins of the 'Forty-Five,* xxiiin.
[7] James to O'Brien, Aug. 1, W.S.P. 199, no. 151.
[8] Cecil to James, July 7, *ibid.,* no. 4.
[9] W.S.P. 198, no. 92. See Maclachlan, *Trade and Peace with Old Spain* (Cambridge, 1940), 146–154.
[10] General Gordon had been a major-general in the Russian service, which he entered in 1693, and had commanded Mar's army in the interval between Mar's embarcation and its dissolution in 1716. He was too old to come out in 1745, and died in 1752. Blaikie, 25n.
[11] *Ibid.;* Glenbucket's memorial to James, W.S.P. 204, no. 114.

mind that it might lead James astray,[12] but without grounds. When James received Glenbucket at Rome, in January 1738, he wrote to O'Brien, who was now more at home in French than in English, "Je trouve quil ne porte rien de positif & de solide, que de ce qui regarde les Montagnards. . . Il n'apporte quasi aucun message ou assurance particuliere d'aucun de la Noblesse du Plat Pais" nor from the Presbyterians or other doubtful groups. Therefore he sent Glenbucket back to Scotland with an independent agent, who would scout the Lowlands for friends, and also get in touch with the English Jacobites.[13]

This agent was William Hay, a brother of Inverness who had gone to Russia to treat with Peter the Great a dozen years back. His instructions, dated February 19, 1738, were "to see as many considerable people as possible & as few as can be of others," to estimate the strength of the "Patriot party," and to speak to prominent Presbyterians of an assurance that the religious establishment would be referred to a free parliament. An attempt must be made to gauge the strength of support expected in a rising with, or without, foreign regulars, and to reach agreement with as many factions as possible.[14] From this mission can be traced the catena of circumstances which led slowly and deviously to the Rebellion of 1745.

The Pretender had never relaxed his efforts to use his friends in Parliament to show not only the weakness of Walpole, but in the nation "a direct inclination to my Person & Family." Cecil was to lead the "honest men" in Parliament and the City of London to demonstrate as violently as possible in favor of the claims made against Spain by merchants trading in the West Indies, which would lead to war with Philip V and all that it might bring with it.[15] In this way James had always been an enemy to the peace of Europe. That the claims could cause war was a shrewd judgment, at a distance of eighteen months, but a state of war could not create a powerful Spanish navy, nor make Jacobites of Spanish ministers: Alberoni and Ripperda had

[12] W.S.P. 202, no. 105.
[13] James to O'Brien, Rome, Jan. 20, 1738, W.S.P. 204, no. 55.
[14] W.S.P. 205, no. 6.
[15] James to Cecil, Dec. 10, 1737, W.S.P. 203, no. 4.

fallen in turn, and Liria-Berwick, once a powerful favorite, was dying of tuberculosis in the south of Italy; [16] the present ministers were not those formerly advised by Lawless, or Sir Toby Bourke.[17] So little desirous were they to be linked with the Pretender that Pierre de Tencin, archbishop of Embrun, then being considered for the French embassy at Madrid, was passed over because his Jacobite connections were not pleasing to the court of the Catholic King.[18]

These feelings did not interfere with the Marquis of La Mina's flirting with O'Brien to discover the Pretender's strength and plans. The Jacobite agent had interviews with the Spanish ambassador to France at Paris on January 7 and 8, 1738.[19] O'Brien prepared a memorial lamenting that the standing army of England obstructed the almost unanimous desire of the nation to seat James III on the throne of his ancestors, and recalling opportunities let slip by France in recent years. Now, he said, the Highlanders and Scottish lords had deputed a man of great importance (who could only have been Glenbucket) to concert a rising with the Pretender at Rome. Ten or twelve thousand men would be sufficient, with the addition of Scottish and English volunteers, to overthrow the government of George II, as he attempts to show by an enumeration of the English army.[20] La Mina took this document and said nothing; at a later interview he stipulated that James must promise to restore Gibraltar and Port Mahon, and must get Fleury to be a party to the invasion, although England and Spain would combine afterward to force France to keep its obligations under the settlement of Utrecht. O'Brien and James both agreed to this,[21] but O'Brien found his conferences with Fleury, Amelot (the French minister for foreign affairs),[22] and

---

[16] James Edward Francis Fitzjames, Duke of Liria and Berwick, Earl of Tynemouth, and grandee of Spain, born 1696, died near Naples in June 1738. Lart, I, 39; W.S.P. 207, nos. 65, 78.

[17] Morel-Fatio, *Recueil des instructions . . . Espagne*, III, 47, 423–24.

[18] *Ibid.*, III, 189n.

[19] O'Brien to James, Paris, Jan. 9, W.S.P. 203, no. 165.

[20] *Ibid.*, no. 166.

[21] O'Brien to James, Paris, Jan. 13, W.S.P. 204, no. 17A; James to O'Brien, April 16, W.S.P. 206, no. 33.

[22] J.-J. Amelot de Chaillou (1689–1749), Secretary of State for Foreign Affairs, 1737–44.

Pecquet, Amelot's *premier commis,* perfectly fruitless.[23] La Mina had obtained all the information he needed without giving anything in return.

The Pretender knew, and acknowledged to Ormonde in April, that he could not do without regular troops whatever Captain Hay might report, and that Fleury was unwilling to supply them or to allow Spain to supply them, so that the best thing to do was to persuade the Spanish ministers to make a bargain independent of French inclinations.[24] Since a small force was to be had more easily than a large one, O'Brien showed a way in which he thought that nine thousand men could carry the enterprise by simultaneous landings at Milford Haven and in Scotland.[25] The Spanish ambassador then at London, Thomas Geraldino (formerly Fitzgerald) could be applied to by Cecil to build up the Spanish opinion of the party.[26]

Captain William Hay returned to Paris from England in June 1738, saw O'Brien, and went on to Rome,[27] leaving behind him material which either convinced the Spanish ambassador or found him willing to seem so. The agent at Paris asked for ten thousand men, and actually received an offer, sincere or not, of twice that number, to be embarked under cover of an expedition to Africa or of reinforcement of Spanish garrisons in Italy.[28] This was beyond O'Brien's hopes, but on the strength of it he made plans which allotted a large force for encouragement of the timid English, with a secondary effort to be made in Scotland.[29]

Hay's report, made when he reached Rome, was cautious: the Lowlands would be hard to raise; arms were scarce in the Highlands; the "patriot party," otherwise opposition Whigs, would be governed entirely by their own interests, joining in a rising only when certain of success; the Presbyterians, however, might be neutral; the Drummond influence was both great and favor-

---

[23] O'Brien to James, Paris, April 21, W.S.P. 206, no. 57.
[24] Letter of April 22, *ibid.,* no. 62.
[25] Memorial of May 5, *ibid.,* no. 108.
[26] James to Cecil, May 28, W.S.P. 207, no. 43. Geraldino was on good terms with the opposition in general. Coxe, I, 577.
[27] O'Brien to James, June 13, W.S.P. 207, no. 83.
[28] *Ibid.,* no. 89.
[29] *Ibid.,* no. 123.

able; and Urquhart was in high regard and very able.[30] Ormonde had been informed of Hay's account and suggested that a rebellion ought to have more definite information for a beginning, and that accredited envoys to France and Spain must use it, when available, to get troops.[31]

Hay was followed by the adventurer, Drummond of Balhaldy or Bohaldy,[32] who pretended to carry such information as Ormonde thought necessary, representing an association of Scotsmen, of whom the most important were the third Duke of Perth [33] and his uncle "old Lord John" Drummond.[34] Another faction, a smaller one, sent its leader, "young Lord John," Perth's brother,[35] whose abstention from the association was probably caused by Balhaldy's inclusion. The latter was a man of little or no reputation, characterized by Lord Elcho as "a low-lifed fellow, void of truth." [36] On his arrival at Rome early in December, he submitted a memorial from the members of the association, with assurances from the "most considerable of the clans," and especially from old Lord Lovat of the Scots plot of 1704, whose ambitions, now extending to a dukedom, once more lured him into trouble. The association had divided Scotland into districts, each under its supervisor — Argyllshire for Sir James Campbell of Auchinbreck, "the Island Clans and those about him" for Cameron of Lochiel, "the bréas of the highlands" for Perth, and "those he vouches for" for Lovat, who was canny to the last. Lord Linton, eldest son of the Earl of Traquair,[37] was also a member. The whole association supported Lovat's desire for promotion in the peerage.[38]

"Young Lord John" reached Rome in early February with in-

[30] W.S.P. 208, no. 87.

[31] *Ibid.*, no. 85.

[32] Drummond's proscribed real name was Macgregor, but he was generally known by this place name, sometimes spelled Balhady, Bochaldy, or Bohadie.

[33] James Drummond, Duke of Perth (1713–1746).

[34] John Drummond (1679–1757) succeeded his nephews in their titular · dukedom in 1747.

[35] John Drummond (1714–1747) succeeded as fourth duke in 1746.

[36] John Murray of Broughton, *Memorials* (Edinburgh, 1898), 51.

[37] Charles Stewart, styled Lord Linton (d. 1764), succeeded his father in 1741 as fifth Earl of Traquair.

[38] W.S.P. 212, nos. 79–79C.

formation [39] in agreement with Hay's report; James wrote to O'Brien on February 15, "Je voye avec peine quil y a peu d'union parmis mes amis en Ecosse, Cependant Je ne doute point quils ne s'unissent touts pour me servir, quand une bonne occasion s'en presentera. Mais pour pouvoir faire cela efficacement, il leur faut un appuy certain où d'Angleterre où de Troupes etrangeres." [40] At the moment the signature of the convention of January 14, 1739, appeared to postpone indefinitely the whole affair,[41] for England and Spain by its terms agreed to settle, on rather low terms for England, the claims of her merchants against Spain for the depredations, or legitimate operations, of Spain's coast guards in the New World.

To offset this major disappointment there were two minor but very satisfying successes. The disputed estate of Prince James Sobieski, who had died in 1737, was the first of these. By Polish law, foreigners could not inherit estates in that country — in 1735 it had been proposed to obtain the "indigenat" for Prince Henry, the titular Duke of York, to secure the Polish portion of the inheritance.[42] But there was no obstacle to the princes' taking their share of the Austrian portion, the estate of Ohlau in Silesia, except the equal claim of the duchesse de Bouillon, Clementina's sister, to the whole inheritance, which was only allowable if the Imperial court had, as it had, a motive for deciding against the house of Stuart, whatever the rights and wrongs of the case might be. Prince James, however, had been persuaded before his death to make over his family jewels, in pawn at Rome, to his Stuart grandchildren, and also his loan of 400,000 Rhenish florins in satisfaction of which he held Ohlau as a fief of the Emperor.[43] When the duchesse de Bouillon contested her father's disposal of his possessions, the two Stuart princes surrendered their claims to the Pope in January 1739,[44] in hopes of eliminating the political aspects of the case, being compensated, presumably, with papal

[39] Dated February 1739, W.S.P. 214, no. 50.
[40] W.S.P. 213, no. 141.
[41] James to Ormonde, March 11, W.S.P. 214, no. 105.
[42] James Keith to Admiral Gordon, Feb. 20 O.S., 1735, H.M.C. *Report* X, app. I, 179.
[43] Digest of the deed of gift, H.M.C. *Report* X, app. VI, 218.
[44] The instruments of this surrender are dated Jan. 24, 1739, *ibid.*, 218–19.

pensions. The jewels were redeemed and divided between Charles and Henry,[45] when they had received enough money to do so from the proceeds of the sale of their Polish claims to Prince Radziwill for 800,000 florins.[46] The Stuarts had now a good bit of ready money to jingle.

The other success was the promotion of Pierre de Tencin to the cardinalate — more important as a sign of the resumption of that prelate into Fleury's favor than as one of the increase of Stuart influence at Rome. Once already, in 1728–1729, he had been nominated by the Pretender,[47] but had seen his advancement blocked by Fleury's objections.[48] On this occasion, the nomination was only made when certain of success. It was dated February 21, 1739,[49] and was followed by the announcement of the promotion two days later; when it was known in France outside Fleury's own circle of ministers, on March 4, it was immediately recognized as a reversal of policy: the self-righteous marquis d'Argenson trumpeted his indignation in the solitude of his journal, "All reason is confounded by this action: the king has certainly put aside his best advisors. Of what policy is this a part, but of vicious expediency. . . ?"[50] Tencin was made *chargé d'affaires* for France at Rome,[51] and was considered to be reinstated in influence. Every facility given him was an advantage to his royal sponsor.

2. THE TEMPTATION OF FLEURY

The Convention of January 1739, far from establishing a firm peace between England and Spain, provoked in Great Britain a strong bellicose reaction. The government of the new colony of Georgia, the City of London, the Merchant Adventurers of Bristol, and merchants of Glasgow, Liverpool and Edinburgh

[45] Agreement for the division, dated Dec. 22, 1742, *ibid.*, 219.
[46] Through their agent in Poland, Father Lascaris. Of this 630,000 florins are said to have been received before January 1741. *Ibid.*, 220.
[47] James to Tencin, Bologna, March 4, 1728, W.S.P. 114, no. 122.
[48] Cardinal Polignac to James, Dec. 14, 1729, W.S.P. 132, no. 117.
[49] W.S.P. 213, no. 165.
[50] d'Argenson, *Journal et mémoires,* ed. J. B. Rathery (Paris, 1859–67), II, 99.
[51] Gabriel Hanotaux, ed., *Recueil des instructions données aux ambassadeurs . . . Rome,* III (Paris, 1913), 182–83.

protested.[52] The City of London showed its displeasure by reject-
ing Sir George Champion, a Member of Parliament, for the
mayoralty at the next election, in favor of one Micajah Perry,
one of the few Lords-Mayors who have gone unknighted, because
Champion had voted in favor of the convention.[53] Very likely
the opposition was foreordained by the state of English politics:
"The Patriots were resolved to damn it, before they knew a word
of it, and to inflame the people against it, which they have done
with great success. They have taught them to expect what they
well know could not be obtained, nor ever can"[54] — a generous
settlement of the claims for damages.

The failure of Spain to pay the modest sum stipulated in the
convention for reparations therefore made the war inevitable.
James was elated with the echo of the English uproar; he predicted accurately in April that there would either be war between
England and Spain or a change of English ministers.[55] In case of
war, his future course was doubtful, but Strafford advised him
from London not to make common cause with the place-hunting
Whig opposition.[56]

Walpole now appears to have approached the Pretender again
by a roundabout way through Avery, who so worked upon the
mind of Thomas Carte that the historian journeyed all the long
way to Rome with vague messages from Winnington and Walpole
to the effect that a conference could be arranged between O'Brien
and the prime minister of George II. He arrived in Rome in July,
and presented, besides Avery's suggestions, lengthy memorials of
his own, with immeasurably complicated schemes of organization
for the party.[57] Patiently James gave him the best answer he
could:

I have no difficulty . . . in putting it in your power to satisfy him
[Walpole] authentically on the two articles about which he is solicitous,

[52] Vaucher, *Robert Walpole,* 272–275.
[53] Bishop Francis Hare to F. Naylor, Oct. 13, 1739, H.M.C. *Report* XIV,
app. IX, 252.
[54] Hare to Naylor, March 14, 1738/9, *ibid.,* 243.
[55] Letter to Ormonde, Rome, April 8, 1739, W.S.P. 215, no. 27.
[56] Strafford to James, in Cecil's hand and cipher, April 18, *ibid.,* no. 61.
[57] W.S.P. 216, nos. 109, 110, 111, and 112. The last two number 41 and 24
octavo pages, respectively.

since, independent of his desires, I am fully resolved to protect and secure the Church of England, according to my reiterated promises. . . As for the Princes of the House of Hanover, I thank God I have no resentment against them, nor against any one living. I shall never repine at their living happily in their own country after I am in possession of my kingdoms; and should they fall into my power upon any attempt for my restoration, I shall certainly not touch a hair of their heads.[58]

Despite the nearness of these two articles to stipulations which Walpole might be expected to make in all honesty, Lord Mahon remarked, "No one, I presume, will here do Walpole the injustice to suspect him of sincerity." [59] Probably not, although I find Mahon's implied laudation of Walpole's lack of scruple disgusting; but there seems to be no reason to doubt the Pretender's sincerity in his promises made at a time when there still remained a high price on his head if he made any visit to his native country.

Carte returned from Rome to London via Paris; Avery brought him into Walpole's presence, where he was told by the minister that there was no authority for such parleys, and then allowed to get out of the country again. Avery continued to speak, in his letters to the bewildered historian, of Walpole's favorable disposition, but Carte was never persuaded to expose himself again.[60] He wrote to James from Paris on October 25 that he had left a letter of the Pretender's with the minister; to this James replied that he expected nothing, but would await direct communication.[61] James wrote to O'Brien on January 26, 1740, "Mr. Walpole se trompe s'il croit de m'en imposer," [62] and was not dismayed when the months went by without further messages. Walpole's design had probably been to divide the opposition; he had been unsuccessful in convincing the court at Rome, but his plan was quite well executed at London, as we shall see.

With the war, efforts to bring Spain to invade England were

[58] Dated July 10, 1739. The original among the Stuart Papers has disappeared. I use here Lord Mahon's extract (III, 67–68), retaining his spelling and punctuation.

[59] Mahon, *ibid.*, note, mentions a copy of this letter found by Archdeacon Coxe, which that worthy cleric did not find convenient to use or print in his life of Walpole.

[60] Vaucher, *Robert Walpole*, 455–58.

[61] Carte's letter does not survive. The reply is dated Nov. 11, 1739. W.S.P. 218, no. 40.

[62] W.S.P. 220, no. 36.

redoubled. James assumed that he was the natural instrument for retaliation against the Hanoverian dynasty, as indeed he was, though a two-edged tool. After the restoration of the Stuarts Spain could hope for anything in reason, because the grateful King of England would be limited in his compliance with Spanish designs only by strong public opinion.

In January 1740, then, in response to a Spanish suggestion, he sent Ormonde to the court of Philip V, dragging him from his rest at Avignon; [63] and the Earl Marischal, then at Valencia, was summoned to meet the duke at court before the end of the month.[64]

Marischal doubted the reality of the preparations in Galicia for an embarcation, because he knew through his own acquaintances that a genuine expedition was being made ready at Barcelona, probably for an attack on Port Mahon, and he was sure that two such exertions would be beyond Spanish resources.[65] Also, James was aware that French neutrality, at least, was indispensable to success,[66] and Fleury was as unlikely to promise it as ever. On evidence available to him, the Pretender concluded in the middle of February that the armament at Corunna which Ormonde and Marischal were asked to command was a feint [67] to lead Walpole's government to keep the English fleet out of the Mediterranean. At any rate, Ormonde's departure from Avignon was not kept from the English,[68] and surprise was out of the question. Also, if James were to be restored, it is odd that his little Spanish pension went unpaid, as usual.[69] Marischal and Ormonde were ordered by Montemar, Philip V's minister, to Corunna; they refused to obey, because of the certainty of giving Walpole the alarm.[70] The arrival

[63] James to Francis Sempill, Jan. 13, W.S.P. 219, nos. 152–152A; J. Edgar to "Sir Charles" Wogan, Jan. 17, ibid., no. 165.

[64] Marischal, "Two Fragments of an Autobiography," ed. J. Y. T. Greig, Miscellany of the Scottish History Society, V (Edinburgh, 1933), 362; James to O'Brien, Jan. 26, W.S.P. 36.

[65] Marischal, 362.

[66] W.S.P. 220, nos. 36, 42.

[67] James to Ormonde, Rome, Feb. 16, ibid., no. 128.

[68] Horatio Walpole to Robert Trevor, Cockpit, Jan. 11, H.M.C. Report, XIV, app. IX, 38.

[69] James to "Inverness," March 9, W.S.P. 221, no. 39.

[70] Marischal's letters to James, April 1 and 29, 1740, W.S.P. 221, no. 127 and vol. 222, no. 16.

of Admiral Haddock's squadron made impossible any Spanish venture in the Mediterranean,[71] leaving no further need for the Corunna feint. Late in June Ormonde and Marischal asked leave to retire from Madrid.[72] Ormonde returned to Avignon, but Marischal retained his commission in Spain, because James could not support him properly.[73]

The Earl of Barrymore,[74] a Jacobite of Queen Anne's day, and once a lieutenant-general in the English army, came over in the spring of 1740 to undermine Fleury's determination to give the Pretender no help, as many another had done in the past. It was evident to him, as to James, that the English were not going to do anything without foreign help.[75] Returning to England in June, he left an impression on Fleury's mind of English attachment to the Stuart family which the cardinal decided to check by means of an agent of his own. This agent was a comte or marquis de Clermont,[76] an unlucky choice for Barrymore's friends, since he seems to have had acquaintances in England hostile to the party, including some of Bolingbroke's associates.[77]

There were two reasons for Fleury to give unusual consideration to Barrymore's representations, and his consequent employment of a method probably unused since Hooke's time. The first was that the Duke of Argyll, the first magnate and one of the most able men in Scotland, was said to be disaffected. A few incidents, at least, had given some basis to the rumor. For instance, James Keith, brother of Lord Marischal, had been in the Russian service since 1728, had been wounded in 1739, and had been given leave to recuperate in France. Allowed by the government to spend part of 1740 in England, despite his Jacobite affiliations, he was received in the highest circles, especially of the Opposition. In London he had interviews with Argyll, but did not discuss politics until one day when the duke received a troublesome mes-

[71] Marischal, 363.
[72] W.S.P. 224, no. 17.
[73] W.S.P. 225, no. 28; Vol. 226, no. 79.
[74] James Barry, 4th Earl of Barrymore in Ireland (1667–1747/8), M.P. for Wigan.
[75] Barrymore to James, Paris, May 23, W.S.P. 222, no. 128.
[76] W.S.P. 223, no. 67; vol. 224, no. 14; vol. 234, no. 169.
[77] Col. Arthur Bret to James, Paris, Jan. 7, 1741, W.S.P. 230, no. 3.

sage while in his company; "he said on reading it, *Mr. Keith*, fall flat, fall edge we must get rid of these people." But after this outburst he said no more.[78] The incident, related in its original form here, was repeated by all who heard of it, and was magnified into the conversion of the entire Opposition to treasonable views.[79]

The other reason was that motives entirely French poised Fleury on the verge of war with England. Maria Theresa's accession in Austria, followed by the election, over the opposition of her husband, of Elector Charles of Bavaria to be Emperor, the last non-Habsburg chosen, precipitated that year a war between Austria on the one hand and Prussia, Bavaria, and France on the other; [80] England was simultaneously at war with Spain, but not yet with France; Holland was neutral, but benevolent toward England and Austria; and Prussia was to make peace and re-enter the war before its close.

This complex division of Europe into camps was certain to be simplified by motives of common interest into broader alliances for more general purposes, as it was in fact in 1743–1744. Fleury was already alarmed by the danger of loss of the Spanish West Indies to England, a menace to the French sugar colonies in the region of the Caribbean; but the Spaniards themselves seemed unable to defend them. In spite of his earlier commitments in Germany and his eagerness to keep England and Hanover neutral, Fleury prepared an expedition, which sailed under the command of d'Antin in early September 1740, with secret instructions to attack the English and support Spain in the West Indies. Had d'Antin obeyed his orders, war would undoubtedly have followed, but an English squadron sent out at the same time overawed him, and he returned to France in the spring of 1741 without having done anything, and thus postponed the war to which the Pretender looked for his opportunity. It is best to say "looked," for Fleury had directed Amelot to give the strongest assurances to the

[78] Marischal to James, Madrid, June 15, 1740, W.S.P. 223, no. 142. Italics are deciphered by a code clerk.

[79] E.g. "young Lord John" Drummond's version, O'Brien to James, Paris, Sept. 12, W.S.P. 226, no. 56A.

[80] France at first only lent her armies as auxiliaries, and did not enter the war formally until April 27, 1744. Nevertheless she was in the thick of it.

Dutch that war in the West Indies would not lead to an attack on the Hanoverian dynasty.[81]

Whatever they had promised, Fleury and Amelot were acquainted with plans being made at the time. Balhaldy came back to Paris that spring with a project for the conquest of Scotland — "in all respects the most beautiful that I ever heard or read of," was the judgment of Francis Sempill,[82] who had moved to Paris and taken to himself the management of some of O'Brien's former cares late in 1739. Sempill and Balhaldy are accused of forming a partnership, and it may be so, because that plan included the levy of 20,000 men in Scotland, a chimera. Money was needed, as for all plans, and worse than ever before. James offered through O'Brien the reduction of his claim against Sweden for money advanced to Charles XII in 1716–1717 from 175,000 to 130,000 livres as a premium for ready payment, but it does not appear that Sweden paid him even on these favorable terms.[83] Fleury was inclined to let the Pretender spend the money now involved in litigation in Austria rather than supply him from the French treasury, if the need should arise; when the marquis de Mirepoix, representing Louis XV at Vienna, seemed to have taken the side of the duchesse de Bouillon in her lawsuit,[84] he was probably stunned to receive as brusque a letter from Amelot, his chief, as an ambassador ever had from such a quarter.[85] Fleury pretended to the Nuncio at Vienna that he could not believe Mirepoix to have been so rash.[86]

The agent, comte or marquis de Clermont, returned from England before September 5, 1740, and gave his account direct to Fleury, who seemed to be balancing on the question of an invasion.[87] At first it was thought that the report was favorable, because it was reported that Fleury had said to Prince Campo Florido, the Spanish envoy at Paris, that Spain and France might now

[81] Vaucher, *Robert Walpole*, 338–39.
[82] W.S.P. 222, no. 9.
[83] O'Brien to James, June 20, 1740, W.S.P. 224, nos. 8A–8B; James to O'Brien, Rome, July 6, *ibid.*, no. 176.
[84] James to O'Rourke, Jan. 22, 1740, W.S.P. 220, no. 18; O'Brien to Fleury, July 1, Corr. Pol. Autriche 224, fol. 96v.
[85] Letter of July 6, 1740, *ibid.*, fol. 111.
[86] W.S.P. 225, no. 79.
[87] Sempill to James, Sept. 5, W.S.P. 226, no. 20.

unite for the Stuarts; [88] but a favorable report could have no basis in fact, for the Duchess of Buckingham's group was breaking up (Lord Cornbury burning his compromising papers as a mark of withdrawal from the movement),[89] and Argyll was now known to be as loyal to Hanover as ever he had been. George Robinson, an agent then in Holland, wrote to Colonel Bret on Argyll's opposition: "My friend [an informant in England] says positively that it is against Sr. Robt. only and that the Elector is sure of him, I repeat sure of him, so that I beg you will acquaint the King with this because it has really given me a great deal of concern. . ." [90] Marischal conceded: "My brother may perhaps be mistaken as to *The Duke of Argyle* appearance is one thing and hopes are another, we have seen odder changes." [91]

Fleury's designs, if d'Antin should meet action in the New World, seemed diversionary rather than effective: he inclined toward an invasion of Scotland, although he had himself thought many months earlier that no such thing could be successful without a landing by regular troops in England; [92] of course, this change of view was noticed. Marischal recalled the French minister's use of Stanislas Leczynski, and hinted at collusion by the new group at Paris. Had James and others not received advices from "a very honest man" of Balhaldy's character? He judged that Fleury only intended to use a small force to begin a civil war in Scotland, to distract England and bring Spain into alliance with France; the damage done to England's well-being would be satisfactory to the cardinal, since "no *French ministry will* ever *wish them* [the three kingdoms] *to be powerful.*" [93] He warned that the Lowlanders would not be brought out by *"any little body."* [94]

O'Brien was sure, after a discussion with Campo Florido, that

[88] James to Sempill, Albano, Oct. 26, W.S.P. 227, no. 172.

[89] Cornbury to O'Brien, Paris, undated as to time, received Nov. 4, W.S.P. 228, no. 66.

[90] W.S.P. 227, no. 44.

[91] Letter to Edgar, Sept. 15, W.S.P. 226, no. 79. Italics are deciphered by a code clerk.

[92] James to Ormonde and Marischal, Rome, Jan. 27, 1740, W.S.P. 220, no. 42; Sempill to James, Nov. 21, W.S.P. 228, no. 160.

[93] Letter from Madrid, Nov. 30, *ibid.,* no. 184. Italics are deciphered.

[94] Letter of Dec. 18, W.S.P. 229, no. 75. Italics are deciphered.

there was no concert between France and Spain; [95] and no great expedition was possible without one. James warned Sempill on January 9 that if he had any part in Fleury's plans, "It is certain I shall Always be against a small expedition into Scotland, which could only tend to destruction, & that I could not answer it either to God or man, if I should anyways authorize or concurr in such an enterprise. . ."; he repeated the caution in the following month.[96]

Why the cardinal had taken this tack was not disclosed until January, when Colonel Bret informed the Pretender that the report of Clermont had been unfavorable, and that to counterbalance it Bret was now required to return to England to procure plans and promises. Bret suggested that James attach himself to the pro-Spanish party, and particularly to a lady whom I conjecture to be the comtesse de Toulouse.[97] James did not follow this advice, which would have implied abandoning Fleury altogether. Bret returned to England; and Balhaldy, having nothing to do in Paris, went to Scotland to make a show of consultation with the associators.

3. THE FALL OF WALPOLE

Sempill, originally employed by James at the instance of some of his friends in England, was unwilling to allow anyone else to correspond there, particularly O'Brien, whose services, if not showy, were at least reliable and prudent; nevertheless, the English agent neglected his work badly, and was reprimanded by his master,[98] but too late to prevent the temporary loss of the object of years of endeavor — the destruction of the Walpole ministry. A great attack was made on Walpole on the motion of Sandys on February 13, 1741. The Opposition was present in great strength, and the course of the war had persuaded some of the ministerial

[95] Letter to James, Paris, Dec. 19, *ibid.*, no. 79A.
[96] W.S.P. 230, nos. 25, 170A.
[97] Described as the mother of the "chief supercargo of the bales of goods" in the Indies. If this uninterpreted cant term means commander of the fleet there, she was Mme. de Toulouse, who was d'Antin's mother, and a prominent figure in France. Bret to James, Jan. 7, 1741; W.S.P. 230, no. 3.
[98] James to Sempill, Dec. 28, 1740, W.S.P. 229, no. 118; *ibid.*, no. 121.

party to desert, but a group of Jacobites and other Tories led by William Shippen, thirty-two in number, left the House of Commons, and a few startling secessions from Opposition to Government occurred, including those of Lord Cornbury and Micajah Perry.[99] The motion was defeated by 290 to 106.

There are two stories of Shippen's motives. One is that of Archdeacon Coxe, undocumented, that a friend of Shippen was detected in treasonable correspondence, and was spared by Walpole in return for a promise of support on the next important occasion.[100] Another, for which we can say more, is that the Jacobites in Parliament were working at cross-purposes with the Chevalier de St.-Georges. Walpole's relations with Cecil, as related by Dr. King, show how this could sometimes be. In 1741 James's own letters took too long to arrive, and Sempill had neglected to instruct his correspondents; they thus were easily led astray. James did not lose his temper, but wrote to Marischal his second thoughts on March 22: "You will hear how Walpole has got the better of the great attack made against him in Parliament, & I think on the whole that it is better for my intrest that it has ended so." [101]

Why? He probably expected to be approached by the Opposition for the support of his friends. Possibly he even desired Walpole to make advances, although he would probably not have trusted him. He was wooed, in fact, by both at the same time. Avery now talked to Carte, who had been at work with manuscripts at the Scots College in Paris,[102] and conveyed to O'Brien by his means a new message from Walpole. Free use was made of Winnington's name, and Walpole's "grandes et bonnes vues pour le *Roy*" were exposed; the message ended with the proposal that O'Brien and Winnington meet in Flanders. O'Brien agreed to do so, and to meet Avery again in a week's time,[103] but neither of

[99] Lord Guernsey, Sir James Dashwood, and Edward Harley left the House with Shippen. *Gentleman's Magazine,* 11:232 (May 1741).

[100] Coxe, I, 670–71.

[101] W.S.P. 231, no. 114. A full Jacobite account of the division is that of Carte, W.S.P. 232, no. 13. Carte reverses the digits of the number of M.P.'s leaving the house, giving 23, instead of the probable 32.

[102] W.S.P. 226, no. 123; vol. 227, no. 99; vol. 228, no. 120.

[103] O'Brien to James, Paris, April 10, 1741, W.S.P. 231, no. 189. Italics are deciphered.

these two conferences took place, and O'Brien was never able to find out more of the matter.

Approaches from the Opposition, more serious, were made through Mar's brother, James Erskine, styled Lord Grange, one of the Opposition leaders. Balhaldy returned from Scotland in the spring, with a paper from Grange, to the effect that the Opposition would be willing to work for the Pretender and for Jacobitism, purged of absolutist doctrines, if James III would regulate the conduct of his supporters.[104] James was willing, having already determined to fall in with that side; his answer, dated March 24, was ready:

> We have been now more than 50 years out of our Country, we have been bred & lived in the School of Adversity . . . long experience teaches us how little we can depend on the friendship of fforeign Powers. . . But should it happen that any Forreign Power contributed to place me on the Throne, it must be visible to all thinking men that I can neither hope to keep it, nor enjoy peace & happiness upon it, but by gaining the love & affection of my Subjects. I am far from approving the mistakes of Former Reigns, I see, I feel the effects of them. . . Therefore I do not entertain ye least thought of assuming [?] the government on the same footing my family left it, I am fully resolved to make the law ye rule of my government & absolutely disclaim any pretentions to a dispencing power.[105]

After this he summarizes the terms of his last declaration, with which he did not expect Grange to be familiar, because it had never been printed. Copies of this letter were sent to other Englishmen and Scots; [106] it was principally intended for England, but failed of its effect because the bulk of the English Opposition cared not a rap for James or his utterances.

A good instance of the usage James experienced from foreign powers was given that summer by Spain. Campo Florido apprised O'Brien in July of a decision taken for providing the Pretender with troops, provided that France would throw her own forces

---

[104] Two copies of Sempill's translation of this paper into French, admittedly a free one, are W.S.P. 231, no. 137 and vol. 233, no. 202. One copy is Affaires Etrangeres, Mémoires et documents, Angleterre 76, foll. 104–06.

[105] W.S.P. 232, no. 160–160A.

[106] James to Sempill, June 28, 1741, W.S.P. 234, no. 2; Edgar to Murray of Broughton, June 29, ibid., no. 15.

into the balance.[107] A few days later he added that twenty Spanish vessels awaited French consent to embark men for Scotland.[108] The return of d'Antin without action, and the failure of Bret in his mission to England [109] were ample reasons for Fleury to withhold agreement, and Spain's sincerity was in doubt from the beginning. Lord Marischal had given up any faith he had in it, seeking and obtaining leave to retire from Spain to France,[110] which would surely not have been permitted if Campo Florido's conferences with the agent at Paris had been anything but politic maneuvres. But, as James said to Bret of Fleury (and it applies equally to Spain), "His resolutions in regard to my intrest, do not depend on his receiving a little more or less encouragement from England, But rather on the situation of affairs abroad . . . he will not undertake a War merely on my account . . ."[111]

Balhaldy did not understand these calculations, based on a half-century of experience, and turned out new projects as if by machinery. He submitted a scheme for a descent by a small French force in Scotland,[112] which we have seen that James could not approve, and requested authority to demand General Keith's resignation of his Russian appointments to free him for a very remote invasion day.[113] The Pretender would only entrust to Sempill, not to Balhaldy, a letter to be forwarded to Keith when Cardinal Fleury should make a definite and irrevocable decision.[114]

A general election was held in England in 1741, which reduced Walpole's majority to almost nothing. James had aligned his friends with the Opposition, probably on the principle that any government loyal to George II must be continually disturbed: he had been deeply disappointed by Shippen and the seceders in February, and took steps to prevent Jacobites from feeling so free in the future. Reasons of dubious relevance have been

[107] O'Brien to James, Paris, July 3, ibid., no. 72.
[108] O'Brien to James, Paris, July 10, ibid., no. 127.
[109] Sempill and Balhaldy's letters to James, July 17, ibid., nos. 165, 168.
[110] Marischal to James, Valencia, Aug. 5, 1741, W.S.P. 235, no. 63.
[111] Letter of Sept. 6, ibid., no. 169.
[112] Ibid., no. 70.
[113] W.S.P. 234, nos. 80, 82.
[114] James to Sempill, July 19, W.S.P. 234, no. 177; James to Keith, July 18, ibid., no. 172.

assigned for these precautions, especially that Lord Chesterfield's visit to Avignon in the summer of 1741 was the determining event, some sort of bargain being made then and there by Chesterfield and Ormonde.[115] Ormonde's correspondence does not bear out that conjecture; [116] Lady Mary Wortley Montagu said in 1742 that the visit was "insignificant"; and James himself wrote to the Duchess of Buckingham on November 15, 1741, "I have no manner of private deallings or Correspondence with Lord Bolingbroke, Pultney or Walpole." [117] It may well be that the meeting was arranged for family reasons.[118]

Be that as it may, James wrote many letters to his friends in England ordering them to oppose Walpole on all occasions: "What distresses the Governing party cannot but be still of advantage to my Cause." [119] Cecil and the duchess were both instructed, against their wills, to lead their friends in Parliament into the ranks of the Opposition.[120] O'Brien wrote to James that the duchess disagreed,[121] which his master thought was a quibble.[122] Nevertheless, he did not allow Sempill to discredit the aging and crotchety English managers as he attempted to do,[123] so that he could monopolize authority at Paris: "Balhaldy & you can act more boldly in what relates to Scotland, but when England is concerned it is no ways fit to advance or sollicite any thing, but in concert with those lately come from thence," he said.[124]

Sempill's jealousy was occasioned by the decline of his own popularity among the English group since his first commission to act for it some years back, and also by his belief that the cardinal was about to go to war to restore the Stuart line, so that what these odd people in England thought meant little, in the pres-

---

[115] Vaucher, *Robert Walpole*, 418–19.
[116] His letters in W.S.P. 234–237 number only six, from June to October, and do not refer to Chesterfield at all.
[117] W.S.P. 238, no. 41.
[118] Ormonde was Chesterfield's uncle by marriage.
[119] James to Sempill, Sept. 27, 1741, W.S.P. 236, no. 72A.
[120] W.S.P. 236, nos. 73, 76.
[121] O'Brien to James, Paris, Oct. 21, W.S.P. 237, no. 61.
[122] Letter to O'Brien, Nov. 7, *ibid.*, no. 195.
[123] Sempill to James, Oct. 30, *ibid.*, no. 126.
[124] James to Sempill, Nov. 1, *ibid.*, no. 150.

ence of a large army of regular troops; promises of a general loyalty and readiness to serve could be exaggerated into assurances of a more exact kind. He could not recognize that careful organization was required to make good his careless statements and to prepare the ground for the ejection of George II, either by rebellion or with foreign forces of the size James was likely to obtain; therefore he did not trouble himself about it. There was no able leader in England, as he and Balhaldy knew,[125] but they did not try to find one, and only quarreled with the less able ones who presented themselves. Since James, a thousand miles away, could not be his own parliamentary leader, his party line could not be flexible: in early 1742 Walpole fell and the Jacobites were in the swim for a few days, but they could not agree, and did not know what to do. Thus the new ministry was as unfavorable to them as the last. Balhaldy had foreseen the difficulty and obtained leave from Rome, in December 1741, to go over to London to concert an arrangement with the Opposition through Lord Grange.[126]

The new Parliament started well, in December, with the Jacobite members accommodating their own discordant views to the directions of their master, to his delight, as he wrote when his last word was of the Christmas adjournment.[127] In spite of a warning from Balhaldy that the Jacobites were leaderless and that some opposed a coalition,[128] he had great expectations when the news of Walpole's fall arrived, in Sempill's letter of February 26 New Style,[129] until one dated March 12 informed him of the constituents of the new Cabinet. No Jacobites were included.

The new ministers were, for the most part, the old Whig Opposition, with some relics of Walpole's Cabinet. Pulteney, Argyll, and Sir John Hynde Cotton were conspicuous omissions. Cotton was a known Jacobite already, and Pulteney was made an

[125] "You have there ane excellent old watch, Not a wheel or a pin a wanting, had it a good Spring to set it in motion, but alass that is old worn out and rusty. . . " Balhaldy to Edgar, London, Feb. 6 O.S., 1741/2, W.S.P. 239, no. 177.
[126] W.S.P. 237, no. 190; vol. 238, nos. 98A and 133.
[127] Letter to Sempill, Feb. 1, 1742, W.S.P. 239, no. 154.
[128] Ibid., no. 177.
[129] W.S.P. 240, no. 66.

earl by George II, but a rumor ran around once again, as in 1718, 1720,[130] and 1740, that Argyll was disaffected. The Pretender wrote to Colonel Cecil at the end of April that he desired, if possible, to be restored by his subjects, without foreign troops,[131] and enclosed a note in his own hand to be given to Argyll (though not addressed to him),[132] when circumstances should be right for delivery. In July, Cecil played the fool with the note, and sent it without prior sounding to Argyll's lodgings in London; immediately the duke forwarded it to George II as a demonstration of loyalty.[133] The second Earl of Orrery, heir of his father's consideration in the party, had warned Cecil, but vainly, that something of the sort would happen.[134] Fortunately Sempill, who had crossed to England in late March or early April,[135] had returned in June; or he might have been apprehended.

On the strength of information obtained in discussions with Lord Grange, Sempill threw himself upon Campo Florido, anxious to be told, as he was, that Spain would supply troops for a descent in Scotland if France would enter the war against England. Fleury pretended to be in favor of a descent, but feared that an invasion of England would bring in the Dutch.[136] James feared that Sempill was being amused: "Les officiers en $\frac{\text{Espagne}}{\text{Delf}}$ meurent de faim, que peut on donc attendre de $\frac{\text{cette cour}}{\text{Nicholas}}$?" he had asked a few months before.[137] Sempill also approached Fleury's subordinate ministers, in expectation of the cardinal's death. Here again the Pretender's own insight was better than Sempill's: "As for Messrs. Amelot & Maurepas way of thinking, tho' it be always good to have them our friends, yet it matters little what their private opinion be, as long as he who is their chief . . . thinks other ways."[138] Did he know that neither of

[130] Lockhart, II, 10–16, 31–34.
[131] Letter of April 25, W.S.P. 241, no. 57.
[132] *Ibid.*, no. 58.
[133] J. Robinson to James, Paris, July 16, W.S.P. 243, no. 20.
[134] Sempill to James, July 16, *ibid.*, no. 21.
[135] W.S.P. 241, no. 13.
[136] Sempill to James, June 18, 1742, W.S.P. 242, no. 77.
[137] James to O'Brien, Sept. 20, 1741, W.S.P. 236, no. 28. Decipherment is mine, by comparison with other letters of James and O'Brien.
[138] James to Sempill, July 4, 1742, W.S.P. 242, no. 176.

them was of the caliber to take the cardinal's place? Nor were
the favorable dispatches of Bussy, French minister at London, as
important as they might have been: if they were correct, England
was near to open revolt in June.[139] Seldom has an envoy more
clearly shown his unfitness to measure public opinion.

4. ALARMS AND ANTICIPATIONS

The Jacobites were not incredulous. The Pretender began to
lay plans for either his own voyage or Charles's to France when
one of them should be summoned.[140] This expectation had its
origin in Cardinal Tencin's recall to be a member of the French
Council of State; of that prelate there were high hopes, but not
unreasonable ones: "I take his being called thither at this time a
clear proof that the French stand in no awe of the English
Governmt. & are not disposed to observe certain managements
with them," but "were Cardl. Tencin actually first Minister, I
dont see how he could do great matters for us at the present
moment." [141] Marischal agreed, and went further, writing from
Rheims in November, "Cardl. Fleury has never been sparing of
good words nor Lord Sempil shy in receiving such wares, I need
not repeat to your Majestys [sic] my opinion of them." [142] He
need not; after long experience of Sempill's eagerness to believe,
the Pretender had him superseded by O'Brien, leaving only those
who had a positive preference for Sempill to communicate with
James by his means. O'Brien had lived forty years and more
abroad, and was unknown to many members of the party; but
though he was not au courant in England, he was trustworthy,
and had obtained the sole confidence of Marischal and others.[143]
Tencin did not forget his benefactor, but actively furthered his
designs in the Council of State.[144] It may have been because of

---

[139] O'Brien to James, Paris, July 25, W.S.P. 243, no. 55. Bussy had previously
exaggerated the significance of the actions of cliques, as in the case of the Lord
Mayor's banquet of 1740. Corr. Pol. Ang. 408, fol. 213r and v.
[140] W.S.P. 243, no. 159.
[141] James to Sempill, Sept. 10, W.S.P. 244, no. 34.
[142] W.S.P. 245, no. 71. Italics are deciphered.
[143] W.S.P. 237, no. 94; vol. 245, no. 106.
[144] Sempill to James, Nov. 12, 1742, W.S.P. 245, no. 115.

such demonstrations as this that Balhaldy took it upon himself to write to the Scottish Association warning them of a descent in the following spring.[145] Since the admission of John Murray of Broughton, who had succeeded Urquhart as principal agent for Scotland in 1741,[146] the Association had been "maturing," that is, had done nothing except swear friends of its members to loyalty and secrecy; Murray's attempts to raise money in late 1741 had completely failed.[147] Young Lord John Drummond had wasted much effort in journeys to and from France because of Balhaldy's jealousy; yet he was to recruit a Scottish regiment for Prince Charles, first organized in the French service, when Sempill and Balhaldy were doing nothing.

Balhaldy's letter threw the group into panic, and led some to wonder how they could have been so foolish; as weeks went by without further word the panic was sharpened by suspicion. In the end Murray of Broughton was dispatched to Paris to clear up the misunderstanding. He departed in the middle of January 1743,[148] and arrived in Paris in early February,[149] almost at the same time that Fleury died.

Of this visit there are three accounts — Balhaldy's, that Murray saw Amelot and Tencin and was delighted with what they had to say; [150] Murray's, in the *Memorials* written in self-justification after Culloden, that he immediately felt distrust when he met Amelot, through Balhaldy's means; [151] and that of Murray as a young man, drawn from the letters he wrote during his stay, which falls somewhat between the other two, but closer to Balhaldy's than to his own later one. It is to this that I incline, because Balhaldy was defensive in 1743, and Murray was even more so after 1746, when he was ostracized by his friends.

Murray's first letter to James Edgar, of February 18, conveys his satisfaction at having found at London a letter which Bal-

[145] Murray, *Memorials*, 32.
[146] Edgar to Murray, April 27, 1741, W.S.P. 232, no. 54.
[147] Murray, 18–22.
[148] Murray's papers, in Blaikie, *Origins*, 6.
[149] Before the 4th N.S. (W.S.P. 247, no. 80). Ewald (I, 80), using the *Genuine Memoirs* of Murray, a spurious account, says that Murray was sent to Paris *from Rome* in early 1742. He is wrong.
[150] W.S.P. 247, no. 80.
[151] Murray, 44–45.

haldy had written, which would have relieved the Association of its anxiety had it not been delayed.[152] Murray does not mention this discovery in his later story. Again, the Scottish emissary took sides with Sempill against Lord Marischal on the question of the latter's residence at Boulogne.[153] He did not approach Daniel O'Brien, leaving him ignorant of the bare fact of his arrival until Tencin let it out in late February.[154] Furthermore, he wrote to James in March 4, "After two weeks attendance, I had the honour to be presented to Mr. *Amelot,* who said in The *K. of France's* name, all that the present Situation of affairs, would in my humble opinion allow off; which will certainly give great Satisfaction to *Your Mtys friends* att my return to *Scotland.*" [155] In the later version he said that this interview disappointed him, and that news of it depressed his accomplices.[156] Murray actually seems to have gone away pleased as far as London. There he saw Cecil, who had lost faith in Sempill, and probably said so, as Murray later recounted.[157] In another account he tells of meeting the Duke of Perth, brother of Young Lord John, who expressed distress at the report he brought. Probably he acquired from Cecil and Perth the feeling of disillusion which he thought later to have been instinctive and instantaneous.

"Lord Kenmure" [158] approached him on his arrival in Scotland with a tale of dissatisfaction with George II among the Cameronians, the extreme wing of Presbyterianism. Murray communicated it to the old Chevalier so convincingly that he immediately "promised to take them under his protection, and to allow them unrestrained liberty of conscience, with a yearly sallary to each of their preachers." Balhaldy undertook to procure a commission for Captain Cramon, who, with Sir Thomas Gordon of Earlston,[159] spoke for the Cameronians.[160] The Earl of Traquair, one

---

[152] W.S.P. 247, no. 148. Murray seldom wrote to James III directly.
[153] Letter to Edgar, Feb. 25, *ibid.,* no. 174.
[154] *Ibid.,* no. 187.   [155] W.S.P. 248, no. 4.
[156] *Memorials,* 44–45.
[157] *Ibid.,* 47.
[158] John Gordon (1713–1769), but for his father's forfeiture in 1716, eighth Viscount Kenmure.
[159] Sir Thomas Gordon of Earlston in Kirkcudbright, third Bart. (1685–1769).
[160] Murray, 53–55.

of the associators, went to meet Balhaldy at London, and make a grand concert there between Jacobites of the two nations, Murray having now received word from Rome that an attempt was near.[161] Traquair fell under Balhaldy's influence, and retained a letter which he was supposed to have forwarded to Marischal, in which Murray asked for the honest earl's judgment; [162] perhaps Balhaldy knew what it would be.

Neither Murray nor James heard much of what went on in London until Sempill wrote to Rome that Amelot, who had now no superior in the government but Louis XV, since there was no chief minister, was looking for a man to send to England to test the Pretender's friends.[163] He did not find one at once; it was only on August 19 that James Butler, an equerry of Louis XV, was instructed and sent off to Balhaldy for introduction to those he had been in touch with; and Butler began badly by blabbing something of his mission to the receptive Carte days before his departure. The result was that Colonel Cecil was said to have known by the 19th that an agent was coming, and had, according to Sempill and Balhaldy, told so many people that the government was probably fully informed.[164] Sempill was foolish to believe that he could keep Cecil, the confidant of many who despised the monopolists of business at Paris, in the dark until the last minute; he had actually striven to give the French government a different opinion of the colonel, describing him as "une personne qui pourroit lui [Butler or another agent] donner toutes les lumieres et les eclaircissements désirables." [165]

Butler's mission was ostensibly the purchase of horses for the stables of Louis XV and, despite leaks to Carte and Cecil, Balhaldy was at least able to pretend that that was all the English government knew. One high point of his visit was a stay at London, where he attended a great dinner at which between twenty

---

[161] *Ibid.*, 52, 54.
[162] Blaikie, 27–28. The letter was probably of early April 1743.
[163] W.S.P. 251, no. 32.
[164] W.S.P. 252, nos. 40, 57.
[165] Jean Colin, *Louis XV et les jacobites, le projet de débarquement en Angleterre de 1743–1744* (Paris, 1901), 15. See also Mém. et doc., Ang. 77, fol. 266.

and forty citizens were present,[166] and with Balhaldy prepared a list of the City's liverymen, which indicated that 186 of 236 favored the cause, including ten aldermen, one of the Sheriffs (William Benn), and the Lord Mayor, Wilmott.[167] Another, probably the climax of Butler's visit to England, was a race meeting at Lichfield, where scores of drunken gentlemen spoke indiscreetly and were solemnly set down, although they refused to sign anything,[168] as "Jacobites zélés." Nor can we believe that all of those listed, in a memorial submitted to Amelot on Butler's return, committed themselves at all. It would be useless to name them all. Three hundred and nineteen are put down for the counties of England and Wales; second or further listings being subtracted, 291 distinct persons, including a great number of lords (some of Jacobite creation, like Lord Caryll, listed for Sussex) remain.[169] Some were undoubtedly Jacobites — Lords Abingdon, Lichfield, Orrery, Thanet, Guernsey and Barrymore, and Sir John Hynde Cotton among them; others — Lords Petre, Exeter, Waldegrave, and Chesterfield, for instance — had Jacobite relations. Still others — Lords Masham and Oxford, Sir John St. Aubin, the Foleys and the Gowers, were still Tories, at least. The presence of many of the names, however, is inexplicable. How can one account for Shrewsbury,[170] Shaftesbury, and Somerset? Only by remembering the teeming brains of Sempill and Balhaldy.

---

[166] Mém. et doc., Ang. 77, fol. 46.

[167] The aldermen named were Daniel Lambert, Robert Westley, Henry Marshall, Richard Hoare, Robert Ladbroke, William Calvert, Walter Barnard, —— Gibbon, John Blackford, and William Benn. Lambert had been Lord Mayor in 1741; Westley, Marshall, Hoare, Benn (never knighted), Ladbroke, and Calvert were Lords Mayors 1744–49. "A List of the Names. . . " W.S.P. 254, no. 154.

[168] Mém. et doc., Ang. 77, fol. 46.

[169] Balhaldy's memorial, Oct. 25, 1743, W.S.P. 253, no. 51; another copy, in French, is Mém. et doc., Ang. 76, foll. 203–07. It would be a useful and an interesting task, but not mine, to trace the Jacobite connections of this list, which undoubtedly includes more Jacobite names than were ever listed at once on any other occasion.

[170] Unless this title refers to the Jesuit Gilbert Talbot, de jure Earl of Shrewsbury, seventy years old at the time. See G. E. Cokayne, Complete Peerage, article "Shrewsbury." Gilbert Talbot, at any rate, would not have been at Lichfield.

5. THE ATTEMPT OF 1744

Balhaldy and Butler returned to Paris on or about October 20, 1743.[171] The equerry was enthusiastic; he had been only too well entertained. "I discover'd, during my stay in that Kingdom," he wrote to the Chevalier on November 21, "a very fair prospect of success, to any undertaking in favour of your Majesty; which I have represented, and shall continue repeating here . . . what chiefly grounds my hopes . . . is to see your Majesty's affairs in such good hands, and carry'd on with the strictest secrecy, activity, discretion and prudence." [172] Which is nonsense, for Sempill, Cecil, and others had capacities of a very feeble order. What chiefly grounded the hopes of all informed men was the signature of the second Family Compact [173] by France and Spain on October 25 in answer to the treaty of Worms, concluded on September 13, 1743 by Austria, Sardinia, and England — the camps were formed. Of course, the French government, having determined on war, was more ready to accept Butler's report than it would have been otherwise. Orders were given on November 15 for the concentration of transports and war-vessels,[174] and at the commencement of December Balhaldy was accredited to James by the King of France and sent off [175] to obtain leave for Prince Charles to go to France and join an expedition being prepared at Dunkirk.[176]

There the comte de Saxe, soon to be made marshal of France, was to command the troops under Charles: 9000 of these were actually assembled at the port, and the necessary ships were equipped in the road there.[177] The arms normally allotted to such a body were supplemented by six twelve-pounders and 8000 fusils.[178] It was hoped that Charles could be embarked, if secrecy

[171] Balhaldy to James, Nov. 13, W.S.P. 253, no. 154.
[172] *Ibid.*, no. 189.
[173] The treaty of Fontainebleau.
[174] Colin, 33.
[175] Father Giulio Cordara, "Commentary on the Expedition to Scotland," Sir Bruce Seton, ed., *Miscellany of the Scottish History Society*, IV (Edinburgh, 1926), 25.
[176] The preference for Charles over his father had been established earlier. O'Brien to James, Paris, Aug. 18, 1743, W.S.P. 252, no. 39.
[177] Marischal, 365.
[178] Colin, 41–42.

were maintained and the journey from Rome quickly made, before January 10, 1744.[179] The King of Spain was informed of the project by a personal letter from Louis XV of December 10.[180] The secret seems to have been well kept: at least for a time the English were deluded as to the destination of the force,[181] leaving the way open for the landing had the "Young Pretender" arrived in time.

Balhaldy, however, was not in Rome until December 19. He and Sir John Graeme, who had accompanied him, assured James and Charles "that all difficulties had been smoothed away and the whole thing would be easy to carry out." [182] The Pretender was too old in disappointment to believe all he was told: Balhaldy was known to him and to most of his friends. Charles was his elder son, and so far as England was concerned, his only one, for Prince Henry's inherited devotion and preoccupation with salvation plainly unfitted him for the throne, or even for life in a Protestant country.[183] His own experience of the French since 1715 had been that of a tool in the hands of rough workmen, and he felt no confidence in men whose interests governed them alike in war, finance, and diplomacy.[184]

In consideration for the rights of his heir, he left the decision to Prince Charles, who accepted the offer and prepared to escape the surveillance of English spies and break away to France. Balhaldy almost immediately returned with this message. James issued declarations thought appropriate on December 23, 1743.[185] Aside from a declaration that Charles was now Regent in James III's absence, they are of little interest: that to Scotland promises dissolution of the Union and abolition of the Malt Tax; the one

[179] Orders to Roquefeuil, Dec. 21: "Je dois vous prévenir que vous partiriez *trop tard,* si vous ne sortiriez du port que le 10 du mois prochain. . . " Colin, 47.

[180] *Ibid.,* 35.

[181] General Cope was only sent to Scotland in early February, O.S. Omond, 119.

[182] Cordara, 25–26.

[183] Dunbar's description of Henry's way of life, W.S.P. 246, no. 139, is imperfectly printed by A. and H. Tayler, *The Stuart Papers at Windsor,* 106f.

[184] James to Sempill, March 28, 1743, W.S.P. 248, no. 136.

[185] Originals are W.S.P. 254, nos. 92–93. They are printed in *A Collection of Declarations, Proclamations, and other Valuable Papers, published by authority at Edinburgh in the Years 1745 and 1746* (n. pl., 1748), 3–7, 10–15.

to England concedes the sanctity of the Habeas Corpus Act, and the undesirability of heavy and unnecessary taxes, with special attention paid to "foreign Excises." The Church of England is promised protection and support, while party distinctions are renounced to allow promotion as a reward for ecclesiastical service and merit alone.

According to Father Cordara, the only Roman source, Charles left home on January 9, ostensibly on a hunting trip; his failure to return was accounted for by a cock and bull story of an injury in a remote village. The pretence was kept up for eleven days. During that time the Prince had sailed for France, by way of Massa in Liguria, Finale, and Antibes, where he arrived on January 23, 1744.[186] At Avignon he met Ormonde, then set off for Paris. Suspicion was already general in Rome when the Pretender broke silence and told Benedict XIII the truth, but although a spy is reported to have written to England on the 18th,[187] the Prince arrived in France without injury, but regrettably late.

Word having been sent to England of Louis XV's decision, replies were received by Sempill which he represented as overjoyed.[188] O'Brien was kept ignorant until February.[189] On the other side, Murray of Broughton and his colleagues vainly awaited news from Balhaldy. Lord Traquair (formerly Lord Linton) was probably pledged to silence about Butler, for when he returned to Scotland he mentioned only a few country visits and the Lichfield race-meeting, but nothing of Butler's report, so that Murray actually came to think that Butler had come principally to buy horses.[190] The general message brought by Traquair from Balhaldy, that the English were optimistic, did not make

[186] Cordara, 34–44; James Maxwell of Kirkconnell, *Narrative*, ed. W. Buchanan (Edinburgh, 1841), 11–13; Colin, 54–55; Mém. et doc., Ang. 77, fol. 37.

[187] A French informant, who knew nothing of his government's plans, sent word on that day. Mém. et doc., Ang. 77, fol. 33.

[188] "Extrait [in Sempill's hand] d'une lettre du Sieur *Barry*," Dec. 19. Mém et doc., Ang. 76, fol. 219; Sempill to [Amelot?], Jan. 28, 1744, Mém. et doc., Ang. 77, fol. 44. Peter Barry was a physician of Craven Street, in the Strand, London. *Ibid.*, fol. 143; Sir Bruce Seton and J. G. Arnot, *Prisoners of the 'Forty-Five* (Edinburgh, 1928–29), 28–29.

[189] Mém. et doc., Ang. 77, foll. 65–66.

[190] Blaikie, 47–48; Murray, 55, 61.

sense to him.[191] The first word he received of French actions was a letter from the shifty Scotsman dated December 1743, but not delivered until February.[192] The expedition, he learned, was to consist of two forces, one, under Charles, of twelve thousand men, to land in England; the other, of three thousand commanded by Marischal, was designed for Scotland.[193] It is to be seen that Balhaldy was not telling the truth. Marischal was told nothing until the sailing date, and even then was never assigned a definite group of battalions, or paid.[194] When Charles was at Paris, "kept private as possible," Marischal was excluded from talk with him, probably by Balhaldy and Sempill.[195]

From Paris Charles went to Dunkirk in February. It was now proposed to land the force at Blackwall, near London in the Thames estuary, which caused some delay in finding pilots, but word came to Sempill on the nineteenth that good ones would report to Dunkirk very soon.[196] From the instructions issued at the time, there appears to be no question that the descent was not to be a feint.[197] Sixteen battalions of foot (at least one much under strength, however [198]) and one of dragoons were made ready; the total assembled were 334 officers and 9,695 men.[199] To serve under Marischal, three battalions of Irish were to move to Dunkirk,[200] but he never learned of them, so that he, in agreement with the Jesuit Cordara of all people, concluded that the Jacobites had been deceived. In fact, they were very wrong. Saxe pleaded with the minister of war, the comte d'Argenson, brother of the marquis of that name soon to replace Amelot, saying that the English were alert, that surprise was lost and invasion impracticable; [201] d'Argenson held him to his task without wavering.

[191] Murray, 56.
[192] *Ibid.*, 61; Blaikie, 48.
[193] Murray, 62.
[194] Marischal, 360, 365–66; David, Lord Elcho, *A Short Account of the Affairs of Scotland, 1744–46,* Hon. Evan Charteris, ed. (Edinburgh, 1907), 232.
[195] Marischal, 359; Maxwell, 13.
[196] Mém. et doc., Ang. 77, fol. 84.
[197] Colin, 59–62, 65, 68–73.
[198] Saxe to the comte d'Argenson, Calais, Feb. 24, 1744, *Correspondance du comte d'Argenson, ministre de la guerre* (Paris, 1924), I, 260.
[199] Colin, 77–79.
[200] D'Argenson to Saxe, Versailles, Feb. 29, Colin, 135.
[201] Colin, 118, 126–29.

Bad weather was responsible for several days' delay. Embarcation on March 4 was followed by two successive violent storms, on the nights of 6/7 and 11/12 March. Fourteen vessels were run aground, and others damaged in various ways.[202] Most of the troops were saved, but d'Argenson ordered suspension of the plan on March 8,[203] and on March 16 Saxe received orders to report at Versailles.[204]

Charles returned to Paris in early April, kept his house from chagrin,[205] and waited for the French to turn up something else for him to do. War between England and France had formally begun on March 15, and, in his mind, surprise was not essential to success. The French government had learned of the arrests of several of the surest Jacobites on the list,[206] however; and the old expert Chavigny, called on for his opinion by Louis XV, reported on March 26: "Il y aura toujours des mécontents; mais quel fond peut-on y faire? J'aurais eu le temps de me désabuser des jacobites si je m'y étais jamais mépris: ils ne sont bons à rien. . ."[207]; his testimony may not have been true of his experience, but could not be without its effect.

Charles was a young man, stubborn, uncultivated,[208] and, on the whole, very selfish. He lacked his father's insight, experience, and loyalty to his religion. His only military knowledge was acquired at Gaeta, as a schoolboy. His best qualities were affability and condescension; his physical courage was great, but sometimes endangered him uselessly. And he lacked temper, to the point of violence. All of these characteristics destined him to be the spark which was to destroy his friends and disrupt the life of a nation; for Scotland was never the same after he left it, as I shall endeavor to make clear.

His egotism was matched by that of the French monarchy. Amelot was dismissed in April from the Ministry of Foreign

---

[202] Ibid., 150–52, 169–71.

[203] D'Argenson, Correspondance, I, 267.

[204] Colin, 181–82.

[205] French Foreign Office Minute, April 1744, printed in Murray, 501.

[206] Col. Cecil, Mr. Charteris (brother of Lord Elcho), the Duke of Perth, Lord Barrymore, and Lord John Drummond. Mém. et doc., Ang. 77, fol. 188.

[207] Colin, 187.

[208] Mahon remarked of Sheridan, the prince's tutor, "History can only acquit him of base perfidy by accusing him of gross neglect." III, 281.

Affairs, and was only replaced in November, by the marquis d'Argenson. The change was made in the first place because Amelot's presence was thought to make peace difficult,[209] and at the end of 1744 peace was thought to be the goal of d'Argenson. Indeed, two agents were charged with preliminary talks in England about that time; and in April 1745 Fournier, a farmer-general, sent to London on an errand about tobacco, was instructed to make overtures of peace, which kept him there until the following November, when French assistance to the Pretender made Fournier's mission a mockery.[210] Even in January 1746 the French had the effrontery to make certain less definite advances.[211]

6. MURRAY AND THE YOUNG PRETENDER

During the early part of his stay at Paris, Charles gave, and was anxious to give, the French no trouble; he was quite naturally kept ignorant of these intrigues. He received little assistance from Louis XV; 3000 livres a month was so far short of his expenditures that during the remainder of 1744 he contracted debts of over 30,000 livres, which the marquis d'Argenson ordered paid.[212] It would have been natural for the prince to take his father for his model, and serve with the French in Flanders, but fears of Dutch intervention in the war led Louis XV's ministers to deny him permission to join the army there.[213] His presence was an embarrassment, and he felt it; visits to his relatives, the ducs de Bouillon and de Fitzjames, at their country-houses, were his only relief from the monotony and poverty of his life in Paris. He did not at first interfere in Sempill's management of his affairs.

That management had been extraordinary. Sempill had not sent word to the Scots of the postponement of action, no doubt because he and Charles still cherished the hope of another at-

[209] Sir Richard Lodge, *Studies in Eighteenth Century Diplomacy, 1740–1748* (London, 1930), 87.
[210] E. Zévort, *Le Marquis d'Argenson et le ministère des affaires étrangères* (Paris, 1880), 246–47, 254, 258.
[211] *Ibid.*, 259.
[212] Mém. et doc., Ang. 75, fol. 209.
[213] *Ibid.*, fol. 208.

tempt,[214] although Lord Elcho and others eventually brought the news, the loyal felt the slight, which carried some danger with it.[215] What the immediate emotions of "honest men" in England may have been we can only conjecture, since Sempill's reports ("Nos amis sont de plus en plus encouragés par l'etat actuel des choses. . ." [216]) were unworthy of credit: perhaps many tippling gentlemen were relieved when they learned that their heat at Lichfield was not to be transformed into energy in arms. The Duchess of Buckingham was recently dead, and Cecil an invalid. Sir John Hynde Cotton was the only considerable Jacobite active at that time, barring Shippen, whose talent was for debate, not for marching and countermarching.

The indignation of the Scots was once more resolved by sending John Murray of Broughton to France. This time he took the route of Ostend and Rotterdam to Paris, meeting Balhaldy on the way. He had warned the former agent of the Association that he was coming, but the news had been withheld from the prince until an attempt had been made to dissuade Murray from coming all the way.[217] It failed, and Murray went on to Paris, seeing "the Prince of Wales" secretly in a stable. It was then that he learned the reason for Balhaldy's anxiety of keep him away — to tempt the French to invade Scotland, Balhaldy had for many months past told them that they could count upon 20,000 Scots, ready to rise at Charles's call.[218] The Scots had no idea that such fantastic estimates had been made in their name; sober judges would have reckoned much less than half that; and Murray felt authorized to promise no more than four thousand,[219] which was slightly more than supported the cause at Prestonpans.[220] For every exaggeration in the total Balhaldy had also introduced several misjudgments of the dispositions of individuals, as Butler's lists show.

[214] Charles to Louis XV, Paris, July 24, 1744, Mém. et doc., Ang. 77, foll. 244–45.
[215] Murray, 70.
[216] Sempill to Amelot, Feb. 23, 1744, Mém. et doc., Ang. 77, fol. 113.
[217] Murray, 78, 83–88.
[218] Ibid., 90; Mém. et doc., Ang. 77, foll. 160–61.
[219] Murray, 93.
[220] Blaikie, Itinerary of Prince Charles Edward Stuart (Edinburgh, 1897), 90–91.

Now that he was undeceived, Charles communicated Murray's advices to the Old Pretender.[221] James was not ignorant of officiousness in that quarter, and of a tendency toward "accepting of good words"; he relieved his son of the burden of dealing with Sempill and Balhaldy. They continued in Paris, grumbling that they had been abandoned.[222]

Murray found it easy to gain his young master's confidence (they were much of an age) before returning to Scotland. He advised him to continue to remind the court of France of the bright prospects of a Europe in which England was separated from her present continental allies, and that France could make those prospects real; money could be raised in Great Britain; [223] and if France refused the use of her troops, Charles promised (or threatened) to come to Scotland in the following summer, "though with a single footman." [224]

Murray went home again in October, stopping for a short while in the Low Countries, he said, to tamper with officers of the Scots Brigade in the Dutch service.[225] He found Traquair's eagerness dimmed by the disgrace of Balhaldy, a friend of his, but with the assistance of Cameron of Lochiel,[226] compelled Traquair to go to England to bring the men of Lichfield into some sort of organization. The earl promised to do this, but did not set out until early in 1745.[227] In the meantime, Murray was very busy borrowing money. The Dukes of Hamilton and Perth, and Mr. Francis Charteris, later Earl of Wemyss, gave fifteen hundred pounds apiece; others gave smaller sums, and the well-inclined, but penniless, promised in writing to rise when called.[228] Not all of these promises were honored, of course.

Murray did not keep from some of the most trusted the prince's intention to come, with or without a foreign force, in the summer

[221] Letter of Sept. 18, 1744, Murray, 375–76.

[222] Sempill was nevertheless given a letter of credence to d'Argenson, dated Feb. 23, 1745. Mém. et doc., Ang. 78, fol. 19.

[223] Murray, 96–97.

[224] Ibid., 93; Elcho, 234.

[225] Murray, 101–02, 428; Elcho, 234. This had been suggested to the French as far back as February. Mém. et doc., Ang. 77, fol. 89.

[226] Donald Cameron, called "Gentle Lochiel" (ca. 1695–1748).

[227] Murray, 104–06, 117.

[228] Ibid., 119–121.

of 1745. "Most of the Gentlemen of that party look'd upon it as a mad project and were utterly against it," Elcho said later, and asserted from hindsight that Murray wished to remedy his "desperate circumstances" at the risk of the party's destruction, by encouraging this intention.[229] Maxwell of Kirkconnell repeated the charge,[230] and the author of the Woodhouselee Manuscript, whoever he was, supported it to the extent of calling Murray of Broughton a bankrupt.[231] For what good it would do him, the defendant denied the allegation, spread, he said, by Macdonald of Glengarry because of an old grudge.[232]

The majority of the "Buck Club," founded at Edinburgh for the promotion of the cause, authorized Murray to draw up a statement of its views for transmission to Charles: he was not on any account to come without at least 6000 regular soldiers, and 30,000 louis d'or to pay them. Murray says that Traquair carried this statement to London to send it from there but, negligent as usual, returned it to its senders in April 1745. Summer being perilously close, "Young Macdonald" of Glengarry, the chief's son, was charged with another message by the frightened Jacobites, who foresaw that Traquair's laziness or obstructionism might cost them their lives. If Glengarry and Murray told the truth, Glengarry did not arrive in time to put off the Young Pretender's departure;[233] if not, as is possible, the prince would not be put off. Lord Elcho believed that Glengarry secretly carried a message opposed to that of the generality.[234] Since any such message was probably verbal, we shall probably never know the facts.

Prince Charles did not await exact information of French advances to England, but he could not have been ignorant of the rumors that ran around Paris. To act independently, he must have money. He wrote to the Old Pretender in March to say that he had borrowed to pay for broadswords to arm his followers,

[229] A short Account, 234.
[230] Narrative, 55.
[231] Steuart, A. F., ed., The Woodhouselee MS. (London and Edinburgh, 1907), 89.
[232] Murray, 107; Blaikie, Origins, 66.
[233] Blaikie, Origins, xlvii–xlviii.
[234] Elcho, 235.

and desired his jewels — probably his share of the Sobieski inheritance — to be sold; "for the Prince [cipher compels the use of the third person] sees almost everything at the French Court sticks at the money, as it did in the last enterprise, which was when the Prince insisted for an invasion of Scotland.[235] He still represented that he wished to work with the French, knowing that his father would probably forbid him to go to Scotland alone.

Balhaldy, when Murray met him in the summer of 1744, had been buying arms in Holland; to add to this store, Charles accumulated swords and guns, borrowing money from the two Paris bankers, father and son, named George Waters, to do so.[236] He procured a ship to carry this cargo — 1500 fusils, 1800 broad swords, powder, ball, flints, 20 light field pieces, and a fund of four thousand louis d'or [237] — and arranged with the proprietor of a French ship of war for escort to Scotland. At Navarre in the middle of June, he wrote a letter to his father explaining his actions and his secrecy. Marischal was accredited to the French court, and a Mr. Stafford was sent to Spain.[238] A letter of excuses for the sudden departure was left to be transmitted to Louis XV; [239] before the letter was delivered, Charles was gone.

Doutelle, the transport, left Nantes with the Prince and a handful of friends on June 22/July 3, 1745, and was joined by the escorting war vessel, *Elisabeth,* at Belleisle after a lapse of several days. The ships were separated by an encounter with H.M.S. *Lion* on July 9, but *Doutelle* got safely to Eriskaig, where it touched on July 23, Old Style. The Scots were not surprised, for Sir Hector Maclean [240] had been sent ahead. They had resolved to do nothing without regulars, but few, when Charles met them face to face, could resist his charm and self-confidence. The rebellion began with a clash at Loch Lochy, which was followed by the raising of the standard at Glenfinnan on August 19.

---

[235] Charles to James, Paris, March 7, 1745, Mahon, III, xi (app.).

[236] Charles to James, Navarre [the country-house of the Duc de Bouillon], June 12, *ibid.,* III, xvi (app.).

[237] *Ibid.,* III, 340.

[238] *Ibid.,* III, 338; Mém. et doc., Ang. 78, foll. 102–03.

[239] Mém. et doc., Ang. 78, fol. 73.

[240] Of Duart, Bart. (1704–51).

7. THE 'FORTY-FIVE

The history of the rebellion is not a part of this study, but there are some aspects of it which may well be considered. In the first place, some of the Highland clans formerly favorable did not rise. Secondly, the rebellion received more support in the Lowlands than has sometimes been supposed, particularly in Edinburgh and the northeastern counties. In spite of Lord Elcho's flat statement, too often followed, that only gentlemen joined at Edinburgh, and that "not one of the Mob who were so fond of him [Charles] Ever ask'd to Enlist in his Service," [241] the thorough list of rebel prisoners now available [242] shows sixty-four residents of Edinburgh, not gentlemen for the most part, who did not plead that they had been forced to join. It may reasonably be assumed that more escaped, and some were killed, while some who were not pressed said that they were. In general, the gentry made a smaller contribution to the Scottish portion of the army than has been supposed: artisans, shopkeepers, farmers, and laborers made up the bulk, many holding commissions of company rank.[243]

Other indices of the strength of Jacobitism are the benevolent neutrality of the *Scots Magazine,* not only during the occupation of Edinburgh, but well into 1746. The attitude, during the occupation, of the Royal Bank of Scotland was also neutral. It carried on business with both sides impartially, removing some of its gold from Edinburgh Castle, held by General Guest for George II, in which it had been placed for safe keeping, to redeem its notes held by the Young Pretender, so that he could pay his troops in hard money.[244] The governor of the castle seems not to have known that he was taking care of money used to feed the enemy. Had the bankers been sure that the rebellion would fail, they could have fled to the fortress to avoid personal seizure by Charles's men, but evidently they were not. The post-Revolu-

---

[241] Elcho, 261.

[242] Sir Bruce Seton and J. G. Arnot, *The Prisoners of the '45.* The count is my own.

[243] *Ibid.,* I, 279–280.

[244] "The Diary of John Campbell," *Miscellany of the Scottish History Society,* I (Edinburgh, 1893), 537–56.

tionary origin of the Banks of England and Scotland marked them for destruction, if the letter of the law were observed; but Charles found it wise, and useful, to proclaim at Edinburgh that he meant the banks no harm.[245] Evidently, within limits, he was believed, for they returned to business, and their financial machinery was an advantage to the rebel army.

Besides reprinting the instruments of his father, the Young Pretender issued others of his own, of which that to the banks was only one. Before his departure from France he had signed one of May 16, 1745,[246] which was so loosely worded as to leave room for the removal of churches, colleges, and schools from the control of the Protestant churches in England, Scotland, and Ireland. I attribute this to inexperience, not ill-will. Perhaps the error was pointed out to Charles, for on October 10, at Holyrood Palace, he issued another,[247] in which he was more definite:

> We therefore hereby, in his Majesty's Name, Declare . . . that Our Present Attempt is not undertaken . . . to impose upon any a Religion which they dislike, but to secure them all the Enjoyment of those which are respectively at present established among them, either in *England, Scotland,* or *Ireland*; and if it be deemed proper, that any further Security be given to the established Church or Clergy, We hereby promise, in his Name, That he shall pass any Law that his Parliament shall judge necessary for that Purpose.

Also, of the national debt,

> That it has been contracted under an unlawful Government, Nobody can disown, no more than that it is now a most heavy Load upon the Nation; yet, in regard that it is for the greatest Part due to those very Subjects whom he promises to protect, cherish, and defend, he is resolved to take the Advice of his Parliament concerning it, in which he thinks he acts the Part of a just Prince. . .

It would be a bold parliament which attempted to cancel the national debt, and an altruistic one, for any conceivable parliament would contain many of the creditors. The debt, then, was safe; as to the Union the Old Pretender was represented as

A Collection of Declarations . . . Published by Authority at Edinburgh, 34.

[245] Proclamation dated Sept. 25, 1745, signed "Charles, P.R.," reprinted in
[246] *Ibid.*, 7–10.
[247] *Ibid.*, 15–19. Elcho attributes it to a gentleman of Edinburgh, who submitted it to Charles for his consideration. *A short Account,* 290.

implacable, "But whatever may be hereafter devised for the joint Benefit of both Nations, the King will most readily comply with the Request of his Parliaments to establish."

Other utterances were issued to meet temporary needs — e.g. the invitation to Presbyterian ministers to resume their functions.[248] These are only practical documents, but they show the responsiveness of the Young Pretender to public opinion. It may have been this sensitivity which suspended the blockade of Edinburgh Castle when the governor threatened to bombard the civilian part of the city, and also prevented the issue of paper money. Yet, if it be true that the expedition seized so much public money in England as to make a profit,[249] conciliation was easy in financial matters.

The invasion of England raises other points. Charles expected, barring mishaps, to meet a French force there in December, headed by Prince Henry, with the duc de Richelieu in charge under him.[250] An alliance, with a mutually favorable commercial clause appended, was concluded by O'Brien with the ministers of Louis XV on October 24, at Fontainebleau.[251] The marquis d'Éguilles had already been sent to Scotland by way of Dunkirk, landing at Montrose on October 6/17.[252] Some arms and a thousand men, including Young Lord John Drummond's Royal Scots Regiment, were landed in Scotland in December,[253] after his departure with the main body of rebels. That was all the assistance he obtained, for, after many delays, the expedition was supposed to pass over into England from Boulogne just after Christmas; but the freezing of the sluices at the port prevented sailing in time to have the advantage of surprise. The eleven thousand men embarked were then used for other purposes. Thus for one

---

[248] *Scots Magazine*, 7:441 (September 1745).

[249] Elcho, 329*n*.

[250] For the story of this plan and its miscarriage, see Mahon, III, xxv (app.); Elcho, 296*n*.; marquis d'Argenson, *Journal et mémoires*, IV, 318–19; Mém. et doc., Ang. 78, foll. 383–84, 402r and v.

[251] Mém. et doc., Ang. 78, foll. 256–57. Printed by James Browne, *A History of the Highlands* (London etc., 2nd ed., 1849), III, 448–50.

[252] Mém. et doc., Ang. 78, foll. 208, 234–35.

[253] Blaikie, *Itinerary*, 84; Mém. et doc., Ang. 78, foll. 196–97. Some 2400 fusils, 2405 sabers, 120,000 cartridges, and other things were added to the rebel stores.

thousand men and arms for twenty-four hundred more, the French obtained the withdrawal of ten battalions from Flanders to England,[254] and no end of other disarrangement of English plans.

Another point about the invasion may seem obvious, but deserves measurement: the English did not rise. Elcho names all the halting places on the march south to Derby and the return, and records that at most of them there were few or no recruits.[255] He does not exaggerate. There was a dribble at Preston, and individual enlistments elsewhere in Lancashire, culminating at Manchester, where the largest number joined; and all English so far raised were constituted into the Manchester Regiment.[256] These Elcho spoke of as "about 200 common fellows who . . . had no subsistence, for they used to say . . . that they had for sometime been resolved to inlist with whichever of the two armies came first to town."[257] It is only fair to add that Maxwell of Kirkconnell thought better of them. Among the members of the regiment eventually captured were a fair proportion of weavers[258] — 27 of 161.

Lancashire was a disappointment, but the rest of England was a flat failure. The titular Lord Clancarty[259] had gone over to France in August, and had delivered a message in the name of the Duke of Beaufort, Lords Lichfield, Barrymore, and Orrery, Sir John Hynde Cotton, and Sir Watkin Williams asking for 10,000 men and 30,000 arms for the rising.[260] Arms for so many implies so many to arm; but there were none, lacking the landing in England, to come to Charles. Letters printed by Mahon from among the Stuart Papers also implicate more clearly the London Jacobites, with the addition to their number of Alderman Heath-

[254] Lord Tweedale to Craigie, Sept. 4, 1745, Elcho, 296n.
[255] Elcho, 323–331.
[256] "John Daniel's Progress," Blaikie, *Origins*, 168–69, 173–4.
[257] Elcho, 331; cf. Maxwell, 70.
[258] Seton and Arnot list occupations where available, but do not distinguish English from Scots in all cases. In this count all members of the Manchester Regiment were included.
[259] Robert Maccarty (1686–1769), but for his father's attainder in 1691, Earl of Clancarty. He had been governor of Newfoundland from 1733 to 1735.
[260] Marischal's mémoire, Mém. et doc., Ang. 78, foll. 126–27, printed in Murray, 510; Sempill to James, Nov. 15, 1745, Browne, III, 436–38.

cote.[261] The mayor and aldermen of York had spoken of ten thousand willing Yorkshiremen,[262] but sent no one.

At Derby the Scots concluded that these assurances were either insincere or exaggerated, and became alarmed at their exposed position. A Council of War forced a decision on Charles by this reasoning: one army was at London, another between Derby and the capital, together reaching thirty thousand men, it was estimated; Charles had 4500 in England with him, and "supposing by a miracle in our favour we should arrive even at the gates of that capital without losing a man, what kind of figure could four thousand five hundred men cut in . . . a city of more than a million and a-half of inhabitants"?[263] The prince yielded with a bad grace. Had any considerable Englishmen joined, it is improbable that he would have done so.

Returning to Scotland, Charles fought and won the battle of Falkirk, lost valuable time in the siege of Stirling, and found himself forced by desertion[264] and the movements of the enemy to move northward to take up a position near Inverness. In arms for him there were now about eight thousand men,[265] including the regulars from France and some clans which had not gone with him to England. The Duke of Cumberland, commanding for his father, George II, approached Inverness in April 1746, and met the rebels with the advantage of their exhaustion by a futile night march at Culloden Moor, and destroyed them. Only five thousand rebels were engaged,[266] of whom probably 1200[267] to 1500[268] were killed in the field or in the pursuit which followed, in consequence of Cumberland's order that no quarter be given. The survivors of the French force, mostly Irish and Scots by birth, surrendered; in the following three months nearly 3000

[261] Mahon, III, 445n.

[262] Murray to James, July 5, 1743, Blaikie, *Origins*, 36–37.

[263] *Memoirs of the Chevalier de Johnstone* (Aberdeen, 1870–71), I, 45–46. Johnstone's figure for the population is, of course, a guess.

[264] Address from the Chiefs to Charles, Jan. 29, 1746, John Home, *History of the Rebellion in the Year 1745* (London, 1802), 352.

[265] As against nearly 9400 Scots alone five months earlier. D'Éguilles' list, Nov. 3, 1745, Mém et doc., Ang. 78, foll. 319–320v.

[266] Blaikie, *Itinerary*, 97.

[267] The estimate accepted by Browne (III, 251).

[268] Wolfe's figure. J. T. Findlay, *Wolfe in Scotland* (London etc., 1928), 106.

Scottish prisoners were taken,[269] most of whom were sent to England for disposal.

8. THE END OF PRACTICAL JACOBITISM

The fate that there awaited these unfortunates was diversiform. Those surviving in prison in 1747 were for the most part discharged. Before that time, according to the compilers of the list of prisoners, 120 were executed; 382 prisoners of war (French subjects) were shortly released; 121 were banished "outside our Dominions" by King George; 92 enlisted under compulsion in the British army, and 936 were transported to America.[270] Of many there is no record beyond some mention that they had been imprisoned. The mortality of the prison ships in the Thames is known to have been shockingly high (a death rate of over 27 per cent in a period of three months is recorded in one convoy)[271] and shows what happened to a great many. Some of the ordinary prisons were little better: at Carlisle 30 were selected for trial; there was an interval of one month between condemnation and execution, yet in that time 5 of these men had died. Confinement in ships went on until the summer of 1747. The total number of deaths must therefore have been very high, unless conditions were substantially improved. One Donald Macleod told Bishop Robert Forbes that no less than 400 men died in three ships opposite Tilbury while he was there, including 60 to 70 of the Glenmoriston Grants.[272] For this we have a measure of corroboration: a historian of the parish of Urquhart and Glenmoriston tells us that baptisms there fell from 32 in 1744 and 30 in 1745 to 18 in 1746 and 12 in 1747.[273] Most of the Glenmoriston men were in prison.

Glenmoriston was especially badly hurt by the ravages after

[269] Seton and Arnot list 3471, including the English captured at Carlisle and the French prisoners of war.

[270] Seton and Arnot, I, 41. Mr. J. Macbeth Forbes accounted for 823 transportations in his *Jacobite Gleanings from State Manuscripts* (Edinburgh, 1903), 43.

[271] Seton and Arnot, I, 163–64.

[272] Forbes, *The Lyon in Mourning* (Edinburgh, 1895–6), I, 181.

[273] William Mackay, *Urquhart and Glenmoriston* (Inverness, 1893), 318n.

Culloden, as well as by death of disease, and by transportation. Bishop Forbes preserves an account of the pillage there, in which even agricultural implements were destroyed.[274] Plunder was done with great thoroughness in the spring and summer of 1746: it was forbidden except in the presence and by command of an officer;[275] the proceeds were divided in set proportions among the persons who executed it, according to rank and rate of pay.[276] In July it became less respectable, for frequent orders were issued against it — so frequent (seven between July 23 and October 11) as to suggest that they were ineffective.[277]

In December 1746 a report[278] was made to Lord Albemarle, commanding in Scotland after Cumberland's departure, on the state of the Highlands, by two spies who had traveled through that region just before. Were it not monotonous it would be shocking. Fifteen villages are burned in Morvern, and six in Appin; the lands of Keppoch and Glen Nevis are all burned. Lochiel is burned, except Fassfern, and also Locharkaig. Glenmoriston has been burned, to the number of twenty villages of Grants; in Glengarry "there is neither houses nor people, only some few huts inhabited by women only in a starving condition." Winter was coming on, and there had been no food raised that year. Cluny Macpherson's country is all burned, and, if the passage at this point means what it says, the whole of the braes of Badenoch. An estimate of the loss of men alone in the Highlands, at the end of the report, states that the Camerons have lost 460 males and the Stewarts (of Appin) 160 of a much smaller clan. Women and children are not counted.

A good study of this devastation has not been made, but with the evidence only of printed sources such as the *Lyon in Mourning*, it can be made out that the living standards of the Highlands suffered a great loss, dipping often below the level at which survival is possible: destruction of farming tools and the wholesale confiscation of cattle, which the plundered were not then

[274] *The Lyon in Mourning*, III, 108.
[275] Order of April 17, 1746, A.N. Campbell-Maclachlan, *William Augustus, Duke of Cumberland* (London, 1876), 301.
[276] Letters of Wolfe, quoted in Findlay, 117.
[277] Campbell-Maclachlan, 336–41.
[278] C. S. Terry, ed., *The Albemarle Papers* (Aberdeen, 1902), I, 331–40.

allowed to buy back for food, must have meant starvation for some; [279] the burning of houses and even huts must have led to death of exposure or disease for many more.[280] When these effects are added to transportations, executions, and deaths in prison and battle, we must believe that the population of the Highlands, always small, fell sharply, and that some places did not regain their former size and prosperity, however insignificant, for many years.

This study can go no further on this subject. Still, it can be safely said that Jacobitism was far more hurt by the extirpation of its human material than by the act for abolition of heritable jurisdictions, often mentioned in this connection. It was force brutally exercised which eradicated loyalty to the Stuarts from the Highlands. This is not to say that the jurisdictions had not sheltered it in some cases, for they had, but they could equally well have sheltered Hanoverian sentiment had the Stuarts ruled — was not the greatest Scottish jurisdiction that of Argyll, the great defender of the Protestant Succession? James III had pledged his word, as he did never lightly, to purchase the jurisdictions gradually, and to reform the feudal land tenure of Scotland, which put so much power into the hands of the magnates. He had such reasons in mind. Come James come George, strengthening of royal justice and centralization of power would have been among the results of the '45. Nevertheless, the abolition of the jurisdictions was meant to be a blow at the Pretender, and it was; in another season, under other circumstances, it would have reconciled some Highlanders who had suffered from the old system to King George. At that time it could not humanly be so. Its social effects were not immediate, for a man cannot be deprived of traditional power by a statute; in this case the law was assisted by the flight of the most important chiefs, not only of the Highlands but of the Lowlands as well. Those who lived to return spent years abroad awaiting permission. Separation did the government's business, and executions, by leaving gaps which only

[279] *Scots Magazine*, 8:287 (1746); Campbell-Maclachlan, 324–25; R. Forbes, I, 176.

[280] Forbes, I, 91, 309; II, 93, 333; *Scots Magazine*, 8:287; W.A.S. Hewins, ed., *The Whitefoord Papers* (Oxford, 1898), 79.

minors could fill, facilitated it: a generation grew up which had never known the legal powers of the chiefs, had known neither the face and voice of the Young, nor the scrawling hand of the Old Pretender. That was the end of Jacobitism in Scotland.

In England, sentimental Jacobitism lingered when the effective force of it had gone. Just when the vital spark was lost is more difficult to say than in the case of Scotland; probably years before 1745, as is evident from the behavior of England at the time. In the last years of Anne it was certainly there in the number of those — Charles Caesar, Orrery, Ormonde, Atterbury, Wyndham, St. John, and Gower, to name a few — who were active, and willing to undertake the restoration of the Pretender when Anne should die, at the risk of their lives and fortunes. These men grew old: many died; some left the party, as did Bolingbroke and Wyndham, to fit themselves uneasily into a political system in which the Pretender was a joke; some were swayed, as were Gower and Wynn, by the desire for office. Their exclusive and principled loyalty was faded by the light and air of conflict with authority, side by side with men whose political actions were as unscrupulous as those of Walpole. In this sense, coalition with the Whig Opposition was a mistake, but it was impossible for the Pretender to avoid it without reducing his party to impotence. In office, Cotton alone had the strength of will to stand two years as the opponent of all the measures of the government which had put him there.

It is possible that the Atterbury trial was the crucial event, for the bishop was the soul of the party in England when he was arrested. Lansdowne was already in France; Lord North and Grey soon followed him into exile; and Wharton made his own return to England impossible by his extravagant conduct: their successors were James Hamilton, Colonel Cecil, and the Duchess of Buckingham. There was no figure in England equivalent to Cameron of Lochiel, Lord George Murray, Young Lord John Drummond, or even the vigorous, if scheming, Murray of Broughton.

Jacobitism in England therefore did not have to be uprooted, for the top was dead. In Scotland it died because its human material was gone, but in England no one had the strength, the touch, or the intellect to use the material available. An English aspirant to insurgent leadership had not the advantage of the authority inherited by a Highland chief; he had to be brilliant, old enough to command respect, young enough to take the field, and used to making instant decisions. Shippen and Cotton were not fools, but they could not satisfy most of these requirements. Of all the parliamentary Jacobites, not one had a mind of the first rank after the departure of Atterbury, and few would have dared to cut themselves boldly away from things as they were, as Atterbury could do.

The "social background" of the leadership had its own influence on the destinies of the party. Here one cannot speak with complete authority, because the composition of the party has never been studied in detail[281] (as it must be), but especially at first, and always to a great degree, Jacobite leaders came from landed, if not titled, families. Of those who held the office of Secretary of State, Melfort, Middleton, and Bolingbroke were peers before they took it. John Hay was the younger son of a Scottish earl (Kinnoull) and James Murray of a viscount (Stormont). John Caryll was a member of a well-to-do old Catholic family in Sussex; Thomas Higgons of a great connection in the western counties. Three of these four commoners received peerages from James II and his son, and the last could have expected a higher title than his knighthood had his capacity been greater. Nagle and "Sir John" Graeme were the least of the series, socially, but were not inconsiderable.

Those who did not hold the seals were for the most part of the same sort: Orrery, North and Grey, Wharton, the Duke of Hamilton, Strafford, Dundonald, Marischal, Pitsligo, Barrymore, Traquair, and many others were peers of one or other of the three kingdoms, and not of Jacobite creation. Tullibardine and Lord George Murray, Marshal James Keith, the Master of Sinclair, Lord Elcho, and the Master of Lovat were among the sons of peers; John Murray of Broughton was the son of a baronet, and eventu-

---

[281] When this passage was written, I had not yet read the work of Mr. G. P. Insh, *The Scottish Jacobite Movement* (London, 1952). So far as it goes, I do not believe that Mr. Insh has invalidated it, although I can no longer say that the party's social structure has not been studied.

ally succeded. The Highland chiefs, however poor the clan, were aristocrats beyond parallel in England.

I have remarked that the patricians lost touch with what we now call the masses, in England by their own mediocrity as a rule, and in Scotland by the depletion of the loyal clans and exile of the chiefs. In the beginning, the lower classes were not averse to "the old cries," but after the flight of Ormonde they were seldom used: assembly at loyal gatherings was restricted by danger of detection or loose talk to gentlemen of staunch principles, who flocked to each other's houses, but forgot to court the mob. That element of the population was excluded, and left to imagine what went on behind closed doors, not without guidance by Whig newspapers and pamphlets. In 1696 it was possible to enlist a good number for service in the regiments to be raised by Lord Montgomery and others; after Ormonde's departure it was not spoken of by responsible people, and may even have been impossible before that time. Layer's absurd recruitment of a few men in Essex led with the shortest possible interval to his arrest and conviction. Exclusion had had its effect, and separation from the leaders added to it, as Ailesbury, Atterbury, Ormonde, and others one by one were forced out of the country.

Again, the weakening of ties binding landlord and tenant in England, which had begun earlier and proceeded more quickly than in Scotland, deprived landed Jacobites of the followings which Scots lowland squires, who had no more legal powers over their tenants than the English, for military purposes, could command. Ormonde, on progress through the West, where many of his estates lay, was lustily greeted, but there is no reason to believe that he could have formed a rebel army from among the cheering standers-by.

The religious composition of the party was mixed. Catholics predominated in numbers abroad, for good reason. A Catholic had more opportunities for employment than a Protestant in the French, Spanish, or Imperial service, and he had less reason to stay at home, especially if he were Irish. He was also more at ease abroad in the Catholic countries usually willing to admit Jacobites, because troublesome inquiries by ecclesiastical authorities were out of the question in his case. Without a foreign sojourn, proper education for ordination and practically all chance of promotion in his church were almost beyond his reach. Abroad there was education of all levels without concealment at Paris, Rome, Madrid, and elsewhere.

In Great Britain the greater number of Jacobites were almost certainly Protestant. The Anglican, even the non-juror, was very comfortable at home, and had little incentive to go abroad after the first curiosity of the Grand Tour had been satisfied. Most Catholics were also unwilling, if they shared the political sentiments of the bolder Protestants (as most of them did), to expose themselves to the enforcement of the usually dormant penal laws. Protestants are the men who flaunt the White Rose, gather to drink the Pretender's health under semi-public conditions, and break windows on anniversaries. The signs of the strength of Jacobitism among Protestants are the existence of the non-juring sect of the Church of England, the acceptance of James III's patronage by the Scottish Episcopal Church, and the constant cultivation of Ormonde, who retained symbolic significance as the grandson of the great Protestant duke in spite of his own inferior intellect; and the struggle for the retention of the Protestant Secretary and the Protestant governor in the years 1725 to 1727 was much less motivated by a desire for new friends than by the absolute necessity of keeping the old ones. Still, we shall never know the exact ratio of Catholic and Protestants, and an estimate can only be drawn from a long study. The populace of the eighteenth century did not take the time for study, but burned at once Pope, Devil, and Pretender without cogitation. Historians followed where party-writers led, and the myth of overwhelming numbers of Catholics in the party has come down to our own day.

That there was no steady stream of publications to offset those of the other side by vindicating the Pretender's honesty and lack of bigotry, as well as the inclinations of his followers, was a great handicap. Charles Leslie's writings were far from the common level. Other writers either so far disguised their feelings as not to be Jacobites, or were completely inept and unconvincing. After 1714 attempts to influence the public by use of the printed word were guarded; fewer people wrote, and fewer read the matter supplied. Often manuscript copies of Jacobite pieces appear to have met the demand.

Indeed, there might have been found among Jacobites abroad men of more ability: they had risen and continued in the second and third generations to rise to very creditable posts in the service of foreign nations. Drummonds, McCarthys, Fitzgeralds, Mahoneys, MacDonalds, MacMahons, and many a Fitzjames attained rank and favor all over Europe. They might have been more useful to the party in England, but they found rewards more certain where they were. Also, they were willing, like Lord Marischal, the greatest of them all, perhaps, to serve in great things, but not in small. When they could not choose their company, or were set to trivial tasks, they found it more pleasant to retire, as he did in 1740, "to live quietly with a great Plutarch in the way I wish, untill there comes an occasion for reall service." [282] In the case of Jacobites born abroad, permanent foreign interests were involved, more weighty (being more immediate) than a loyalty, hereditary but not renewed, to the three kingdoms with which they seemed always to have been at war.

Thus every factor influenced England and Scotland to forget the cause, the principle of loyalty behind it, and the "old cries" by which fidelity was manifested. Even the burning of the Pretender in effigy became a spectacle like that of Guy Fawkes, and ceased to mean anything at all. The old man who departed this world in 1766 had no connection with British reality. Only his son was left to believe that the cause was living, and that son had killed it. The succession of Cardinal York to the Stuart claims in 1788 caused the last enthusiasts to acknowledge only the truth, that Jacobitism was a thing of the past. No one need now or ever regret it:

> These men, and those who opposed them
> And those whom they opposed
> Accept the constitution of silence,
> And are folded in a single party.[283]

Distant sufferings and grievances were better forgotten, with so many near at hand.

---

[282] W.S.P. 224, no. 17.

[283] T. S. Eliot, "Little Gidding," from his *Four Quartets*, by permission of the author and Harcourt, Brace and Company.

APPENDIX

The Authorship of the MS "Political Reflexions"

Three MS tracts — the "Hystorical Account," known to be by Thomas Sheridan the elder; "The King of Great Britain's Case," a narrative of the events preceding the Revolution, identified by a passage in the "Hystorical Account" (p. 71 in the MS) as Sheridan's work; and "Political Reflexions," a tract similar to these in hand, in details of narration, and in thought — are preserved in the Royal Archives of Windsor. By comparison of these three pamphlet-length works, I have come to the conclusion that they are in fact written by the same man. I have chosen some of the passages which have led me to this conclusion. From the "Hystorical Account" (p. 70; HMC *Stuart Papers*, VI, 64) comes this story of Melfort's misintelligence before La Hogue:

His Lop had persuaded the Court of ffrance, that none of the first or second rate would be ready to sail before the 10th of June Old Stile; and that Carter's squadron woud joyn the french & declare for the King. Which made the K. of ffrance order Tourville to fight fort oufoible; but the whole fleet was out; and in the engagement wch happened the 19th of May old stile, Carter fought as heartily as any of the English . . . within 2 hours after the contrary [of the information on the first and second rates] was found true; as one Mr. Clark sent purposely by Lord Peterborow had before affirmd & for his reward was confin'd at La Hogue as a false intelligencer.

In the "Political Reflexions" (p. 94) it is related thus:

In spring following Melfort's return the expedition of La Hogue was undertaken; upon this Lords assurance, that none of the second-rate-ships would be out before the 10th of June old stile; and that a Squadron of the Fleet, commanded by Carter, wou'd declare for our King and joyn the French; to wch story the King of France giving credit, orderd Tourville fort ou foible to fight.

and from page 95 of the same tract:

On Fryday i' th' evening the K. from a hil had a view of the Fleet; Sir Randle mcDonnal assur'd him the first and second-Rates were out and the Britannia in the head of them. This had been affirm'd eight days before by one Clark, sent by Lord Peterborow to give them notice, and for his pains was confin'd as a Spy by Melfort; who next morning persisting in the contrary opinion, said before the Duke of Berwick, Lord Lucan, Sir Randle mcDonnal, and Mr. Sheridan there was not one of those ships at Sea. Sir Randle made answer, that as sure as he then saw him, he saw the Britannia wth the flag the night before; but in two hours after, this ship, wth the whole Fleet, came into the Bay.

Plainly Sheridan was one of the few witnesses of this conversation, which accounts for its occurrence in the "Hystorical Account." There are other similarities in the two relations of British intelligence in France in 1696: The "Hystorical Account" (p. 77; HMC *Stuart Papers*, VI, 73) gives it thus:

> In two or three days after the Kr departure [for Calais] it was found, the design was al discover'd to the P of O. Whereupon ye Q.[ueen] sent for Sher[idan] and before Mr Carryll told him, the K. of France had desir'd an Apology might be written in English, to vindicate both him and his Brother of England, from what was most falsly given out, that they both had contriv'd the Murder and assassination of the Usurper; and that she had pitched upon him to Write it. . . . but in two days after the Q. told Sher. the K. of ffrance said such a thing would not now be fit, Since the Holland Gazet had publish'd that there was a paper a writing to exculpat the two Ks from having any hand in the Murder of P. of O.

The "Political Reflexions" are much the same (p. 109):

> The King of France (our King being at Calais) advisd the Queen to get a manifest written in English to free them from so false and horrid an imputation; but of this so early notice was given, that wthin three days after her Majestie had commanded Sheridan to write it, it was in the Holland Gazette that a writing was directed to be made to disculpat them from the crime.

Again from the "Hystorical Account" (pp. 77–78; HMC *Stuart Papers*, VI, 73):

> Sheridan was afterwards told, the K. had dispatched fr. Plowden from Calais to England without the privity of any but Ld Middn and fr. Sanders; yet this was discoverd to the Earl of Shrewsbury Secretary of State, and a warrant by him given to seize fr Plowden; who made his escape into Scotland. Not long after fr. Mansel was privatly sent to the Emperor; of which the P. of O. had notice from some of his spies about our K.

The "Political Reflexions" follow this (p. 110):

> . . . I have heard . . . in particular, that his [James's] sending fr. Plowden a Jesuit from Calais to London, to wch, (as was said) none were privy, except fr Sanders, the confessor, and Lord Middn, was discoverd to Lord Shrewsbury, and a Warrant in the Messenger's hand to seize him; of wch receiving notice by a great chance, he escap'd being taken by flying into Scotland. After the King's return from Calais, he sent father Mansel to the Emperor's Court, of wch the Prince of O. had early notice, as he also had of Mr Sheridan's journy, employ'd the Winter before, to the Elector Palatine . . .

There are also similarities to link the "King of Great Britain's Case," acknowledged by Sheridan as his own, and the "Political Reflexions." The "Case" says of parliaments (p. 105):

> And not only their results, thus confirm'd and approv'd, Stampt with his

Fiat become Laws, are call'd the King's Laws, but the very Parliament also, is called ye King's Parliament.

The "Reflexions" say it more shortly (p. 131):

The Parliament is the King's; and his Fiat makes the laws, as his Stamp makes the Coyn.

Since "Fiat" was not the formula of the King's assent, the coincidence is worthy of remark.

Still again, the "Case" relates (pp. 112–3) of the English constitution:

By one of the most fundamental Maxims in our Laws, the *King never dies* . . . For tho' the natural person of our King dies, his political person, the Kingship, or Royal Authority never do's; this, like water in a conduit, continually running in the same Channel, or blood, and passing in one and the same instant from father, or predecessor, to the son, or next heir, makes the decease not to be called the death, but in our Law-Language, the Demise. . . And over and above the last maxim, our Laws teach us another, equally fundamental, *The King can do no wrong*: that is, no mismanagements in Gover'ment, are to be imputed to him; never his, but whenever happening the faults of his Ministers, who onely are punishable. . .

The "Reflexions" follow this too:

There are in our Laws two fundamental maxims; 1st that the King never dies. 2d that the King can do no wrong. The first proves, Our Monarchy is hereditary, & that therefore the Throne can never be vacant either by death, or abdication; as so long as there is any one of the Royal-line left to fill it: for this reason, the decease, in our law-phrase, is not calld the death, but the demise. . . . The second maxim demonstrats that our Kings are not accountable before any Tribunal on earth: whatever happens to be don amiss in their Government, their Ministers, not they are answerable for it.

All this gives very solid grounds for believing that Sheridan is the author of the "Reflexions"; there remains the bare possibility that some other person used his papers as a basis for a new tract; but the "Reflexions" are dated 1709, while Sheridan was still living: if the three papers were retained by him until his death in 1712, taken by the younger Thomas and with the rest of his letters and papers fell into the general collection of Stuart Papers, their *provenance* is explained. Otherwise it is obscure. Sheridan was very jealous of other pamphleteers: in the "Hystorical Account" he has no good words for any of them; it is improbable that he would have trusted his own writings to them to alter and dilute (for they were very strong) as they liked. Altogether, then, the supposition that Sheridan wrote the "Reflexions" is supported by the evidence, and can be taken for granted unless some definite proof of the contrary is found.

BIBLIOGRAPHY

I. MANUSCRIPT SOURCES

1. The Stuart Papers in the Royal Archives at Windsor Castle. This collection includes most of the voluminous correspondence, memoranda, and accounts of James II and his descendants in the male line, and consists of about 600 volumes in all, arranged for the most part chronologically. Those for the latter part of my period (after 1718) are substantially unpublished and unknown to history. I have frequently cited this collection as W.S.P. The story of the provenance of these papers is printed in the Historical Manuscripts Commission's *Stuart Papers*, introduction to volume I.

2. The Nairne Papers, a portion of the Carte Collection in the Bodleian Library at Oxford. David Nairne, a senior clerk employed by Melfort and Middleton, kept about a dozen volumes of manuscripts, mostly copies and originals of the correspondence of the Secretaries of State. These were deposited at the Scots College at Paris in 1741 by George and Thomas Inese, with the exception of one volume, which Nairne's daughter was allowed to retain (it contained only personal papers). For this transaction I rely on W.S.P. 238, no. 50, and W.S.P. 239, no. 39. It was therefore at some time after early 1742 that Thomas Carte procured them by theft or bribery, certainly not by James III's permission, from the College to join his other acquisitions, with which they passed to his widow and thence to the Bodleian Library, after some extracts and abridgments had already been printed in James Macpherson's *Original Papers* (see below, among printed sources). History has so far been written from this imperfect, though honest, edition. I have gone to the originals, which have much more than Macpherson prints, and differ in small but important points from his version in many cases.

3. The Gualterio Papers, among the Additional Manuscripts of the British Museum. The correspondence and other papers of the Cardinal Protector cover a great range of subjects over a period of many years. Some of them, having to do with England and the Pretender, fill gaps in the other two collections. There are many duplications, and many volumes are not useful at all. Those cited in my notes include Add. MSS. 20,292–93; 20,295; 20,303; 20,310–12; 20,318; and 20,322.

4. Carte Papers other than those collected by Nairne. Of these there is a great miscellaneous bulk, dealing with most imaginable subjects of English or Irish history up to Carte's own old age. To any historian of this period, whether interested in Jacobitism or not, Carte's notes of his interviews with various personages of the time, usually dealing with

occurrences of the reigns of William III and Anne, in Carte MSS. 231, 237, and 266 could be of great use. In general the chronological calendar compiled with great labor by Mr. Edward Edwards is of the greatest convenience in the use of the collection, and is reasonably accurate.

5. The Rawlinson Collection, also of the Bodleian Library. This is of even greater bulk than Carte's, and is of more miscellaneous character. It has never been properly used, except in such writings as those of Thomas Hearne, and contains much interesting and useful matter. Letters of the most important non-jurors are included. I have used several volumes (there are over a thousand), but particularly Rawlinson MSS. A. 311.

6. A small volume of letters by Bolingbroke in the Bodleian volume MSS. French d. 18.

7. The archives of the Ministère des affaires étrangères at Paris. Here I must caution the reader that I have not exhausted the material available there, which would have called for a period of study double the time allotted to the preparation of this book, with only slight reward in clarifying the history of Jacobitism *from the inside,* which is my purpose. It was essential that I should consult, as I have done, the two series, Correspondance politique, Angleterre, and Mémoires et documents, Angleterre, for the years 1733, 1740, 1741, 1743, 1744, and 1745.

II. PRINTED SOURCES

The Historical Manuscripts Commission has printed many documents from private collections, none more important than the seven volumes of *Stuart Papers,* published from 1902 to 1923. An eighth volume brought to the stage of manuscript extracts and abridgments arranged in chronological order has not been published as yet. The manuscript has been deposited at the Public Record Office. If printed, it will make available almost all of the Stuart Papers to the end of the year 1719.

Other publications of the Commission cited in my notes are Report IX, appendix, part II; Report X, app., parts I, IV, and VI; Report XI, app., part IV; Report XII, app., part VIII; Report XIII, app., part II; Report XIV, app., parts III, IV, and IX; Report XV, parts II, IV, and VI: also the *Lords MSS.,* New Series, vols. VII and VIII; and the Portland Papers, vol. VI.

H. M. Stationery Office has also provided a good quantity of printed material in the *Calendar of State Papers, Domestic Series* (cited here as Cal. S. P. Dom.), of which thirteen volumes for this period have appeared as of this time.

Other collections of printed sources follow:

Alberoni, Giulio, Cardinal, *Lettres intimes addressées au comte I. Rocca, ministre des finances du duc de Parme,* ed. Émile Bourgeois, Annales de l'université de Lyon, vol. IV (Lyon, 1892).

D'Argenson, Marc-René, comte de, *Correspondance*, ed. marquis d'Argenson (Paris, 1924).

Bourgogne, Louis, duc de, *Lettres . . . au roi d'Espagne*, ed. A. Baudrillart and L. Lecestre, 2 vols. (Paris: Société de l'histoire de France, 1912–1916).

Brosses, Charles de, *L'Italie il y a cent ans* (Paris, 1836).

Campana de Cavelli, Emilia, marquise, ed., *Les Derniers Stuarts à Saint-Germain-en-Laye*, 2 vols. (Paris, 1871).

Clement XI, *Opera Omnia* (Frankfurt, 1729).

Cole, Christian, ed., *Memoirs of Affairs of State; containing letters written by ministers employed in foreign negotiations from . . . 1697 to . . . 1708* (London, 1733).

A Collection of Declarations, Proclamations, and other valuable Papers, published by Authority at Edinburgh, in the Years 1745 and 1746 (n. pl., 1748).

A Collection of Original Papers about the Scots Plot (London, 1704).

Dickson, W. K., ed., *The Jacobite Attempt of 1719*, Publications of the Scottish History Society, vol. XIX (Edinburgh, 1895).

Dickson, W. K., and Wood, M., eds., *The Warrender Letters*, Publications of the Scottish History Society, 3rd series, vol. XXV (Edinburgh, 1935).

Forbes, Duncan G., ed., *The Culloden Papers* (London, 1815).

Granville, Denis, *Remains*, ed. George Ornsby, Publications of the Surtees Society, vol. XLVII (Durham, 1865).

Granville, Denis, *Remains*, ed. George Ornsby, Publications of the Surtees Society, vol. XXXVII, 1860 (Durham, 1861).

Grimblot, Paul, ed., *Letters of William III and Louis XIV and of their ministers . . . 1697–1700*, 2 vols. (London, 1848).

Hanotaux, Gabriel, ed., *Recueil des instructions données aux ambassadeurs et ministres de France . . . Rome*, vol. III, (Paris, 1913).

Hardwicke, Philip Yorke, Earl, ed., *Miscellaneous State Papers . . . ,* 2 vols. (London, 1778).

Hewins, W. A. S., ed., *The Whitefoord Papers* (Oxford, 1898).

Hogan, James, ed., *Les Négociations de M. le comte d'Avaux en Irlande, 1689–90* (Dublin: Irish Manuscripts Commission, 1934).

Hooke, Nathaniel, *Secret History of Colonel Hooke's Negotiations in Scotland in 1707* (Edinburgh, 1760).

Lart, C. E., ed., *The Parochial Registers of Saint-Germain-en-Laye, Jacobite Extracts . . . ,* 2 vols. (London, 1910–1912).

Legg, L. G. W., ed., "Jacobite Correspondence, 1712–1714," *English Historical Review*, 30:501–518 (July 1915).

McCormick, Joseph, ed., *State Papers and Letters addressed to William Carstares* (Edinburgh, 1774).

Macpherson, James, ed., *Original Papers, containing the secret history of Great Britain from the Restoration, to the accession of the house of Hanover*, 2 vols. (London, 1775).

Macray, W. D., *Correspondence of Col. Nathaniel Hooke, . . . 1703–1707*, 2 vols. (London: Roxburghe Club, 1870–71).

Mar, John Erskine, Earl of, "The Earl of Mar's Legacies to Scotland . . . ," ed. Hon. Stuart Erskine, *Wariston's Diary: Mar's Legacies: etc.*, Publications of the Scottish History Society, vol. XXVI (Edinburgh, 1896).

Morel-Fatio, A., and Léonardon, H., eds., *Recueil des instructions données aux ambassadeurs . . . Espagne*, 3 vols. (Paris, 1894–99).

Omond, G. W. T., *The Arniston Memoirs* (Edinburgh, 1887).

Prideaux, Humphrey, *Letters . . . to John Ellis, . . . 1674–1722*, ed. E. M. Thompson, Publications of the Camden Society, New Series, vol. XV (Westminster, 1875).

Rancé, Armand-Jean le Bouthilier de, *Lettres*, ed. B. Gonod (Paris, 1846).

Ravaisson, François, ed., *Archives de la Bastille, documents inédits . . .*, 18 vols. (Paris, 1866–1903).

Rose, Sir George H., ed., *A Selection from the Papers of the Earls of Marchmont*, 3 vols. (London, 1831).

Tayler, Alistair and Henrietta, eds., *The Stuart Papers at Windsor* (London, 1939).

Tayler, Henrietta, ed., "Jacobite Papers at Avignon," *Miscellany of the Scottish History Society*, vol. V (Edinburgh, 1933).

Terry, C. S., ed., *The Albemarle Papers*, 2 vols. (Aberdeen: New Spalding Club, 1902).

Terry, C. S., ed., *The Chevalier de St. George* (London etc., 1901).

Trevelyan, G. M., "The 'Jersey Period' of Negotiations Leading to the Peace of Utrecht," *English Historical Review*, 49:100–105 (January 1934).

Vault, François-Eugène de, *Mémoires militaires relatifs à la succession d'Espagne sous Louis XIV*, 11 vols., Collection de documents inédits sur l'histoire de France (Paris, 1835–62).

III. CONTEMPORARY ACCOUNTS

Ailesbury, Thomas Bruce, Earl of, *Memoirs*, ed. W. E. Buckley, 2 vols. (Westminster: Roxburghe Club, 1890).

D'Argenson, René Louis, marquis, *Journal et mémoires . . .*, ed. E. J. B. Rathery, 9 vols. (Paris: Société de l'histoire de France 1859–67).

Balcarres, Colin Lindsay, Earl of, *Memoirs Touching the Revolution in Scotland, 1688–1690*, ed. A. W. C. Lindsay (Edinburgh: Bannatyne Club, 1841).

Beamont, William, ed., *The Jacobite Trials at Manchester in 1694*, Publications of the Chetham Society, vol. XXVIII (Manchester, 1853).

Bernardi, John, "The most Sad and Deplorable *Case* of Robert Blackburne, John Bernardi, and Robert Cassills" (single sheet, London, 1727).

Bernardi, John, *A short History of the Life of Major John Bernardi, written by himself in Newgate* (London, 1729).

Berwick, James FitzJames, Duke of, *Mémoires . . . écrits par lui-même*, 2 vols. (Paris, 1778). Readers must be particularly careful to avoid confusion with the *Mémoires du maréchal de Berwik, duc et pair de France*, 2 vols. (La Haye, 1737), not written by Berwick, and differing in many essentials from the genuine ones.

Blackmore, Sir Richard, *A true and impartial History of the Conspiracy against the Person and Government of King William III . . . 1695* (London, 1723).

Blaikie, W. B., ed., *Origins of the 'Forty-Five, and other papers. . .* , Publications of the Scottish History Society, 2nd series, vol. II (Edinburgh, 1916). This volume contains, *inter alia*, "Papers of John Murray of Broughton found after Culloden," and John Daniel's "Progress with Prince Charles."

Bolingbroke, Henry St. John, Viscount, *A Letter to Sir William Windham* (London, 1753).

Caylus, Marie-Marguérite le Valois, comtesse de, *Souvenirs et correspondance*, ed. E. Raunié (Paris, 1881).

Clarendon, Henry Hyde, Earl of, *The Correspondence of Henry Hyde, Earl of Clarendon . . . with the diary of Lord Clarendon from 1687 to 1690*, ed. S. W. Singer, 2 vols. (London, 1828).

Clarke, J. S., ed., *Life of James II, King of England, . . . writ of his own hand*, 2 vols. (London, 1816).

Cordara, Giulio Cesare, S.J., "Commentary on the expedition to Scotland," ed. Sir Bruce Seton, *Miscellany of the Scottish History Society*, vol. IV (Edinburgh, 1926).

Dangeau, Philippe de Courcillon, marquis de, *Journal publiée en entier. . .* , ed. Soulié and others, 19 vols. (Paris, 1854–60).

Deane, J. M., *Journal of a Campaign in Flanders, A.D. 1708*, ed. J. B. Deane (privately printed, n. pl., 1846).

Elcho, David Wemyss, styled Lord, *A short Account of the Affairs of Scotland in the years 1744, 1745, 1746*, ed. Hon. Evan Charteris (Edinburgh, 1907).

Forbes, Bishop Robert, ed., *The Lyon in Mourning, or a Collection of Speeches, Letters, Journals, etc., relative to the Affairs of Prince Charles Edward Stuart 1746–1775*, Publications of the Scottish History Society, vols. XX–XXII, (Edinburgh, 1895–96).

Forbin, Claude, comte de, *Mémoires*, 2 vols., in the *Collection des mémoires relatifs à l'histoire de France*, ed. Claude Bernard Petitot, vols. LXXIV–LXXV (Paris, 1829).

Foucault, Nicolas-Joseph de, *Mémoires*, ed. F. Baudry, *Collection des documents inédits sur l'histoire de France* (Paris, 1862).

Goss, Alexander, D. D., ed., *An Account of the Tryalls at Manchester, October 1694*, Chetham Soc., vol. LXI (Manchester, 1864).

Johnstone, James, chevalier de, *Memoirs*, trans, and ed. Charles Winchester, 3 vols. (Aberdeen, 1870–71).

Keith, Field-Marshal James, *A Fragment of a Memoir* . . . (Edinburgh: Spalding Club, 1843).

Ker of Kersland, John, *Memoirs*, 3 vols. (London, 1726–27).

King, Dr. William, *Political and Literary Anecdotes of his own Times* (London, 1818).

Lockhart of Carnwath, George, *The Lockhart Papers*, 2 vols. (London, 1817).

Mackay, Hugh, *Memoirs of the war carried on in Scotland and Ireland, 1689–91*, ed. J. M. Hog and others (Edinburgh: Bannatyne Club, 1833).

Macky, John, *Memoirs of the Secret Services of John Macky* (London: Roxburghe Club, 1895).

Marischal, George Keith, Earl, "Two Fragments of Autobiography," ed. J. Y. T. Greig, *Miscellany of the Scottish History Society*, vol. V (Edinburgh, 1933).

Maxwell of Kirkconnell, James, *Narrative of Charles, Prince of Wales' Expedition to Scotland in the Year 1745*, ed. Walter Buchanan (Edinburgh: Maitland Club, 1841).

Murray of Broughton, John, *Memorials of John Murray of Broughton*, ed. R. Fitzroy Bell, Publications of the Scottish History Society, vol. XXVII (Edinburgh, 1898).

O'Kelly, Charles, "Macariae Excidium, or the Destruction of Cyprus," ed. T. C. Croker, *Narratives Illustrative of the Contests in Ireland*, Publications of the Camden Society, vol. XIV (London, 1841).

Paton, Henry, ed., "Papers about the Rebellions of 1715 and 1745," *Miscellany of the Scottish History Society*, vol. I (Edinburgh, 1893). This includes "Leaves from the Diary of John Campbell, an Edinburgh Banker in 1745."

Quincy, Joseph Sévin, chevalier de, *Mémoires*, ed. L. Lecestre, 3 vols. (Paris: Société de l'histoire de France, 1898–1901).

Rae, Peter, *A History of the Late Rebellion* (Dumfries, 1718).

A Report from the Committee appointed by the House of Commons . . . [to examine Christopher Layer] (London, 1722).

[Sage, Bishop John,] *The Case of the Present Afflicted Episcopal Clergy in Scotland* (London, 1690).

St.-Simon, Louis de Rouvroy, duc de, *Mémoires*, ed. A. de Boislisle, 41 vols. (Paris, 1879–1928).

The Scots Magazine, vols. VII, VIII (Edinburgh, 1745–46).

Sheridan, Thomas, *Historical Account*, H.M.C. *Stuart Papers*, vol. VI (London, 1916).

Sourches, Louis-François du Bouchet, marquis de, *Mémoires sur le règne de Louis XIV*, ed. G. J., comte de Cosnac and E. Pontal, 13 vols. (Paris, 1882–93).

Spanheim, Ezechiel, *Relation de la cour de France en 1690,* ed. Ch. Schefer (Paris: Société de l'histoire de France, 1882).

Spottiswoode Miscellany, vol. II, (Edinburgh: Spottiswoode Society, 1845). This volume includes a reprinting of *A Short Account of the Grievances of the Episcopal Clergy in Scotland,* and one of John, master of Sinclair's *A true Account of the Proceedings at Perth* (first printed London, 1716).

Steuart, A. F., ed., *The Woodhouselee MS.* (London and Edinburgh, 1907).

Tayler, Henrietta, ed., *The Jacobite Court at Rome in 1719,* Publications of the Scottish History Society, 3rd series, vol. XXXI (Edinburgh, 1938). The center of this volume is the narrative of Alexander, Lord Forbes of Pitsligo.

Villars, C. L. Hector, maréchal de, *Mémoires,* ed. C. J. M., marquis de Voguë, 6 vols. (Paris: Société de l'histoire de France, 1884–1904).

The Whole Proceeding upon the Arraignment, Tryal, Conviction, and Attainder of Christopher Layer (London, 1722).

IV. SECONDARY WORKS

A. BOOKS

Blaikie, W. B., *Itinerary of Prince Charles Edward Stuart from his landing in Scotland July 1745 to his Departure in September 1746,* Publications of the Scottish History Society, vol. XXIII (Edinburgh, 1897).

Blanchet, A., and Dieudonné, A., *Manuel de numismatique française,* 4 vols. (Paris, 1912–1936).

Bourgeois, Émile, *La Diplomatie secrète au XVIIIe siècle,* 3 vols. (Paris, 1909).

Boutry, Maurice, *Intrigues et missions du cardinal de Tencin* (Paris, 1902).

Browne, James, *A History of the Highlands and of the Highland Clans,* 2nd ed., 4 vols. (London, 1849).

Campbell-Maclachlan, A. N., *William Augustus, Duke of Cumberland* (London, 1876).

Chambers, Robert, *History of the Rebellion in Scotland in 1745, 1746,* 7th ed. (London and Edinburgh, 1869).

Churchill, W. S., *Marlborough, his Life and Times,* new ed., 2 vols. (London, 1947).

Colin, Jean, *Louis XV et les jacobites: le projet de débarquement en Angleterre de 1743–1744* (Paris, 1901).

Coxe, William, *Memoirs of the Life and Administration of Sir Robert Walpole, Earl of Orford,* 3 vols. (London, 1798).

Dalrymple, Sir John, *Memoirs of Great Britain and Ireland . . . ,* 3 vols. (London and Edinburgh, 1771–1788).

Dureng, Jean, *Le duc de Bourbon et l'Angleterre* (*1723–1726*) (Toulouse, 1911?).

Ewald, A. C., *The Life and Times of Prince Charles Stuart, Count of Albany*, 2 vols. (London, 1875).

Feiling, K. G., *A History of the Tory Party, 1640–1714* (Oxford, 1924).

Findlay, J. T., *Wolfe in Scotland in the '45 and from 1749 to 1753* (London etc., 1928).

Forbes, J. Macbeth, *Jacobite Gleanings from State Manuscripts* (Edinburgh and London, 1903).

Graham, J. M., *Annals and Correspondence of the Viscount and the first and second Earls of Stair*, 2 vols. (Edinburgh, 1875).

Handasyde, Frances Elizabeth, *Granville the Polite* (Oxford etc., 1933).

Hanson, Laurence, *Government and the Press, 1695–1763* (London, 1936).

Home, John, *The History of the Rebellion in the Year 1745* (London, 1802).

Insh, G. P., *The Scottish Jacobite Movement* (London, 1952).

Klopp, Onno, *Der Fall des Hauses Stuart und die Succession des Hauses Hannover in Gross-Britannien und Irland . . .* , 14 vols. (Vienna, 1875–88).

Lang, Andrew, *Prince Charles Edward Stuart . . .* , 2nd ed. (London etc., 1903).

Lémontey, P. E., *Histoire de la régence et de la minorité de Louis XV, jusqu'au ministère du cardinal de Fleury*, 2 vols. (Paris, 1832).

Lodge, Sir Richard, *The History of England from the Restoration to the Death of William III* (London etc., 1910).

Lodge, Sir Richard, *Studies in Eighteenth Century Diplomacy, 1740–1748* (London, 1930).

Mackay, William, *Urquhart and Glenmoriston* (Inverness, 1893).

Mackenzie, W. C., *Simon Fraser, Lord Lovat, his Life and Times* (London, 1908).

Macknight, Thomas, *The Life of Henry St. John, Viscount Bolingbroke . . .* (London, 1863).

Maclachlan, J. O., *Trade and Peace with Old Spain* (Cambridge, 1940).

Mahon, Philip Henry Stanhope, styled Lord (later Earl Stanhope), *History of England from the Peace of Utrecht to the Peace of Aix-la-Chapelle*, lengthened to the Peace of Versailles, 7 vols. (London, 1836–54).

Michael, Wolfgang, *England under George I*, trans. A. and G. E. MacGregor, 2 vols. (London, 1936–39).

Noorden, Carl von, *Europäische Geschichte im achtzehnten Jahrhundert*, 3 vols. (Düsseldorf and Leipzig, 1870–82).

Owen, J. H., *War at Sea under Queen Anne, 1702–1708* (Cambridge, 1938).

Ranke, Leopold von, *History of England, Principally in the Seven-*

teenth Century, trans. G. W. Kitchin and others, ed. C. W. Boase and G. W. Kitchin, 6 vols. (Oxford, 1875).

Salomon, Felix, *Geschichte des letzten Ministeriums Königin Annas von England und der englischen Thronfolgefrage* (Gotha, 1894).

Seton, Sir Bruce, and Arnot, J. G., *The Prisoners of the '45*, Publications of the Scottish History Society, 3rd series, vols. XIII–XV (Edinburgh, 1928–29).

Sorel, Albert, *L'Europe et la révolution française*, new printing, 8 vols. (Paris, 1946–49).

Thornton, Percy M., *The Stuart Dynasty, Short Studies of its Rise, Course, and Early Exile* (London, 1890).

Tindal, Nicholas, "Continuation" of P. Rapin de Thoyras' *History of England*, 3rd ed. of Tindal's trans. of Rapin, 4 vols. in 5 (London, 1743–45).

Trevelyan, G. M., *England under Queen Anne*, 3 vols. (London etc., 1930–34).

Vaucher, Paul, *La Crise du ministère Walpole en 1733–1734* (Paris, 1924).

Vaucher, Paul, *Robert Walpole et la politique de Fleury* (Paris, 1924).

Wiesener, Louis, *Le Régent, l'abbé Dubois, et les Anglais, d'après les sources britanniques*, 3 vols. (Paris, 1891–99).

Yorke, Philip, *The Life and Correspondence of Philip Yorke, Earl of Hardwicke*, 3 vols. (Cambridge, 1913).

Zévort, Edgar, *Le Marquis d'Argenson et le ministère des affaires étrangères* (Paris, 1880).

B. ARTICLES

Bruce, M. W., "The Duke of Mar in Exile," *Transactions of the Royal Historical Society*, 4th series, 20:61–82 (London, 1937).

Bruce, M. W., "Jacobite Relations with Peter the Great," *Slavonic Review*, 14:343–62 (January 1936).

Chance, J. F., "The 'Swedish Plot' of 1716–17," *Eng. Hist. Rev.*, 18:81–106 (January 1903).

Davies, Godfrey, "Macpherson and the Nairne Papers," *E.H.R.*, 35:367–376 (July 1920).

Du Hamel de Breuil, comte Jean, "Le Mariage du Prétendant," *Revue d'histoire diplomatique*, 9:53–90 (1895).

Fieldhouse, H. N., "Bolingbroke and the d'Iberville Correspondence, August, 1714 – June, 1715," *E.H.R.*, 52:673–682 (October 1937).

Fieldhouse, H. N., "Bolingbroke's Share in the Jacobite Intrigue of 1710–14," *E.H.R.*, 52:443–459 (July 1937).

Fieldhouse, H. N., "Oxford, Bolingbroke, and the Pretender's Place of Residence, 1711–14," *E.H.R.*, 52:289–296 (April 1937).

Jenkinson, Sir Hilary, "What Happened to the Great Seal of James II," *Antiquaries' Journal*, 23:1–13 (April 1943).

Lloyd, E. M., "Marlborough and the Brest Expedition, 1694," *E.H.R.*, 9:130–132 (January 1894).

Parnell, Arthur, "James Macpherson and the Nairne Papers," *E.H.R.*, 12:254–284 (April 1897).

Petrie, Sir Charles, "Jacobite Activities in South and West England in the Summer of 1715," *Transactions of the Royal Historical Society*, 4th series, 18:85–106 (London, 1935).

Walcott, Robert, Jr., "English Party Politics (1688–1714)," *Essays in Modern English History in Honor of Wilbur Cortez Abbot* (Cambridge, Mass., 1941).

Williams, Basil, "The Foreign Policy of England under Walpole, 1721–27," *E.H.R.*, 15:251–276, 479–494, 665–698 (1900); 16:67–83, 308–327, 439–451 (1901).

Wolff, H. W., "The Pretender at Bar-le-duc," *Blackwood's Magazine*, 156:226–246 (August 1894).

V. TRACTS AND PAPERS

[Harbin, George,] *The Hereditary Right of the Crown of England Asserted* (London, 1713).

Ius Sacrum, or a Discourse wherein it is fully prov'd and Demonstrated, that No Prince ought to be depriv'd of his Natural Right . . . (London, 1712).

Leslie, Charles, *The Finishing Stroke* . . . (London, 1711).

Leslie, Charles, "A Letter from Mr. Leslie to a Member of Parliament in London" (n. pl., 1714), reprinted in *Somers' Tracts*, 4th coll., vol. IV (London, 1751).

Leslie, Charles, *The Rehearsal*, reprinted, 4 vols. (London, 1708–09).

The Loyal Catechism . . . (London, 1713).

Molloy, Charles, and others, *Common Sense, or the Englishman's Journal*, reprinted, 2 vols. (London, 1738–39).

INDEX